Praise for *The End of Work*

'Adam was expelled from the garden of Eden to till the ground in the sweat of his face, so the Bible says, leaving us with centuries of theological argument about how to relate the reality for so many people of work as toil, drudgery and effectively a curse, to the equally familiar experience of work as creative achievement and personal fulfilment. Post-Christian we may now be in Britain, yet in a society still reeling from de-industrialization, with unemployment endemic in certain quarters, with leisure activities expanding vastly, and so on, there is a rich and complex Christian tradition of thinking about the nature of work which John Hughes puts back on the agenda in this provocative book.'

Fergus Kerr, University of Oxford

'John Hughes has written not about work but about the "end" of work. But this is the most far-reaching question imaginable in practical reason. To what end do we exert ourselves at all? What do we hope to achieve? Through a tour of reading in nineteenth- and twentieth-century thinkers that is as subtle and sympathetic as it is diverse and adventurous, he has shown us how the ancient struggle between the fine and the useful has been played out dramatically in the post-industrial West and holds the key to a great deal that we think of as modernity. Here is an exciting new voice contributing to the interpretation of our moral predicaments. I cannot imagine anyone putting Hughes's book down without having learned something important.'

Oliver O'Donovan, University of Edinburgh

D1440944

Illuminations: Theory and Religion

Series editors: Catherine Pickstock, John Milbank and Graham Ward

Religion has a growing visibility in the world at large. Throughout the humanities there is a mounting realization that religion and culture lie so closely together that religion is an unavoidable and fundamental human reality. Consequently, the examination of religion and theology now stands at the centre of any questioning of our western identity, including the question of whether there is such a thing as 'truth'.

ILLUMINATIONS aims both to reflect the diverse elements of these developments and, from them, to produce creative new syntheses. It is unique in exploring the new interaction between theology, philosophy, religious studies, political theory and cultural studies. Despite the theoretical convergence of certain trends they often in practice do not come together. The aim of ILLUMINATIONS is to make this happen, and advance contemporary theoretical discussion.

Published:
Sacrifice and Community: Jewish Offering and Christian Eucharist
Matthew Levering

The Other Calling: Theology, Intellectual Vocation and Truth
Andrew Shanks

The State of the University: Academic Knowledges and the Knowledge of God
Stanley Hauerwas

The End of Work: Theological Critiques of Capitalism
John Hughes

God and the Between
William Desmond

Forthcoming
After Enlightenment: Hamann as Post-Secular Visionary
John Betz

The End of Work
Theological Critiques of Capitalism

John Hughes

Blackwell
Publishing

BLACKWELL PUBLISHING
350 Main Street, Malden, MA 02148-5020, USA
9600 Garsington Road, Oxford OX4 2DQ, UK
550 Swanston Street, Carlton, Victoria 3053, Australia

The right of John Hughes to be identified as the author of this work has been asserted in accordance with the UK Copyright, Designs, and Patents Act 1988.

Designations used by companies to distinguish their products are often claimed as trademarks. All brand names and product names used in this book are trade names, service marks, trademarks, or registered trademarks of their respective owners. The publisher is not associated with any product or vendor mentioned in this book.

This publication is designed to provide accurate and authoritative information in regard to the subject matter covered. It is sold on the understanding that the publisher is not engaged in rendering professional services. If professional advice or other expert assistance is required, the services of a competent professional should be sought.

First published 2007 by Blackwell Publishing Ltd

1   2007

Library of Congress Cataloging-in-Publication Data

Hughes, John.
  The end of work : theological critiques of capitalism / John Hughes.
      p. cm.—(Illuminations: theory and religion)
  Includes bibliographical references and index.
  ISBN 978-1-4051-5892-3 (hardcover : alk. paper)—ISBN 978-1-4051-5893-0 (pbk. : alk. paper)
1. Capitalism—Religious aspects—Christianity. 2. Work—Religious aspects—Christianity.
3. Labor—Religious aspects—Christianity. 4. Utility theory. 5. Marx, Karl, 1818–1883. I. Title.

BR115.C3H84 2007
261.8′5—dc22

                                        2007003784

A catalogue record for this title is available from the British Library.

Set in 10.5/12pt Sabon
by SPi Publisher Services, Pondicherry, India
Printed and bound in Singapore
by C.O.S. Printers Pte Ltd

The publisher's policy is to use permanent paper from mills that operate a sustainable forestry policy, and which has been manufactured from pulp processed using acid-free and elementary chlorine-free practices. Furthermore, the publisher ensures that the text paper and cover board used have met acceptable environmental accreditation standards.

For further information on
Blackwell Publishing, visit our website:
www.blackwellpublishing.com

'*Art and Prudence*', Eric Gill. By kind permission of the Estate
of Eric Gill / The Bridgeman Art Library.

To my parents

                         ... We don't know the ins and outs
how can we? how shall we?
What did our mothers tell us? What did their mothers tell them?
What the earth-mother told to them? But what did the queen of
heaven tell *her*? ...

                                       The Wall, David Jones

Contents

Foreword

This book considers the 'problem of labour' from a theological perspective. While it is obviously aimed at theologians concerned with how Christianity might engage in social criticism (particularly by building on recent interest in theological aesthetics to show the non-utilitarian roots of the British Christian Socialist tradition), it is also aimed at secular philosophers and political theorists who have in recent times shown a greater openness to the historical and theoretical connections between the Marxist tradition and Christianity. More specifically it seeks to draw attention to the potential contribution of neglected resources in romantic philosophy and theology to the reconceiving of the task of social criticism after the collapse of state-centralist utilitarian socialism in Eastern Europe. It is aimed at those of at least higher undergraduate level in these disciplines.

I begin with a survey of twentieth century theologies of work, contrasting differing approaches to the contemporary reality of work, and the relation between divine and human work. I go on to explore the nineteenth and twentieth century debates about labour under capitalism. Through a reading of Weber's *Protestant Work Ethic*, I argue that the triumph of the 'spirit of utility' is crucial to understanding notions of modern work, and that this is bound up historically with an anti-theological agenda. In exploring Marx's critique of labour, I argue that the very possibility of critique was premised upon a vision of unalienated labour which Marx derived from the quasi-theological traditions of German Romanticism. This critique was however compromised when these sources were suppressed in favour of the anti-theological prejudices of political economy, creating contradictions that have continued to haunt the Marxist tradition, as illustrated in the work of the Frankfurt School. The English Romantic tradition of social criticism, as represented by Ruskin and Morris, represents another critique of labour, which was more explicit about its theological presuppositions, criticizing contemporary labour conditions on the basis of a vision of true work as art, like God's work in creation. Finally I turn to various twentieth century Catholic thinkers who supplement this aesthetic tradition with classical metaphysical categories which help them to think through the nature of art and the relationship between utility and non-utility in work. Such a perspective enables us to see the ultimate nothingness of utility, and how non-utility can be not only defended against work, but also extended to transform work so that it participates more fully in divine work, and so becomes a liturgical offering.

Preface

Of the more concrete conclusions of this book, one of which I am particularly convinced at its completion is the claim that work is made more delightful by company and cooperation. Doctoral dissertations are in some ways negative illustrations of this, in that their tediousness often results from the reclusive existence encouraged by notions of originality and independence in research. No thought of course can be completely private, and fortunately the reality of doctoral work is greatly eased by the great cloud of those who accompany one along the way, whether intellectually or more broadly.

My debt of thanks must begin with my supervisors, with both of whom I have been unbelievably fortunate. It is difficult to find words appropriate for my gratitude to Catherine Pickstock: for inspiring me in my undergraduate years, for bringing light out of the initial chaos of my proposals, for being tireless in her detailed and regular reading of my work even from across the world and long after she had ceased to be my official supervisor, and most especially for generating the enthusiasm and joy without which this dissertation would never have been possible. Few people would be capable of following this act, yet when Catherine left on maternity leave, Jeremy Morris was brave enough to take over supervising this dissertation which seemed not quite to fit in the usual disciplinary boundaries. His historian's eye for detail and context, and knowledge of the nineteenth century, were crucial in the final year, while his breadth of intellectual interests meant that he in no way resisted the less historical, more philosophical direction of the argument. I could not have wanted more from either of them.

Among my companions along the way, special mention should be made of Matthew Bullimore, who shared with me the curious amphibious existence of being simultaneously a doctoral student and an ordinand; in addition to being the most frequent audience to my rambling thoughts and influencing my thinking in myriad ways over the years, he also provided me with more cups of tea during moments of tedium than I dare to recall. Others who have read sections of the dissertation and provided helpful comments and criticisms include Andrew Davison, David Grumett, Mark Berry, Alice Wood, Chad Pecknold, James

Lawson, Althea Pipe, Frances Arnold and my mother. More broadly I am grateful for the support and encouragement of my family, the extraordinary 'redoubtable cell' of John Munns, Anna Matthews, Rob Mackley, Russell Dewhurst and Andrew Davison, and of all my friends from Westcott House. From Emmanuel College, I would particularly like to thank Jeremy Caddick for all his help, and the Choir, especially Claire Cousens, Jen Spencer, Ben Martin and Rowena Bayliss, for brightening up the gloomier slog of the final year. Among my fellow graduates, I am particularly grateful for conversations with Karl Hefty, Adrian Pabst, Rachel Greene, Jim Walters, Brutus Green, Scott Moringiello, Ed Morgan and Ben Fulford. The finishing touches were put to this book after my ordination and I would like to thank my Vicar, John Henton, and the people of St David's and St Michael's for the support and friendship they have given me as I have made the transition to a different sort of work.

Among my longer-term academic debts I should begin by acknowledging John Milbank, who, in addition to being very generous towards me, has perhaps been my primary theological inspiration and with whom I often feel I am simply writing extended footnotes to his asides. Janet Soskice, Nick Adams, Pete Candler, Simon Oliver and Ben Quash all fuelled a passion for philosophical and political theology in the peculiar Cambridge style during my undergraduate studies. Tim Jenkins has also helped in a rather different way by keeping me ever-vigilant towards the dangers of aspects of this style! From my Oxford days I appreciated the distinct but related perspectives of Oliver O'Donovan, Bernd Wannenwetsch and John Webster, which perhaps made me a *little* more self-critical in my Romanticism …

Cooperation is however no excuse for the abdication of personal responsibility, and the opinions and mistakes of this dissertation are my own. While I believe that theologians should consider all things in relation to God and so have no safe 'ground' to themselves, this nomadic and often parasitic existence involves a certain vulnerability. I am conscious that I have strayed across many different fields and authors, without really being a 'specialist' in any of them. Similarly, some may be dissatisfied by the fact that I have sought to address myself to a number of audiences with very different starting positions: secular social critics and theorists who regard religion as at best an irrelevance and at worst reactionary; Christian socialists, who seem to have lost sight of the distinctiveness of their social vision; and the Church more generally, which often regards social criticism as an optional extra.

While we may not live by bread alone, it certainly helps; and at the material level I am grateful for the support of the Arts and Humanities Research Board, the C. S. Gray and Gwyn funds at Emmanuel, the Newton Scholarship Fund, the Diocese of Exeter, the Ministry Division of the Archbishops' Council, the Zelie Timms and Bernard Maitlock funds at Jesus College, the Cleaver Trustees, the Toc H and All Hallows Trust, and the Dean and Chapter of Exeter Cathedral.

Finally, if my thanks are to be more than flattery and vanity, they must find their meaning within the movement of total gratitude towards the One from whom we receive all things, and back to whom all our work is offered: '*quia per incarnati verbi mysterium nova mentis nostrae oculis lux tuae claritatis infulsit.*'

The Parish of St David with St Michael and All Angels, Exeter,
St Frideswide, 2006

Come to me, all who labour and are heavy laden, and I will give you rest.

*Et ideo ipse solus est maxime liberalis,
quia non agit propter suam utilitatem, sed solum propter suam bonitatem*

Consider the lilies of the field, how they grow; they neither toil nor spin.

Introduction

Work in the Christian Tradition

> The Lord God took the man and put him in the garden of Eden to till it and keep it

> Cursed is the ground because of you; in toil you shall eat of it all the days of your life . . . in the sweat of your face you shall eat bread till you return to the ground, for out of it you were taken.

> 'Blessed indeed' says the Spirit, 'that they may rest from their labours, for their works follow them.'

> Work: begot in man by an animal need, and, at the same time, a tool by which to lift himself above animality. A hard bondage and a liberating force. Today still it remains marked by this ambiguous character.[1]

Why write a book about work now? In recent years there has been a considerable number of books, by theologians and others, that seek to offer analyses and critiques of contemporary capitalism. Yet these books start from the presupposition that capitalism as we now know it is very different from how it was even 50 years ago. Talk of 'late capitalism' indicates an awareness of how the current economic order is marked by various features distinguishing it from the period of classical capitalism in the nineteenth and early twentieth centuries: the withering of the role of the nation state, the globalization of finance capital, the emergence of international corporate monopolies with ever-increasing hyper-profits, the replacement of traditional manufacturing industry by information and finance as the driving engines of the global economy, an ever-increasing gap between the rich and the poor, spiralling debt, and the disabling of any opposition to this order by its absorption into the system.[2] Late capitalism, on this account, is more fluid, more virtual than what came before. It is defined more by consumption than production, by the apparently infinite stimulation of desire and exchange of

---

[1] Henri de Lubac, *Paradoxes of Faith* (San Francisco: Ignatius Press, 1987), p. 149.
[2] See particularly, Ernest Mandel, *Late Capitalism* (London: Verso, 1999), and Frederic Jameson, *Postmodernism, or, the Logic of Late Capitalism* (London: Verso, 1991).

signs that the market has become. In such a situation, writing about work seems decidedly passé. Mechanization and the out-sourcing of manufacture to third world countries with cheap labour markets has meant that work in the traditional sense of manual labour, as it was pictured by the philosophers of antiquity or the classical economists, has largely disappeared from view in Western societies, relegated to an invisible underclass. While there might be some interest in the changed working conditions that this new economic situation has produced for the educated Westerner (the need for greater flexibility and so forth), there is little sense that work might be the key to understanding our economic situation. The 'problem of work' sounds to contemporary ears to be a nineteenth- and early twentieth-century problem, compared with more contemporary concerns such as globalization, ecological crisis, the media construction of desire, and the economy of symbolic exchange. The situation of late twentieth- and early twenty-first century capitalism seems better understood through complex cultural-aesthetic categories than through narrowly economic ones.

Most of the authors I will be considering here are either nineteenth- or early twentieth-century writers. However it is my claim that the two traditions that I will be exploring – the Marxists and the British Romantics – have critiques of labour under capitalism that are sensitive to exactly these 'cultural-aesthetic' questions which have become prominent in more recent years. I will argue that these traditions, particularly when read alongside each other, point towards the 'aesthetic' origins of *any* critique of capitalism, and may help us to set forth a non-utilitarian socialism better suited to the problems of our own day. Furthermore, it is my claim that these 'aesthetic' roots of the critiques of capitalism are in fact a form of thinly disguised theology, more or less indebted to the Christian tradition. It is, therefore, my hope that this book might be of general interest to intellectual historians, political theorists and social critics, and that in particular it might alert them to the neglected role that theology has played in social criticism. On the other hand, I hope that theologians and the Church might engage in a deeper and bolder conversation with the traditions of social criticism which are, in some sense, products of the Christian tradition, rather than borrowing uncritically from them. Before embarking on this discussion, it is perhaps useful to give some sort of brief overview of the main elements of the views of work in the pre-modern Christian tradition.

Human work has been viewed as having a profoundly ambiguous nature throughout the Christian tradition. In the Scriptures apparently differing views lie side by side, and cannot easily be separated. It is an oversimplification, for example, to say that the Old Testament has a positive view of labour but regards it as purely this-worldly, while the New Testament is uninterested in 'secular employment', but has much to say about spiritual 'works'. Already in the traditions which make up the first two chapters of Genesis we see tensions: humanity is commanded by God to 'subdue' the earth and to have 'dominion' over all living creatures, we are given the task of 'tilling and keeping' the garden, and then after the primordial disobedience we are told that our labouring for food will be characterized from now on by 'toil' and the 'sweat' of our face.[3] Work in some sense seems to be inseparable from the nature of humanity in its aboriginal goodness, yet this seems not to be necessarily the same as the work that is characterized by toil and struggle. The people of Israel continued to know this twofold character of work in its life and its imagination: in the slavery of the people in Egypt, in the vision of the promised land as so abundant as to require minimal effort in cultivation, in the Wisdom writers' account of the vanity of work, and in their condemnation of idleness, in the prophetic polemic against the fabrication of idols, and in the account of cultic liturgical work as 'Spirit-inspired'.[4] The institution of the Sabbath provided a profound focus for such thinking, relativizing the ultimacy of labour beneath a higher reality of rest. In the Sabbath the resting from ordinary labour was linked with the deliverance from slave labour in Egypt, and even more dramatically with the divine rest from creation on the seventh day.[5] This latter point already introduces the question of some sort of analogy between human action and *God's* action, which will remain a crucial albeit difficult feature of the tradition since. Other texts through-out the Old Testament speak of God's formative and redemptive 'works' and also of the analogy between human artisanship and divine creation, the 'work of his hands'.[6] In the New Testament Christ himself uses many images of labourers in his parables, while at the same time, particularly in the Sermon on the Mount, he appears to have more to say about the

---

[3] Genesis 1:28 (*kbsh* and *rd* – from the Priestly tradition), 2:15 (*shmr* and *'bd* – from the Yahwist tradition), and 3:17 (*'tsbwn*). For overviews of the perspectives on work in the Bible, see: Paul Beauchamp, 'Travail: Théologie Biblique' in Jean-Yves Lacoste (ed.), *Dictionnaire Critique de Théologie* (Paris: Presses Universitaires de France, 2002) and Alan Richardson, *The Biblical Doctrine of Work* (London: SCM, 1952), especially pp. 25–9 for the views in Genesis. I am also grateful to Diana Lipton for conversations on the meaning of these texts.

[4] Exodus 1:11–14 (*sbl* and *'bdh*), Deuteronomy 11:10–11, Ecclesiastes 2:1–18 (*'ml*), Job 7:1–11 (*tsb'*), Proverbs 6:6, Isaiah 40:19, Exodus 35:31 (*ml'kh* here). For detailed philological analysis, see G. Johannes Botterweck and Helmer Ringren (eds.), *The Theological Dictionary of the Old Testament*, trans. John T. Willis (Grand Rapids: Eerdmans, 1975-); particularly vol. VIII, pp. 325–31, for *ml'kh* and its primary sense of work as skilled artisanship, including cultic crafts, but also its later linking with manual labour through opposition to the Sabbath; and vol. X, pp. 376–405, for *'bd* and its wide range of meanings from slavery, through agricultural work and royal service, to cultic ministrations.

[5] Deuteronomy 5:14–15, Exodus 20:9–11, Genesis 2:1–3 (*ml'kh* is used of human work in all three cases, and an analogy between divine and human *rest* is made in the latter two cases, while only the Priestly author in Genesis uses *ml'kh* of both divine and human work in this context).

[6] For example, Psalm 8:3, 9:1, 19:1, 26:7, 40:5, 66:5, 78:7, 86:8, 92:4,104:24, 111:7, 145:4, where the most common words used are *p'l* and *m'sh*, for which, see: Botterweck and Ringren (eds.), vols. XI, pp. 387–403, and XII, pp. 38–44; Jeremiah 18:3–6 (*ml'kh* again), Isaiah 64:8, Job 10:8, Genesis 2:7 (*ytsr*). On the divine 'work' of creation, see Richardson, pp. 14–16.

liberation from toil and labouring, and a pronounced hostility towards trading and the accruing of riches.[7] John and Paul have more interest in spiritual works and their relation to the works of God, while Paul also has a strong critique of those who think they will be saved by the works of the law, and strict warnings for those who will not work to support themselves.[8] Finally Christ's controversial teaching about the Sabbath can be seen as an extension of the Old Testament view of cultic work to provide a radically new liturgical foundation and goal to all activity, although this is to pre-empt our journey somewhat.[9]

For various reasons, whether of class or eschatological expectation, the early church afforded little reflection to physical labour, other than to condemn idleness and certain specific occupations, although they continued to develop notions of spiritual work. With the rise of asceticism this tradition developed into an elaborate reflection on the links between prayer and physical work, as seen for example in the Rule of Benedict.[10] During the same period Greek notions of the philosophical life as founded upon *otium*, leisure, began to enter into Christian thinking, finding their fullest expression in the Scholastic account of the supremacy of the *vita contemplativa* over the *vita activa*, and the justification of the existence of entire non-labouring classes in the monasteries in terms of their contribution to the work of prayer, which was also the *opus dei*, God's work.[11] Meanwhile the tradition of 'spiritual works' had developed into a vast and often corrupt system of the bartering of human labour with God. The Reformation overturned much of this perspective by rejecting the monastic life and the priority of contemplation as idleness and paganism. Luther's insistence upon justification by grace

[7]   Matthew 20:1–16, 6:24–33 (*kopia*), 11:28 (*kopiontes*), et al; cf. Matthew 19:24, 21:12–13, et al. For *kopos* and its derivatives, see Gerhard Kittel (ed.), *The Theological Dictionary of the New Testament*, trans Geoffrey W. Bromiley (Grand Rapids: Eerdmans, 1964-), vol. III, pp. 827–30.

[8]   For example, John 5:17, 6:28, 9:4, 14:12, 1Corinthians 3:9–13, 9:1, 12:6, 16:10, Ephesians 2:10, Romans 3:20–4:6. 11:6, Galatians 2:16, 2Thessalonians 3:6–13. In the majority of these cases the less negative *ergon* and its derivatives are used, for which see: Kittel, vol. II, pp. 635–53. The Johannine usage in relation to divine works was probably building upon the Septuagint translation of the Psalmic *m'sh* with *ergon*, while Paul's usage seems more indebted to post-exilic and Rabbinic language of works in terms of the keeping of the law. See also Richardson, pp. 30–48.

[9]   Matthew 12:5, John 5:17, 7:22; cf. Beauchamp: 'L'agir cotidien rejoint le service liturgique, non finalise par le produit: "…le jour du sabbat, les prêtres dans le Temple violent le sabbat sans être en faute". Cet ordre nouveau n'est ni un état, ni a proprement parler une fin à atteindre, mais un commencement posé.'

[10] See St Augustine, 'On the Work of Monks', in Philip Schaff (ed.), *Nicene and Post-Nicene Fathers*, vol. 3 (Peabody, MA: Hendrickson, 1999), and St Benedict, *The Rule of St Benedict*, trans. Cardinal Gasquet (London: Chatto and Windus, 1936).

[11] See e.g., St Thomas Aquinas, *Summa Theologiae*, trans. The English Dominican Province (London: Eyre and Spottiswoode, 1963), IIa IIae, q. 182. In the Greek philosophical tradition, Plato and Aristotle already regarded work in ways we might call 'proto-theological', by linking it with ontological teleology; see Kittel, vol. II, p. 636.

not works led to the depreciation of any talk of 'spiritual works', while analogical relations between human and divine work were equally suspect. Secular occupations might be allocated by God, but their goals were entirely this-worldly.[12]

It was however in the eighteenth and nineteenth centuries that the rise of industrial labour and a new consciousness of the condition of the 'working classes' produced much reflection, from within and without the Christian Church, on the problem or nature of labour. Here, especially in the political economists and in Marx, work becomes a serious subject in its own right, and we can begin to discern what might be called 'ontologies of labour', theories which attempted to understand the very nature of labour, and often to make sense of humanity and society through these labour-theories. This is the situation to which most modern theologies of work seek to respond. They normally seek to offer some theological ontology of labour, linking divine and human work, and then to draw some conclusions from this to apply to the practical problem of labour. This problem of labour is primarily then a *modern* one, although as we will discover, we cannot ignore the views that preceded it if we wish to understand it fully. As we shall see, most contemporary theologies of work seem to simply respond to the modern debate about the problem of labour, treating it as a given, and not always a terribly critically considered given (chapter 1). Theology is then brought into conversation with these debates as an external other. My approach here by contrast will be to enter a little more deeply into these debates and to interrogate their inherent relation to theology. It is my contention that these debates did not emerge in a theological vacuum, but were themselves driven by quite specific, albeit complex, theological and anti-theological currents. Only when these are grasped can theologians properly engage with them. In the subsequent chapters I will seek to show that modern work under capitalism can be understood as characterized by a spirit of utility which is at heart anti-theological (chapter 2). I will then argue that even secular critiques of modern labour are founded upon an awareness of the ambiguity of labour, of its potential to transcend utility as well as serve it, which is at heart theological (chapters 3 and 5). Finally I will develop a critique of utility based upon a theological-aesthetic vision of the analogy between human work as art and God's work (chapters 4, 6 and 7).

---

[12] Jean-Yves Lacoste, 'Travail: Théologie Historique' in *Dictionnaire Critique de Théologie*.

What must we do to be working the works of God?

1

Twentieth-Century Theologies of Work

Karl Barth, Marie-Dominique Chenu, John Paul II and Miroslav Volf

Our explorations in the theology of work will begin with a brief overview of the writings of four twentieth-century theologians on 'work'. We will consider two books: one by a Roman Catholic, Chenu's *Theology of Work* from the early 1960s, and the other by a Protestant (Croatian Pentecostalist when he wrote this book, although now an Episcopalian), Miroslav Volf's *Work in the Spirit* (1991). We will also explore the major ecclesiastical teaching document on work, John Paul II's *Laborem Exercens*, and the treatment of work in the greatest twentieth-century work of Protestant systematic theology, Barth's *Church Dogmatics*. Across these texts we will see various historical and confessional patterns of addressing major theological questions such as the relationship between divine and human action and the gravity of the effects of the Fall. All of them engage with various Scriptural foci appropriate to the consideration of work: Eden and the Fall, the Sabbath and Hebrew Law in relation to work, Wisdom literature, the teaching of Christ in the Gospels, and of St Paul, particularly in the Thessalonian correspondence, and the relation of work to the Final End of all things. Yet behind all their discussions lurks the 'problem of labour' as it has arisen in secular debates in the nineteenth and twentieth centuries, and to which they are all, more or less explicitly, responding. I will argue that the failure of all four authors to engage adequately these debates accords a quasi-naturalist autonomy to 'work' in their thought, to which theology must then respond, weakening its capacity for deeper critical engagement.

KARL BARTH: THE SABBATH AND THE REFORMED RESISTANCE TO THE IDOLATRY OF WORK

Barth's treatment of work in the *Church Dogmatics* is the earliest of my four texts (1951) and the most dogmatic and exegetical. In this Barth follows the classical Protestant treatments of work and generally avoids the particular socio-economic situation of the modern world. Yet there are some surprises: Barth places work within his doctrine of creation

(III/4) which is where he locates his ethics, under the exposition of the Sabbath – a typically Barthian tactic to avoid any possible idolatry of human work and to stress the absolute priority of divine work. The command to rest is seen as not simply a concession to working for the rest of the week, rather it is the precondition of all other work and its true meaning: 'the Sabbath commandment explains all the other commandments . . . it points [man] away from everything that he himself can will and achieve and back to what God is for him and will do for him.'[1] It is this day which gives meaning to the working week rather than vice versa, rest which is somehow prior to, the necessary precondition of our work. 'Is not this interruption the true time from which alone he can have other time? Is not the paradoxical "activity" of the holy day the origin of all the other activity which seems to have better reason for this designation?'[2] The Sabbath is not a day of inactivity, let alone time 'for ourselves'. Barth is scathing of the modern secular justification of the Sabbath in terms of the value of 'leisure': 'Is there anything more depressing' he bewails 'than the sight of obviously very bored male and female humanity wandering about our streets on a Sunday afternoon around three o'clock all dressed up and pushing prams? What is the point of it all?'[3] Any humanitarian advantages that the Sabbath provides are secondary to its true meaning: to join with God in resting, celebrating over Creation. Against any attempt to see human work as somehow an extension of God's creation, Barth sets work against the background of the 'always already' completed divine work. In classic Protestant terms: works do not merit salvation but rather follow from God's 'work'.

When Barth does consider the 'active life', he refuses to characterize it under the term 'work', using instead the term 'service' for the task that God's Word commands of us.[4] Activity is not in itself a response to the redemptive Word of God, but frequently just a form of self-preservation. Work certainly has its place within the life of faith, but it is not in itself the whole of the active life God requires of humanity. 'Work' for Barth can be defined as 'man addressing himself to the physical and spiritual cosmos, terrestrial matter'. Work in this fundamental, anthropological sense is essentially 'this worldly'.[5]

---

[1] Karl Barth, *Church Dogmatics III/4,* – hereafter CD III/4 – ed. G. W. Bromiley and T. F. Torrance (Edinburgh: T. & T. Clark, 1961), p. 53. One of the best summaries of Barth's 'theology of work' is: Gordon Preece, 'Barth's Theology of Work and Vocation for a Postmodern World', in Geoff Thompson and Christiaan Mostert (eds.), *Karl Barth: A Future for Postmodern Theology?* (Adelaide: Australian Theological Forum, 2000). Preece sees less discontinuity between work and the active life in Barth than I do, and is more optimistic in finding a Christocentric *analogia actionis*; however he accords more importance to the criticisms of Barth made by Volf and Ellul than I would.

[2] CD III/4, p. 51.

[3] Ibid., p. 61.

[4] Ibid., p. 475.

[5] Ibid., p. 471.

Barth then proceeds to demonstrate the unimportance and secularity of 'work' from scripture: He points first to the absence of teaching from Christ on employment or vocation and that if anything he calls his disciples *from* their work rather than to it. Christ's own craft, whatever *tekton* (Mark 6:3) is taken to mean, does not seem to have continued during his ministry. Paul, admittedly has more to say on work and its importance and we are told that he supported himself through such work (Acts 18:3, 2 Thess. 3:8, 1 Cor. 4:12 et al.). Yet even here, as Barth points out, work is marginal to Paul's apostolate and to his ethical teaching. Even in the Old Testament with its more obviously 'this-worldly' concerns, Barth insists too much has been read into Gen. 1:28 if we think this means that cultivation is the real task God has laid upon humanity.[6] Work, as it is presented in the psalms for example, is a self-evident necessity of life (Ps. 104:23) and idleness is condemned by the example of the ant (Prov. 6:6–11), but this is not because of some inherent value of work in terms of personality or culture; rather it is that, without working, people will starve. The necessity of work, Barth insists, is very much a *post*-lapsarian reality (Gen. 3:17), and we should remember that in the Decalogue there is an explicit commandment *not* to work, but nothing explicitly enjoining work.

Why is Barth so opposed to seeing work as salvific? Why does he insist that it is an almost unnatural grim necessity rather than a holy obligation and part of the fulfilment of our being? This is not just Protestant neurosis about 'works', because Barth's dogmatics are not just an exercise in timeless theology unaware of the contemporary situation. The small print sections reveal that this anti-work dogmatics is directed against specific currents in nineteenth- and twentieth-century liberal Protestant thought: Barth is writing to refute the glib identification of Protestant ideology with capitalist modernity. Thus he writes concerning work: 'the biblical witness enjoins greater reserve, and as we might also add, greater relaxation, than has become customary in Protestant ethics generally, not so much under biblical influences, but under the pressure of recent developments in European economy and economics.'[7] Chiding Brunner, he insists that Luther's sanctifying of non-monastic vocations is not the laudable advent of the ideal of work which has dominated European civilization (Weber must surely also be in the background here). Indeed Protestants may have succumbed to a 'great deal of exaggeration' here, even an excessive elevation of the secular, as in the exalting of matrimony over celibacy. The work of Christ, as it is spoken of in John's gospel especially, is not 'cultural activity' and human work can never be purely *for itself*, but only ever to the Glory of God.[8]

Despite this anti-liberal concern, Barth goes on to make it clear that God *does* command the active life of service, we are to set our minds to

---

[6] Ibid., p. 472.
[7] Ibid., p. 473.
[8] Ibid., pp. 486, 520.

things and do them, because our mere existence is not an end in itself and the active life testifies to this. Such is the partial truth of the Protestant 'ethic of work' against the distorted exaltation of the *vita contemplativa*, when it becomes simply the 'indolence of the sublime' as in the worst of the late medieval monasteries (although Barth is surprisingly generous to the monastic ideal).[9] In their attempt to reinstate the significance of the *vita activa*, the Reformers and their successors exalted *mere* work in the narrow sense of secular vocation, or employment as we might say; thus simultaneously over-rating this, and under-rating the rest of the *vita activa*.

Here then, despite all the earlier caveats, Barth is prepared to allow for some sort of *analogia actionis* when he says that the *vita activa* involves the 'restoration of a correspondence' between divine and human action. Nevertheless he still reminds us firmly that this is a correspondence, not a continuation or development which would be idolatrous, for we are concerned with sanctification not deification (which he claims, rather unecumenically, is the property of pagans and fanatics!).[10] Barth is adamant on this one: we do not become co-creators, co-saviours, co-regents or co-Gods.[11] Yet once again Barth qualifies his proscription with much positive comment on the *vita active*, for the active life of service (*diakonia*), placing ourselves at God's disposal, has been radic-alized under the New Covenant: Jesus's response to the question of the sons of Zebedee, that we, like Christ, should be lords of all by serving all (Matt. 20:25) reveals how we *can* in fact become an imitator, *mimetes* of God (Eph. 5:1) and even a co-worker, *synergos* of the Kingdom (Col. 4:11) doing the works of God, *ergon tou Theou* in his field and vine-yard.[12] In this context Barth mentions cultic service (*latria*, Rom. 1:9 and *leitourgia*, Phil. 2:17) as the supreme expression of this active life of service, because it is the most intense expression of the decision that is manifest in the entire life. In another pregnant suggestion, Barth advises that modern man would do well to take God more seriously and himself somewhat less seriously and thus to learn how work might become a sort of 'play'.[13]

Within this service of faith and obedience which is humanity's *opus proprium*, there remains room for 'work' in the lesser secular sense, although this is *restricted* to the task of 'self-preservation', meeting our basic needs (Aquinas is cited with approval: ST IIa:IIae q. 187 a.3). This animality should not be glossed over with idealizations of work, rather it is a check to our hubristic idolatry of work.[14] Work, for Barth, properly belongs to the order of creation rather than that of redemption. It is the

[9] CD III/4, p. 473.
[10] Ibid., p. 474.
[11] Ibid., p. 482.
[12] Ibid., pp. 477, 487.
[13] Ibid., p. 553.
[14] Ibid., pp. 524–5.

apparent autonomy of this natural realm from the order of salvation, that raises certain problems.

We might conclude by saying Barth's determination to distinguish work, in the sense of employment, belonging to the natural order, from the service of God, which constitutes the active life of our response to his great work, provides a profound critique of the glib liberal celebration of capitalism and its work-ethic. Yet perhaps this very distinction, alongside his hostility to seeing even our service as somehow participatory in God's work, encourages precisely the secularity of work for its own sake which he seeks to resist. This apparent disinterest in the redemption and transformation of labour is all the more striking given Barth's sympathy for the Christian Socialists and involvement in the trade union movement during his time at Safenwil.

MARIE-DOMINIQUE CHENU: CATHOLIC MODERNISM

My second text is *The Theology of Work: An Exploration* by Marie-Dominique Chenu. Written by a Dominican, within twenty years of Barth, this book has a very different agenda, much more imbued with a certain cultural optimism. Whereas Barth's writings have an anti-liberal programme, critical of modernity and reserved about the ultimate significance of work, Chenu is more in the spirit of the *'aggiornamiento'* which was gathering force in the Roman Catholic Church at this time: he is in favour of embracing modernity and re-valuing the importance of work.

Chenu is clear that modern work is a new phenomenon for which the current resources of the Church are insufficient to comprehend, and which therefore demands a new task: the elaboration of a proper 'theology of work'. Work in the machine age, he tells us, is 'a reality lacking anything in common with its previous character',[15] we now exist in a 'new age of man in the universe'.[16] The Biblical images of 'potter, blacksmith and peasant' cannot simply be stretched to accommodate this reality. Chenu feels such starting points doom us to a Luddite 'resentment against the machine' and a 'debatable praise of craft-working' which he regards as 'bad theology and vain romanticism' (although he does concede a certain legitimate protest underlying this against the commodification of labour).[17] The theologian can neither retreat

---

[15]   Marie-Dominique Chenu, *The Theology of Work: An Exploration* (Dublin: Gill and Son, 1963), p. 6. Part of the background to Chenu writing about work is the debate in France over the prêtres ouvriers, who flourished with considerable backing from the Dominicans from the mid-forties until the mid-fifties when they were effectively suppressed on the orders of the Vatican. See: Oscar Arnal, *Priests in Working-class Blue: The History of the Worker Priests (1943–1954)* (New York: Paulist Press, 1986), and Chenu, 'La sacerdoce des prêtres ouvriers', *La Vie Intellectuelle* February 1954, pp. 175–81.

[16]   Chenu, *The Theology of Work*, p. 10.

[17]   Ibid., p. 6.

into a interiorized spiritualism which ignores the external world of socio-economic realities (something he attributes to modern followers of Augustine, Descartes and Plato[18]); nor magisterially pronounce upon these realities without first paying attention to what they are. It is necessary, therefore, that '*sileant theologi in munere alieno*' – theologians should shut up about the affairs of others – allowing these areas a 'scientific autonomy' and awaiting the conclusions of the specialists (for example respecting the economist's choice of methods and not discussing the nature of capitalism).[19] Chenu has a definite historical model in mind for such an engagement with 'new science': the absorption of Aristotle by scholastic thought, which enables him to hold up Thomas Aquinas as a paradigm of good theological method.[20] Thomas's anthropology is celebrated for overcoming the alleged dualism of the Augustinian Platonic tradition, which is accused of instrumentalizing all material activities, ignoring their proper integrity.[21]

Within Chenu's preferred anthropology, work has 'its own value, for its own integrity' and is not merely a means to some spiritual end.[22] Work should properly possess a certain 'objectivity' without being dehumanizing, what Chenu calls a 'metaphysical disinterestedness'. Here he is reiterating the scholastic insistence that the worker should labour for the work's sake and not his own, so that the worker even learns selflessness in becoming subject to his work, the thing made.[23] This sounds similar to the modest place Barth reserves for work, yet there are significant differences in Chenu's account.

Chenu, against Barth, insists that work is not just about 'providing daily bread', meeting our basic needs for sustenance, but rather does transform personality and society, it has a cultural product, it 'creates a kind of social energy'.[24] Here, in his confidence in cultural production and progress, Chenu is obviously more sympathetic to both Whiggish Liberalism and classical Marxism than Barth. From the transition from solitary craftsman to mass production in factories, and from small business to international globalization, Chenu sees the basic law of 'socialization' at work.

This is not merely a transformation of humanity, but something much larger, even cosmic, for Chenu. Work is the means of the transformation, the humanization, of nature: 'The cosmos enters into this economy through man as a transforming force'[25] accomplishing nothing less than the 'synthesis of man and nature'[26] which will culminate in the

18 Chenu, *The Theology of Work*, p. 21.
19 Ibid., pp. 26, 42.
20 Ibid., p. 33.
21 Ibid., pp. 21–2.
22 Ibid., p. 22.
23 Ibid., pp. 19–20.
24 Ibid., p.10.
25 Ibid., p. 17.
26 Ibid., p. 29.

'complete assumption of the universe by man'.[27] Yet at the same time this humanization of nature through work is itself the fulfilment of a basic law of nature, so that Chenu can say, following Teilhard de Chardin, that the collectivization of humanity is the 'culmination of a fundamental process of grouping in the progressive elaboration of or-ganised matter', even a 'higher form of molecular cohesion on the surface of the planet'![28] Here it is difficult to avoid the overtones of somewhat far-fetched pseudo-science and an uncritical, almost social-Darwinian, celebration of 'progress'. Yet Chenu is seeking to avoid both a cold 'artificial' technology imposed upon a hostile nature, and a romantic naturalism that, reacting against this, abandons all technology. Against the latter viewpoint he insists, after Mounier, that 'man is naturally artificial'[29], his nature as *homo faber* is to make things and thus these things are properly 'natural' to him. This is presented as a new, dynamic, evolutionary understanding of the Thomist account of the relationship between Nature and Grace, and for all the unhelpful paths it leads him down, this account of humanity as naturally artificial is still an area where Chenu seems to have grasped something Barth lacked. We will return to this question of cultural production in future chapters.

The cosmic account of *homo faber* leads Chenu into territory that would have appalled Barth, to the language of co-creation. For Chenu, man *is* a 'collaborator in creation',[30] the 'co-creator... of the universe',[31] which is a 'continuous creation' rather than one completed on the sixth day.[32] The Hegelian and pantheistic overtones are hard to miss here, and the potential for this to dissolve into Fichtean celebration of the human will that even generates God is never far from the surface in passages such as the following: 'Day by day, man incorporates spirit in matter, according to his own nature, and, within the moving tide of history, *creates* the rock of eternity'.[33]

Such an account also generates an uncritical celebration of technology, modernity and progress. The hubris of claims such as 'Man fulfils himself by dominating' seems careless in the light of ecological debates, let alone the conflicts of the twentieth century. Is it really true that 'The worst setbacks and the most blameworthy misdeeds cannot halt this destiny'? Likewise Chenu is quite content to pass over phenomeno-logical critiques of the effects of industrialization such as determinism, repetition, working to time, standardization, and fatigue, dismissing them as mere 'psychological changes'.[34] He speaks without hesitation

27 Ibid., p. 73.
28 Ibid., p. 67.
29 Ibid., p. 7.
30 Ibid., p. 17.
31 Ibid., p. 73.
32 Ibid., p. 14.
33 Ibid., p. 47 (my italics).
34 Ibid., p. 19.

of 'victories over time and space' as if either was something to be 'conquered' from a Christian perspective, and goes on to celebrate the 'rationalisation of time' as obviously positive because reason is 'the highest and most certain mark of God.'[35] The only concessions to this unbridled optimism is a grudging admittance that there might be a need to 'define the limits' of the machine[36] along with the recognition that socialization can lead to an ant-heap dehumanizing existence.[37] This is to be supplemented by Christians, who are to provide the 'soul' of this socialization through a 'community consciousness' transcending competition.

Nevertheless, despite these moments of Christian humanist surface transformation, we might conclude that Chenu's earlier partial gagging of the theologians in the face of the pure 'science' of economics makes it difficult to see how one might undertake these tasks without falling into the very ideological 'spiritualizing' veneer that he condemned. More fundamentally, his rather naïve dismissal of the critical value of the tradition, combined with an implicit view of progress which virtually amounts to the historicist immanentizing of teleology, make it difficult to see how and according to which criteria one might distinguish 'bad' progress from 'good'. This last problem will emerge more acutely in our discussion of Marx. Despite these difficulties, Chenu has raised the crucial question of cultural production, which we will return to later in the work of other twentieth-century Roman Catholic writers.

LABOREM EXERCENS: THE NATURAL LAW PERSONALISM OF JOHN PAUL II

The next text we will consider is the Papal Encyclical *Laborem Exercens* issued by John Paul II (Karol Wojtyla) in 1981. This encyclical can be recognized as from the same tradition as Chenu, in the sense of its similarly 'catholic', optimistic account of human agency and correspondingly high view of the value of work. Nevertheless, there are significant differences where John Paul II seems to move towards Barth: he moderates the optimism of Chenu, and outlines a more critical stance on contemporary work and the relation between divine and human labour.

The encyclical has a very general definition of work ('any activity by man'[38]) which is then developed through a Christian humanist personalism. Thus we are told that work is unique to humans among all the animals, and that it possesses 'a particular mark of man and of

---

[35]   Chenu, *The Theology of Work*, pp. 8–9.
[36]   Ibid., p. 9.
[37]   Ibid., pp. 65, 68.
[38]   John Paul II, *Laborem Exercens* – hereafter LE – (London: Catholic Truth Society, 1981), Preface. For the personalist background to this encyclical, see Emmanuel Mounier, *Personalism*, trans. Philip Mairet (London: Routledge and Paul, 1952) and John Paul II (Karol Wojtyla), *The Acting Person*, trans. Andrzej Potocki

humanity', of a 'person operating within a community of persons'.[39] Such language of the sanctity of personhood runs through the encyclicals of John Paul II and can be traced back into his earlier philosophical writings such as *The Acting Person*, where its roots in transcendental Thomism are evident. Although this is linked with the *imago dei* and the command to subdue the earth in Genesis 1:28, the more Kantian elements of this philosophy, its stress upon rationality and autonomous choice as *definitive* of human nature, are also evident.

On the question of the relation of divine and human labour, Wojtyla is more subtle than Chenu. Even before the language of co-creation is introduced its potential for misconstrual as a Gnostic creation which requires remedying by human labour is guarded against by the reminder that even as man becomes 'more and more the master of the earth' he yet 'remains within the Creator's original ordering'.[40] This important claim sets human labour within a much more *participatory* relationship to divine labour, rather than as an extrinsicist supplementation to God's work. While this may in part be motivated by a curial hostility towards modern progressivism, we can nevertheless see here the beginnings of a correction of the uncritical modernism of Chenu by the reminder that a proper attention to historical development should not abolish our faith in the 'natural' teleology of creation, revealed and restored in Christ, by which such development is to be judged.

This more critical account of the divine-human analogy of works corresponds to a less idealized view of work: in Wojtyla's exegesis of Genesis he recognizes that the Edenic 'original blessing' of work given in the Creator's command, must be set alongside the post-lapsarian curse of Genesis 3:17–19 which sin has brought to work, introducing the element of 'toil'.[41] He continues to maintain, however, that the Fall does not obliterate the original goodness of work, and that even the toil can be redeemed and redemptive, following Aquinas's account of *bonum arduum* and the development of the virtues.[42]

The phenomenology of work is continued through the definition of three objects of labour: production for self-preservation (including familial provision); societal transformation of nature through technological production; and (most important to Wojtyla) transformation of self and society through cultural production. The last of these indicates, despite his differences from Chenu, how far Wojtyla has moved beyond Barth, and indeed Aquinas, in a positive evaluation of cultural production.

(Dordrecht: Reidel, 1979). For a range of responses to the encyclical 20 years later, see: Pontifical Council for Justice and Peace, *Work as Key to the Social Question* (Vatican City: Libreria Editrice Vaticana, 2002).

[39] LE, Preface.

[40] Ibid., # 4.

[41] Ibid., # 27.

[42] Ibid., # 9.

Like Chenu, Wojtyla is interested in the contemporary situation of work ('the objective dimension' as he calls it), or the problem of technology. Yet he differs from him in his insistence that all the changes to work, the great transformations from agriculture to industry to information, from manual to mechanical to intellectual, do not alter the essential meaning of work and, therefore, do not require the development of a new theology of work to supplant the ideas found in the scriptures. Instead he wants to affirm that, despite the experience within industrial society of humanity ceasing to be the agent of work and becoming merely a cog or supervisor of a machine which seems to be the real agent, 'the proper subject of work continues to be man'.[43] Even when it might appear to have taken over, we should not forget that technology is a creature of human making and as such should remain as 'instruments', tools to serve us not to be served. This is a much more careful account recognizing the ambivalence of technology than that of Chenu.

This brings us to the 'subjective dimension of work', the philosophical foundation of the encyclical. Wojtyla implies this 'subjective dimension' is the special prerogative of theologians, from which they can comment upon the scientific conclusions of other specialists who deal with the objective dimension (economists, engineers, historians and so forth). In what does this subjective dimension consist? In the personalist claim that the dignity of work depends not upon the 'kind of work being done' but upon the fact that the agent doing the working is a 'person'.[44] The meaning and value of work, the values informing its properly moral ordering, derive from the meaning of personhood. It is the subjective dimension, not the objective dimension that constitutes the 'very ethical nature of work' for Wojtyla. These dimensions are then hierarchically ordered, according to the priority of mind over matter. This produces the moral imperative at the heart of the encyclical: 'work is "for man" and not man "for work"'.[45]

Again we might detect Kantian overtones in the location of values within the interiority of human subjectivity rather than also in the external world of things, and in the argument that persons are always 'ends in themselves' which must not be instrumentalized. Yet the encyclical regards such ideas as uniquely Christian. Indeed Wojtyla claims that, in this prioritizing of the subjective, Christianity brought about a significant break from the valuation of labour in antiquity.[46] It is even suggested that this transvaluation of values goes right back to Christ, who as a carpenter demonstrated that even God is not above engaging in manual labour.[47] Here the implication is that Christianity is historically responsible for subverting classical class distinctions to generate an egalitarian society.

[43]   LE, Preface, # 5.
[44]   Ibid., # 6.
[45]   Ibid.
[46]   Ibid.
[47]   Ibid.

The personalist phenomenology of work leads Wojtyla to criticize various ideologies and practices under the labels of 'materialism' and 'economism'.[48] Both make the mistake, for Wojtyla, of prioritizing the objective side of work and subordinating the worker, reducing humans to tools, and causing a 'reversal of the order laid down from the beginning by the words of the book of Genesis'.[49] Wojtyla calls this domination of the objective over the subjective the true sense of 'capitalism', whether it issues in the abuse of workers by the tyranny of the liberal free market, or by equally tyrannous state monopolies and collectivism. This is how the Church's position is distinguished from both the 'rigid capitalism' of the West and the state communism of the Eastern bloc countries.[50] Against the Right, Wojtyla affirms the priority of Labour over Capital; and against the Left, the right to private ownership even in the case of the means of production.[51] The right to private property is maintained using personalist arguments – the worker should not be depersonalized by working for some distant end or greater good which is beyond his grasp, as in centralized bureaucratic state enterprises; rather she needs to retain a sense of her own initiative and to experience the fruits of her labour. The right to private property is also not absolute, but, following St Thomas, subordinate to the common good, which generates the imperative to increase the socialization of capital by worker participation and ownership.

This is not all the practical wisdom the encyclical contains. On the basis of Christian humanist values an agenda for reform is set out, using the language of rights and responsibilities. We are told of the right of workers to employment and their obligation to work.[52] Attention is devoted to the duties of direct and indirect employers (businesses and the wider societies respectively), the need for a just wage, the importance of unions, the rights of immigrants and the disabled with respect to work.[53]

The encyclical concludes with the so-called 'spirituality of work'. This is seen as a task of the Church, although it is difficult to pin down exactly what is meant. We have already indicated how the encyclical has been more careful than Chenu over a number of points, but it is now appropriate to raise some criticisms arising from this 'spirituality' section. Given that this is where most of the talk of God and Christ comes in the encyclical, it is difficult to avoid the conclusion that it is tacitly accepting under this term 'spirituality' a modern agenda relegating serious theological reflection to an optional postscriptum for the devout. It is hard to see how the ideas that emerge here have shaped or driven the rest of the discussion, indeed they seem entirely incidental to it, while the

[48] Ibid., # 7.
[49] Ibid.
[50] Ibid., # 14.
[51] Ibid., # 12, 14.
[52] Ibid., # 18, 16.
[53] Ibid., # 17, 19, 20, 22, 23.

rest of the encyclical, with its liberal rights humanism, is capable of standing alone. What we seem to have here is a decadent natural law tradition of moral theology that seeks universal assent by attempting to discover a universally evident moral law, *apart from* Christ and the Church, through a loose appeal to creation and 'the way things are'. Hauerwas is surely right to point to the deistic direction of such a strategy, and we might also be critical of the ethical inadequacies of this Kantian natural law personalism.[54] In defining humanity in terms of rationality and freedom it cannot make sense of the traditional Christian valuation of those who lack the fullness of either, such as children and the disabled.[55] In excessively exalting mind over the material, which is then relegated to an inert realm of 'stuff' devoid of value, the encyclical consolidates the language of 'domination' which not only fails to recognize the legitimate ways in which the worker is shaped by the object of his work, but also has suspicious overtones of tyranny towards the non-human creation. Even the language of rights and responsibilities, where Wojtyla achieves such a positive agenda for the humanization of labour, seems incapable of grasping the full ethical complexity of work, beyond the minimal defending of competing territories of self-interest.

A further question concerns the style of the encyclical, which is basically deontological, setting forth moral imperatives to be obeyed. But because it is claiming that these are founded upon the nature of things, they are presented as descriptive, in a manner that can seem guilty of ideological deception. For example, when we read: 'capital cannot be separated from labour; in no way can labour be opposed to capital or capital to labour'[56] it is unclear whether this is a descriptive claim about what is possible or an affirmation of how things should be. At one level this sentence is protesting against the Marxist insistence upon the necessary opposition of capital and labour which frequently instantiates this opposition. Yet this should not obscure the fact that capital *can* be opposed to labour and often is, and to deny this is simply to encourage it.[57] The encyclical is ambiguous on this point in a way that Hauerwas does not recognize. I am more inclined than he to interpret Wojtyla's assertions as attempts to instantiate the ideals they describe rather than simply re-describe that which is already.[58] Nevertheless one must recognize the undoubted romanticism in some of the

---

[54] Stanley Hauerwas, 'Work as Co-Creation: A Critique of a Remarkably Bad Idea', in John Houck and Oliver Williams (eds.), *Co-Creation and Capitalism* (London: University Press of America, 1983), p. 43.

[55] I think Hauerwas is wrong to accuse Wojtyla of ignoring this question; he would have been wiser to say that because such realities do not make sense within the moral framework underlying the encyclical they require a special provision that thus seems an arbitrary imposition without connection to the rest of the encyclical's thinking.

[56] LE, # 13.

[57] Hauerwas, pp. 53, 54.

[58] Ibid., p. 49; Hauerwas does however welcome what he regards as the more sober remarks on the just wage.

descriptions of work in the encyclical, particularly the language of Christ the carpenter and toil being a participation in the sufferings of Christ, and the underlying danger of thinking that inhuman work need only be transformed 'subjectively'.

In conclusion, Wojtyla offers a more satisfactory framework for thinking the participatory analogy of divine and human labour than Barth or Chenu, and he goes further than either in his detailed critical analysis of and response to contemporary work. Yet we have sought to indicate why his personalism does not go far enough, leaving work as still too 'natural'. The encyclical lacks a full account of the *theological* transformation of work, the difference made for example by the Sabbath, as Barth hinted. As a result the encyclical suffers still from an excessive 'activism', and has nothing to say to the contemporary idolatrous cult of work as the measure of all value. Hence, even if Hauerwas errs too much in the alternative direction of total passivity, there is nevertheless some truth to his claim that the encyclical seems to be saying 'exactly the opposite' of Genesis, the good news of which is a command to *rest*.[59]

MIROSLAV VOLF: PNEUMATOLOGICAL TRANSFORMATION

Miroslav Volf's *Work in the Spirit* is the Protestant equivalent of Chenu, in that it is a book purely about the theology of work. It belongs within the Protestant tradition, yet in contrast to Barth it is more open both to modernity and to more traditionally 'catholic' positions. The book also has a revisionary intention and sets out to replace much traditional Protestant thinking on work. The novel approach, based upon eschatology and pneumatology, God's future and the activity of the Spirit, which Volf sets out seeks to build upon recent philosophies of work, while overcoming their differences. In particular he seems to be attempting to mediate between ideologies of the right and left. The revisionary intention to provide a 'new' theology to respond to the contemporary situation means that, as with Chenu, that situation itself is broadly accepted and not really questioned.

The book begins with a general, pre-theological, account of work, before offering the 'theology' in the second half. We are told that 'the purpose of a theology of work is to interpret, evaluate, and facilitate the transformation of human work'.[60] We shall see that this conception of the project entails the presumption that there is such a general and neutral phenomenon as 'work', prior to interpretation, which theology can 'evaluate' secondarily. It also implies a certain model of transformation, concerned with legislation and the political programmes of central governments.

59 Ibid., p. 45.
60 Miroslav Volf, *Work in the Spirit* (Oxford: Oxford University Press, 1991), p. 7.

The first evidence of this adoption of presuppositions from the main-stream societal debate comes in the opening 'definition' of work, which by its very existence seems to specify in advance the shape of the exploration of the nature of work and foreclose certain avenues of interrogation. The most common popular usage of the term, to signify employment, paid labour or occupation, is rejected for its exclusion of certain forms of labour such as housework, and more fundamentally for its 'alienating' reduction of work to earning; yet there is a persistent sense that it is this modern usage that continues to predominate through-out the book. The actual definition which we are given is:

> Work is honest, purposeful, and methodologically specified social activity whose primary goal is the creation of products or states of affairs that can satisfy the needs of working individuals or their co-creatures, or (if primarily an end in itself) activity that is necessary in order for acting individuals to satisfy their needs apart from the need for the activity itself.[61]

This definition is summarized by the claim that work is 'instrumental activity', which enables the inclusion of pleasant activities that might otherwise be regarded as leisurely, providing they are undertaken not for their own sake. Thus the distinction between work and hobby is located not in the objective form of the activity, nor in the subjective appreci-ation or otherwise of the activity, but in its intention or purpose. Volf admits that this division between work and leisure is somewhat 'blurry' and it will not always be possible to clearly distinguish in every case, yet it is clear that this negative definition (work is not-leisure) remains integral to him.

Volf's basic acceptance of the economic status quo is made explicit when he declares his commitment to market economies and democratic planning. This will be the context of the book's investigation: the eco-nomic and political realities of the Western democracies. Volf is not trying to imagine a fundamentally different economic order, but how to shape a more just national economic policy, informed by Christian ethics. Such a policy will be concerned primarily with individual free-dom, meeting the basic needs of all, and preventing unsustainable dam-age to our natural resources.[62] Volf offers some justification for his support of central planning against the ideologues of the absolute mar-ket, yet is less forthcoming on why he does not interrogate the market's functioning more fundamentally, or why he presumes planning is the appropriate response to its problems.

Volf identifies the contemporary problem of work, similarly to Chenu, as one of rapid, substantial transformation: from societies based upon

[61] Miroslav Volf, *Work in the Spirit* (Oxford: Oxford University Press, 1991), pp. 10–11.
[62] Ibid., pp. 18–20.

agricultural and manual labour, through processes of mechanization and automation, to industrial and finally information economies. The transformation of the worker from artisan to machine operator and then to machine supervisor is traced as often involving 'deskilling' and an increasing detachment from the process of production. These transformations have contributed to a 'crisis of work'[63] manifest in phenomena such as child labour, mass unemployment, discrimination, dehumanization and ecological crisis. Volf rejects any attempts to locate the blame for this crisis primarily in economic systems or technological developments. While admitting that both can facilitate crisis, he maintains they are fundamentally neutral and non-determining; rather, moral responsibility lies ultimately with 'personal causes',[64] that is real human beings, employers, employees, consumers, legislators. Here Volf exhibits a strong moral personalism similar to Wojtyla.

Under dominant understandings of work Volf considers the theories of labour of Adam Smith and Karl Marx, as founding fathers of right and left wing economics respectively. He insists that Marx was no more the enemy of individual freedom and creativity than Smith was an absolute egoist, and also notes the centrality of labour for both thinkers. Nevertheless he also highlights the considerable differences between the two: For Smith work is a necessary evil, a means to an end – the rest that all people would prefer. Hence the division of labour and various sacrifices are necessary and work is useful rather than inherently dignified. Work for Marx by contrast should always be an end in itself rather than just a means, so the division of labour and the sacrifice of self-interest might one day be overcome. Smith's exaltation of self-interest and the virtues of the entrepreneur are rejected by Volf as a debasement of human nature, reducing people to means, while the plausibility of Marx's Romantic overcoming of the division of labour is also questioned.

This leads into Volf's own constructive theology of work. Here he begins, like Chenu, with criticism of much traditional theologizing about work. In particular Volf rejects the subordination of the *vita activa* to the *vita contemplativa* in the classical Christian tradition as an 'illegitimate intrusion of Greek anthropology into Christian theology'.[65]

While not wishing to abandon the best of this tradition, Volf believes it to be too negative and lacking in a truly positive account of the nature of work. Volf proposes his own novel relocation of the theology of work: whereas traditionally it has been placed with much Christian anthropology under the doctrine of creation, Volf suggests we would be better to look to the *new* creation. Here he is following Moltmann's claim that Christian faith is fundamentally eschatological.[66] Such an orientation to

---

[63] Ibid., p. 35.
[64] Ibid., p. 43.
[65] Ibid., p. 70.
[66] Ibid., p. 79. Cf. Jürgen Moltmann, *Theology of Hope*, trans. James Leitch (London: SCM, 1969).

the future rather than the past also helps to make his theology transformative and ethically normative in intent, it is about how work *should* be.

Volf goes on to elaborate his account of eschatology in very physical, corporeal terms, against some modern tendencies to spiritualize or moralize the eschaton. He insists on the 'earthly locale of the kingdom of God', the saints of the book of Revelation dwell not in the new heaven, but in the new earth.[67] Faced with the question of the continuity or discontinuity between this new order and the current old order, Volf argues for the *transformatio mundi* rather than the *annihilatio mundi*, which he claims, along with incorporeal accounts of the soul's life in Heaven, have contributed to a devaluing of God's creation and a neglect of the biblical tradition with its emphasis on the resurrection of the body and the liberation of the whole creation (cf. Romans 8:21).[68] Such a perspective seeks to offer a new and positive angle on our works, in particular through the idea that in some sense our works will follow us into the glorified world (cf. Revelations 14:13 and Ephesians 6:8). Volf asks whether Gutenberg glorified would be Gutenberg without any eschatological relation to his famous discovery[69] and concludes that 'human work is ultimately significant not only because it contributes to the future environment of human beings, but also because it leaves an indelible imprint on their personalities.'[70]

This leads into a discussion of the question of cooperation with God, which, as we have already seen, is a highly contested area. Volf claims that there is a recent consensus on cooperation with God as the deepest meaning of work, before delineating two models of *cooperatio dei*: preservation or cooperation with God in *creatio continua*; and 'proleptic co-operation in God's eschatological *transformatio mundi*.'[71] In keeping with his eschatological orientation to the future, Volf prefers the latter model, although he stresses that they are not really alternatives and that his preference should not be understood as implying that human work can create God's new world, which is a gift coming down from Heaven.[72] However, while the consummation belongs to God alone, our 'waiting' for this is not simply inactive, but rather is itself a form of labouring: '"Kingdom-participation" is not contrary, but complimentary, to "kingdom expectation" and is its necessary consequence.'[73] Volf's preference for the eschatological model of cooperation is justified on the basis that this has been largely ignored previously by the

---

[67] Volf, p. 94.
[68] Ibid., pp. 89–96.
[69] Ibid., p. 97.
[70] Ibid., p. 98.
[71] Ibid., p. 99.
[72] Volf also notes the difference between God's creation *ex nihilo* and our work signified in the Genesis narrative by the difference between *bara* and *asa*, at the same time as a certain participatory analogy between the two is suggested.
[73] Volf, pp. 99–100.

tradition, and, more significantly, that a purely protological theology of work based on creation is inadequate for interpreting modern work, which is more oriented towards endless dynamic transformation than mere static preservation.

This eschatological orientation then leads into the book's key argument: for a pneumatology of work, as implied in the title and perhaps in keeping with the author's Pentecostalist background. Work is properly understood as under the Spirit of God because the Spirit is the 'first fruits' or down payment of the future salvation (cf. Romans 8:23).[74] Volf seeks to resist the restriction of the operation of the Spirit to the interior world in much Protestant thought, which leaves the external world as the sphere of the 'old man', unredeemed. His alternative account of work in the Spirit is then developed through the proposal that the Biblical concept of diverse *charisms*, or gifts, should replace the 'static' protological language of *vocation* which has dominated much Christian thinking about labour and occupations, particularly in the tradition of the magisterial reformers, such as Luther and the *vocatio externa*.[75]

It should be clear that Volf's theology of work is concerned to avoid accusations of being ideology, and so the exalted language of divine cooperation is complemented by the argument that precisely this analogy ensures a divine *judgement* upon human work alongside its heavenly goal, a judgement that concerns not only the intention or the product of the work, but its form as well: 'All work that contradicts the new creation is meaningless; all work that corresponds to the new creation is ultimately meaningful.'[76] This is illustrated by using the Pauline language of the fires of judgement consuming the works of false evangelists like straw, while purifying the works of true evangelists like gold (cf. 1 Corinthians 3:12).[77]

This is an impressive theology of work with much to commend it. The eschatological turn succeeds in moving away from the problems of the Natural Law tradition noted in *Laborem Exercens*, adding a more properly evangelical note throughout. Likewise the critique of the Lutheran *vocatio externa*, itself a radical further secularizing of the Natural Law tradition, with its political quietism and lack of transformative potential, is powerful and persuasive. The account of the survival of works after the eschaton provides a more profound goal or *telos* for our works than the mere satisfaction of animal needs in Barth, without succumbing to the uncritical ideological idolizing of work in Chenu. More impressively the linking of divine and human work follows *Laborem Exercens* in avoiding the absolute disjunction of Barth with

---

[74] Ibid., p. 102.
[75] Ibid., pp. 104–6. He claims the idea of using charisms in this way is suggested in Vatican II's *Gaudium et Spes*, but was not taken up.
[76] Volf, p. 121.
[77] Ibid., p. 120.

his secularizing dualism of work and service, and the promethean identification and supplementation in Chenu.

Yet somehow this theology of the relation of divine and human labour
does not seem significantly to affect Volf's phenomenology of work, or
his proposals for the transformation of work. As we have already seen,
he is willing to bless uncritically the recent transformations from static
life-long 'ontological' vocations towards greater 'charismatic' flexibility
and mobility, without questioning what might be lost in terms of security
and identity. Likewise his rejection of the traditional priority of the
contemplative life over the active life leaves him, like Chenu and to a
lesser extent Wojtyla, without any counsel or comfort to offer to those
ensnared by the idolatry of the world of total work. On mundane work,
Volf fails to deliver the goods of his theological vision. Like Wojtyla, he
has many admirable proposals for the just ordering, limitation and
remuneration of labour, yet these seem to be based purely upon a
naturalist humanism, without any vision of theological transformation
beyond this.[78] The most we have is a few comments towards the end of
the book when, apparently disregarding his initial definition of work,
Volf returns to the problems of technocratic societies and begins to
imagine, following Kant and Marx and against Taylorism, a more
autotelic vision of work beyond instrumentality.[79] Yet disappointingly
these comments are not developed.

'NATURALISTIC' VIEWS OF LABOUR AND THE QUESTION OF NECESSITY AND SUPERFLUITY

Certain patterns emerge from our consideration of the above four figures: On the question of any cooperation or analogy between God's
work and our work, we have on the one side the radical disjunction of
Barth, and on the other Chenu's account of human labour as a continuation or even supplementation of divine labour, corresponding perhaps
to the extremes in the debates between Protestants and Catholics over
salvation and works (although Chenu's position is more immediately
influenced by ontologies of labour in Romanticism and Marxism, and
Barth's by his rejection of the same). Wojtyla and Volf can be seen to
represent something of an ecumenical convergence, with a more participatory account, in keeping with the Biblical and Patristic sources, that
avoids Chenu's divinization of labour on the one hand, and Barth's
secularization on the other.

Barth and Chenu offer phenomenologies of human labour, following
from their theologies, which are equally polarized. For Barth, work (as
distinct from service) serves the purely utilitarian natural end of keeping
us alive; while, for Chenu, work achieves the transformation of the
universe through culture. As is beginning to be evident, the secular

---

[78] Volf, pp. 129–54.
[79] Ibid., pp. 195–201.

debates about labour are usually lurking in the background here. For example, we might say that Barth's view of work as a grim necessity, purely serving subsistence and making possible leisure, has genuine parallels with the views of Adam Smith; while Chenu's account of human labour as creating our nature through the 'surplus' of the cultural has similarities to the position of Marx. Volf and Wojtyla again represent attempts to synthesize or mediate these two perspectives, usually proposing limits to the potential of infinite production by an appeal to the conflicts of 'natural needs'.

Various problems persist in these approaches. None of the authors seem to have engaged sufficiently deeply with the debates to which they are reacting, or to draw out the more radical potential in their own ontological claims for human work. They seem often to leave their concepts of work largely untouched by their theological claims, reverting instead to naturalist and personalist understandings. Chenu, Wojtyla and Volf in particular, despite their stronger sense of the *analogia actionis*, suffer from an uncritical view of progress and an acceptance of the modern dominance of the *vita activa*, which leaves them with very little to say to the modern idolatry of work. Barth alone, despite his apparent secularizing of work, has anything like a distinctively theological critique of modern work through the importance he gives to the Sabbath. If this were to be followed through with a theological vision for the transformation of work, in a manner Barth is unwilling to do, we might begin to see how our very categories of work and rest or work and play, of necessity and excess, of the end for which we are working become transformed and subverted. We will return to these questions later, but for now we must consider more deeply what might be distinctive about the situation of *modern* work to which our authors have been reacting, and what relation theology might have to this situation.

What has a man from all the toil and strain with which he toils beneath the sun? For all his days are full of pain, and his work is a vexation; even in the night his mind does not rest. This also is vanity.

2

Utility as the Spirit of Capitalism

Max Weber's Diagnosis of Modern Work

We have explored the attempts of some twentieth-century theologians from a variety of perspectives to make sense of the phenomenon of work, and have seen how these interpretations were largely responses to the peculiar problems presented by the forms which work has taken in the modern Western world. They are all very specific interventions in contemporary debates about modern and largely Western problems, and in this sense are all theologies of *modern* work. Having suggested some weaknesses in these accounts, I will now shift attention away from theological literature to consider further what might be the distinctive nature of modern work, from a historical and theoretical perspective. In this chapter I will explore Max Weber's account of modern work, given in terms of the 'Spirit of Capitalism', considering the source of this concept, what it means and refers to, how exactly it operates in his thought, and ultimately whether it might be helpful in our efforts to understand our own situation.[1]

I will argue that the 'spirit of capitalism' for Weber is *utility*, and that he derives this idea from the discourse of Political Economy. This discourse seems to be the ideological self-expression of the modern industrialists, and yet in many ways does offer a plausible description of the historical, social and economic processes of modernity. However Weber strips the veneer of 'naturalism' from the Political Economists' account

---

[1]   The literature on Weber is vast, but I am focussing on a close reading of *The Protestant Ethic and the Spirit of Capitalism* – hereafter simply 'Weber' – (London: Routledge, 2001) in order to engage constructively with its characterization of capitalism, rather than offering a systematic account of Weber's thought, or even attempting to cover exhaustively the debate that this text has spawned. Gordon Marshall, *In Search of the Spirit of Capitalism: An Essay on Max Weber's Protestant Ethic Thesis* (Aldershot: Gregg Revivals, 1993) provides a good critical summary of this debate, while Reinhard Bendix, *Max Weber: An Intellectual Portrait* (London: Methuen, 1966) gives a good overview of Weber's thought, and Raymond Aron, *Main Currents in Sociological Thought* (London: Penguin, 1990) provides a helpful comparison of Weber with Durkheim.

of utility by situating it in a historical narrative of the emergence of modernity. Furthermore, he crucially links this rise of the spirit of capitalism with disenchantment and the erosion of traditional accounts of the human good. While Weber's historical thesis has undergone much crude criticism in terms of necessary historical causality, and it is also true that at times he seems to be operating with a grand typology of the triumph of reason over tradition, yet he himself has momentary insights that count against these interpretations of his work. In these moments he points towards the *perennial* nature of the spirit of instrumental rational utility, against any simple discontinuity in modernity. We might develop this, following Tawney, by saying that the real shift in modernity is primarily at the cultural-theoretical level: ideas shift to create a true transvaluation of vice into virtue, which then opens the way to the ever more unchecked rise of utility in socio-economic practice. This in turn deconstructs the simple opposition of reason and tradition that some commentators see in Weber, suggesting rather that instrumental reason is only one form of rationality, and can itself only ever be secondary, parasitic or derivative, operating within a larger cultural framework.

THE REVALUATION OF WORK IN THE REFORMATION

Weber's analysis of modern views of work famously links their emergence with certain religious positions, particularly with the rational-ascetic ethics of second generation Calvinism. We will return later to the question of Weber's primary thesis about the influence of the Protestant work ethic on the production of something which he calls the 'spirit of capitalism'. Meanwhile, it is worth drawing attention to much broader shifts in the *theological* view of work, the valuation of labour, which Weber helpfully highlights and summarizes.

These cultural shifts, documented across a range of literary genres from theological treatises to popular literature, are clearly associated with the Reformation in Europe, although they are not limited to any of its various theological strands. Not only this, but there is at least some evidence that they are not just confined to the Protestant Churches, but also found a home in more diluted forms among various currents of the counter-reformation within the Roman Catholic Church.[2] We are not concerned here either with whether they corresponded to changes of perspective among the non-literary masses of society, or whether they issued in new socio-economic practices, but simply as novel intellectual currents, and as such they are largely incontestable.

The shift consists of a radical revaluation of human labour, evident particularly in comments on the monastic life. It is certainly possible to find many examples of pre-Reformation injunctions to diligence and the avoidance of sloth, just as there remain authors afterwards who exalt a

---

[2] For example, the Jesuits.

life of leisure. Nevertheless, there is an undeniable shift in thinking at this time whereby the almost uncontested ancient and medieval view that the *vita activa* is subordinate to the *vita contemplativa* is gradually abandoned. Whereas previously labour was situated primarily in relation to contemplation and only secondarily against laziness, the life of labour comes to be seen not as an unfortunate necessity for some, but a noble obligation for all. Labour replaces contemplation as the highest form of life, while the latter is demoted to become its antithesis, identified with sloth. Weber does not argue for these shifts, but merely presumes them to be obvious. We encounter these transformations in his chapter on Luther, for instance, where they form the background against which he introduces his controversial thesis about the Protestant idea of 'calling'. One thing, Weber tells us, was 'unquestionably new': 'the valuation of the fulfilment of duty in worldly affairs as the highest form which the moral activity of the individual could assume.'[3] This is a 'central dogma of all Protestant denominations' and is opposed to the traditional Catholic distinction of the ethical life into the obligatory *praecepta* applying to all, and the voluntary and supererogatory *consilia* taken on by the vowed religious.[4] The rejection of monasticism within Protestantism embodied a theoretical shift whereby the otherworldly asceticism that was part of the worldview of medieval Christendom was abolished. Salvation now had to be worked out *in* this world, not by withdrawing from it. For perhaps the first time in history an ideology seemed to have gained the upper hand that reversed the aristocratic-traditional opposition of labour to virtue and nobility, and instead linked them.[5] Weber notes in an important passage that this departure from traditional thinking occurred gradually during Luther's career:

> At first, quite in harmony with the prevailing tradition of the Middle Ages, as represented, for example, by Thomas Aquinas, he thought of activity in the world as a thing of the flesh, even though willed by God. It is the indispensable natural condition of a life of faith, but in itself, like eating and drinking, morally neutral. But with the development of the conception of *sola fide* in all its consequences, and its logical result, the increasingly sharp emphasis against the Catholic *consilia evangelica* of the monks as dictates of the devil, the calling grew in importance. The monastic life is not only quite devoid of value as a means of justification before God, but he also looks upon its renunciation of the duties of this world as the product of selfishness, withdrawing from temporal

[3] Weber, p. 40.
[4] Ibid.
[5] I am grateful to Tim Jenkins's unpublished lecture *Weber, or Tabu, Modernity and the Scientific Mind* for drawing to my attention this anti-aristocratic element to the Protestant view of work according to Weber, and its virus-like quality.

obligations. In contrast, labour in a calling appears to him as the outward expression of brotherly love.[6]

Later Weber sums up the difference in perspective very evocatively by contrasting the conclusion of Dante's *Divine Comedy* with Milton's *Paradise Lost*: whereas the former ends in the contemplation of the Beatific vision, the latter concludes with Adam and Eve setting out into the world that lies before them.[7] The turn from the otherworldly to the this-worldly, from passive contemplation to action, could not be more obvious.

Weber goes on to indicate why this shift in the hierarchies of value does not immediately issue by itself in the 'Protestant work ethic' proper, let alone the 'spirit of capitalism', within the Lutheran tradition. Luther's economic conservatism, emotionalism, and perhaps most especially hostility to 'salvation by works', prevents this developing into the rational this-worldly asceticism that Weber will find in Calvinism. The Calvinist doctrines of predestination and works as proofs of election will, he believes, be preconditions for this further development to take place. Nevertheless the momentous significance of the dethronement of the *vita contemplativa* from the pinnacle of the hierarchy of values by the *vita activa*, can be seen from the earliest days of the Reformation, throughout Protestant thinking.

Thus it is not long before not only monasticism is subjected to the censure of uselessness, but many other 'non-functional' areas of life as well. For later generations of Puritans, Weber observes, 'not leisure and enjoyment, but only activity serves to increase the glory of God.' Thus, waste of time becomes the deadliest of sins: 'Loss of time through sociability, idle talk, luxury, even more sleep than is necessary for health...is worthy of absolute moral condemnation.'[8] Activities that we might characterize as not rationally useful, with little purpose beyond themselves, often notable for immediate quasi-aesthetic, intrinsic pleasurability, are suspect for this worldview.

Whereas these areas of life are devalued, labour, formerly regarded as a misfortune, part of the consequence of the Fall, and the lot of the poor, is exalted. This is not simply the extension of the monastic ethos, for which labour was an ascetic technique for the subduing of the flesh, but something more than this: 'Labour came to be considered in itself the end of life, ordained as such by God...Unwillingness to work is symptomatic of the lack of grace.'[9] As Weber rightly points out, the difference from the standard medieval perspective (or for that matter that of Antiquity) could not be more pronounced. For Thomas Aquinas, the Pauline injunction that 'He who will not work shall not eat' is not

---

[6]   Weber, pp. 40–1.
[7]   Ibid., pp. 46–7.
[8]   Ibid., p. 104.
[9]   Ibid., p. 105.

interpreted as an unconditional obligation for all, as with the Puritans. Rather he argues that this applies to humanity as a whole, not to every individual. Thus those able to live off their own means without working, and of course vowed contemplatives, were explicitly exempt from the command to work.[10] Behind the Protestant insistence on work being required of everyone, the language of the 'calling' being extended to non-religious spheres of life, and the idea of work as a 'proof of election', lies the deeper change of the revaluation of work as something worthwhile *in itself*, not for the sake of something else.

If Weber is correct in his diagnosis of the newly exalted symbolic placing and value accorded to labour at the origins of modernity, then we can proceed to ask what, according to Weber, distinctively characterizes this 'labour', what shape it takes, meaning it has, novelty it possesses. To answer this brings us to the question of the 'spirit of capitalism'.

THE NATURE OF MODERN LABOUR: THE 'SPIRIT OF CAPITALISM'

Weber's account of the spirit of capitalism is consistent, but not systematic, and so must be gathered from various observations. Here we will focus on *The Protestant Work Ethic and the Spirit of Capitalism* to argue that the distinguishing features of modern capitalist labour for Weber are: active-instrumentalism, transcendental-rational formalism, 'unnatural' and anti-eudaemonist asceticism, and anti-traditionalism. Let us look a little further at each of these in turn.

Active-instrumentalism: The active pursuit of profit by any means

To say that labour is active might seem to be tautological, yet we have seen that this elevation of the active was already a departure from the earlier tradition which saw ordinary labour as subordinate to the unchanging active-passive intellectual contemplation of God. This could be further expanded by the observation that modern labour for Weber is concerned with the organization and transformation of material things; it is *technological* rather than the labour of mere subsistence. It is active and oriented towards the world, in a way quite different from, for instance, the passive and otherworldly mysticism and emotivism which Weber sees in Lutheran Pietism.[11] The spirit of capitalism is directed to the sphere of the world, but with a certain detachment from the world that transcends the simultaneity of production and consumption in animal labour. Instrumentality (*Zweckrationalität*) expresses this departure from subsistence well, in that the goal of the activity is no longer immediately present in the action, nor even partially inherent in it, but

---

[10]   Ibid., pp.105–6.
[11]   Ibid., p. 68.

rather utterly extrinsic to it, and often quite distant. The form of the action is completely independent from its goal, and indeed 'means' and 'ends' can be connected quite arbitrarily. Hence labour is *instrumentalized* as merely the means to a certain end. This disjunction is particularly suited to large scale cooperative complex tasks, or to long-term projects, where planning is required. Modern scientific-technological advances are not accidental to the instrumental rationality of modern labour but are, according to Weber, integral to it:

> Now the peculiar modern Western form of capitalism has been, at first sight, strongly influenced by the developments of technical possibilities. Its rationality is today essentially dependent on the calculability of the most important technical factors. But this means fundamentally that it is dependent on the peculiarities of modern science, especially the natural sciences based on mathematics and exact and rational experiment.[12]

The spirit of modern capitalism has a definitely practical orientation, rather than theoretical.

Transcendental-rational formalism: The rationally calculating pursuit of profit

If the spirit of capitalism is practical for Weber, then it is also 'rational'. Instrumental reason is characterized by planning and organization rather than spontaneity or recklessness. This is illustrated in the 'provisional description of the spirit of capitalism' taken from the writings of Benjamin Franklin, which stresses carefulness, punctuality and the quantification of time as money.[13] This is also evident in Weber's later 'author's introduction' (1920) where 'rationalism' is repeatedly used to distinguish what is novel about modern Western capitalism.[14] Here Weber points to rationalization in the development of modern Western legal and administrative structures, as well as the separation of corporate and personal property, a stable continuous market, and modern book-keeping, which all combine with the 'rational ethics of ascetic Protestantism' to bring about the rise of 'a very different form of capitalism which has appeared nowhere else: the rational capitalistic organisation of (formally) free labour.'[15] By this date it can be claimed Weber

---

[12] Weber, p. xxxvii.
[13] Ibid., pp. 14–15.
[14] Ibid., pp. xxxi, xxxii, ff. Gordon Marshall frequently protests against commentators reading the *Protestant Ethic* essay (1909) through the later introduction that Weber added (1920), yet I remain unconvinced by his arguments because the large concerns and qualifications made in the introduction seem not to be as entirely absent from the main essay as he would have us believe.
[15] Weber, pp. xxxix, xxxiv.

had developed some of the intuitions evident in the original *Protestant Ethic* essay, through his studies in the comparative sociology of religions, into a distinctive philosophy of Western history based upon the central idea of 'rationalization'. The emergence of the spirit of capitalism is a 'question of the peculiar rationalism of Western culture.'[16]

In emphasizing the importance of rational calculation (*Rechnenhaftigkeit*) to the spirit of capitalism, Weber was developing an insight he had gained during early studies of the differing patterns of behaviour on the stock exchanges.[17] Here he had noted two different forms of self-interest: that of the risk-taking adventurers, on one hand, and of the cautious, prudential businessmen, on the other. He believed these constituted two quite distinct forms of capitalism. Greed, looting, gambling and exploitation are not original to modernity, indeed 'the greed of the Chinese Mandarin, the old Roman aristocrat, or the modern peasant, can stand up to any comparison'![18] Yet while 'the *auri sacra fames* [the greed for gold] is as old as the history of man', Weber believes that 'those who submitted to it without reserve as an uncontrolled impulse . . . were by no means the representatives of that attitude of mind from which the specifically modern capitalist spirit as a mass phenomenon is derived'.[19] Whereas the adventure capitalist is a phenomenon found in all cultures at all times, Weber claimed the rational bourgeois capitalist is the distinctively modern and Western capitalist: 'the risk-minimising though relentlessly profit-maximalising strategist'.[20] It is he who, as in the writings of Franklin, represents the spirit of modern capitalism for Weber: rational calculation not gambling.

In all this Weber's Neo-Kantian influences (through Rickert and others) can be felt: the spirit of modern capitalism has something like the empty, contentless formalism of Kantian practical reason. All substantive concerns, all value judgements and considerations of communal goods, are excluded from consideration, as are all questions of motivation or desire. The spirit of modern capitalism appears to be utterly value-free, without substantive commitments, neutral with regard to the question of human flourishing. This follows from its pure instrumentality; it is a concern with method regardless of goals, means not ends.

Therefore, when Weber introduces the spirit of capitalism through the illustrations from the writings of Franklin, he speaks of the earning of more and more money as the *summum bonum* of this ethic, before commenting that this 'is thought of so purely as an end in itself, that from the point of view of the happiness of, or utility to, the single individual, it appears entirely transcendental.'[21] The spirit of capitalism

---

[16]   Ibid, p. xxxviii.
[17]   Marshall, pp. 31–2. See also Bendix, pp. 13–48.
[18]   Weber, p. 21.
[19]   Ibid., p. 22.
[20]   Marshall, p. 44; cf. Weber, p. xxxvii.
[21]   Ibid., p. 18.

concerns not so much utility for this or that, but utility itself, the means severed from all concern with ends, becoming itself the end instead: *the pursuit of profit purely for its own sake.*[22] In this account of capitalism as characterized by the transformation of means into ends, Weber was following a long tradition of interpretations of monetarism, most recently in Simmel's *The Philosophy of Money*, which Weber described as 'brilliant', and especially Sombart's *Modern Capitalism*.[23] Yet he departed from their interpretations in his account of the capitalist spirit as a form of asceticism.

'Unnatural' and anti-eudaemonist asceticism: The imperative to pursue profit purely for its own sake, as an end in itself

From this transcendental formalist hostility to substantive teleology it follows, for Weber, that the spirit of modern capitalism is anti-eudae-monist. Happiness, *eudaemonia*, the traditional goal of the good life, is one of the substantive goals that must be excluded, in a radical departure from ancient and medieval visions of human being. Weber insists: 'the *summum bonum* of this ethic, the earning of more and more money, combined with the strict avoidance of all spontaneous enjoyment of life, is above all completely devoid of any eudaemonistic, not to say hedon-istic, admixture.'[24] Instead the pursuit of profit is, for the true capitalist spirit, much more like the pure 'duty' of Kant's categorical imperative.[25] To pursue money for the sake of more possessions, greater luxury and other forms of consumption would compromise the purity of the genu-ine spirit of capitalism which must pursue acquisition utterly disinter-estedly, *for its own sake.* Against the popular idea of capitalism as characterized by an excessive consumption and a love of luxury, Weber insists that at least at its origin and essence it has exactly the opposite spirit: the restriction of consumption, frugality, a loathing of pleasure and luxury as waste; in short, a pronounced heroic asceticism. As he hints in the 1920 introduction: 'Unlimited greed for gain is not in the least identical with capitalism, and is still less its spirit. Capitalism *may* even be identical with the restraint, or at least a rational tempering, of this irrational impulse.'[26]

By insisting that, at its origin and deepest level, the spirit of modern capitalism is not acquisitive greed, but rational restraint, Weber was also departing from the two authors to whom his interpretation of capitalism

---

[22] Marshall, p. 25; cf. pp. 34–5.
[23] Marshall, pp. 36–8. See Georg Simmel, *The Philosophy of Money* (London: Routle-dge, 1990). For an excellent discussion of the relationship of Weber to Werner Sombart, see Talcott Parsons, '"Capitalism" in Recent German Literature: Sombart and Weber', *The Journal of Political Economy*, 36:6, 1928, and 37:1, 1929.
[24] Weber, p. 18.
[25] Ibid., p. 19.
[26] Ibid., p. xxxi; Here Weber saw himself as differing also from Brentano, for whom acquisitive desire for money is alone definitive of capitalism – p. 246, n. 13.

was most indebted: Georg Simmel and Werner Sombart. Both these authors had identified the origins of the capitalist spirit not in the Puritan ethos, but in Judaism. For Simmel this was largely due to the Jewish experience of being an estranged people excluded from the economic practices of feudalism. Sombart's *Modern Capitalism* (1902) highlighted two 'economic value attitudes' which combined with material economic and social conditions to make possible capitalism: unlimited material striving and rational calculation. In his *German Economy in the Nineteenth Century* (1903) it became clear that he believed the Jews to be the source of these attitudes. Weber was rejecting this interpretation of capitalism as Jewish in origin, and with it the first of Sombart's economic value attitudes – unlimited material striving – as integral to capitalism.[27] This corresponds to Weber's distinction, noted above, which he claimed Simmel and Sombart had missed, between traditional adventure capitalism, which *is* characterized by greed and luxury, and modern rational capitalism, which is not.

Sombart's second economic value attitude – rational calculation – remained integral to Weber's thinking about capitalism as we saw above; however he sought to show that this was not combined with greed as Sombart thought, but more coherently with self-restraint. The spirit of capitalism is opposed to any spontaneous 'joy of living':[28] While later generations of capitalists may have succumbed to decadence, luxury and ostentation, the original and, in Weber's terms, the 'ideal type' of the modern capitalist entrepreneur, as represented in the writings of Franklin, 'avoids ostentation and unnecessary expenditure, as well as conscious enjoyment of his power, and is embarrassed by the outward signs of the social recognition which he receives...[he is therefore] distinguished by a certain ascetic tendency'.[29] As noted above, natural pleasures such as 'sociability, idle talk, luxury, even more sleep than is necessary', dancing, sport, the theatre, art, even eating and drinking, indeed all forms of leisure, are suspect for the puritanical spirit of capitalism, which sees them as an unproductive waste of time.[30] They were suspect precisely as irrational and disorganized, the 'spontaneous expression of undisciplined impulses.'[31] So Weber concludes, after discussing the controversies over the *Book of Sports* between the English Puritans and the Stuarts:

> Impulsive enjoyment of life, which leads away from work in a calling and from religion, was as such the enemy of rational asceticism, whether in the form of seigneurial sports or the

---

[27] Marshall, pp. 38–40; Weber, p. 122. Though, as we shall see, Weber did see Hebrew monotheism and the prophets as distant ancestors of capitalist rationality; cf. Bendix, pp. 201–5.

[28] Weber, p. 9.

[29] Ibid., p. 33.

[30] Ibid., p. 104.

[31] Ibid., p. 112.

> enjoyment of the dance hall or the public house of the com-
> mon man . . . Here asceticism descended like a frost on the life
> of 'merrie old England'.[32]

Weber is at pains to stress the 'unnaturalness' of this rational ascetic
spirit of capitalism: In most societies people work because they are
poor and stop working when they become rich. People prefer leisure
to profit; 'the opportunity of earning more was less attractive than
that of working less.'[33] Thus he concludes: 'A man does not "by nature"
wish to earn more and more money, but simply to live as he is accus-
tomed to live and to earn as much as is necessary for that purpose.'[34]
The spirit of capitalism, it seems, is so unnatural that it must be *learnt*,
requiring extraordinary motivation (for Weber this is provided by the
anxiety over salvation created by the Calvinist doctrine of predestination).[35] However, once it is initially established, its extraordinary suc-
cesses can be attributed to its inherent instability: unlike 'natural'
lifestyles which always aim at the stable equilibrium of rest, the spirit
of capitalism always seeks more and is without its own inherent checks,
hence its spread is virus-like, consuming all that stands in its way.

This rationalist asceticism is the last bourgeois heroism, the Stoical
anti-heroic heroism of the Puritan struggling alone against nature and
himself, recognizable in Bunyan's *Pilgrim's Progress* or the American
Founding Fathers.[36] This is a *this-worldly, anti-worldly* asceticism.
What does this mean? Primitive Christianity and later Christian monasticism were both, in Weber's categories, anti-worldly forms of 'salvation
religion' rather than cultural religion, yet they expressed this through
fatalist acceptance of the world and other-worldly withdrawal, respectively. The Puritan asceticism by contrast, which for Weber is at various
moments the source and/or an expression of the capitalist spirit, retained
the disparagement of the world, yet now turned this outwards towards
the world into a form of active 'world mastery'.[37] As Weber puts it in a
memorable passage:

> Christian asceticism, at first fleeing from the world into soli-
> tude had already ruled the world which it had renounced
> from the monastery and through the Church. But it had, on
> the whole, left the naturally spontaneous character of daily

[32] Weber, pp. 112–13.

[33] Ibid., p. 24.

[34] Ibid. The quotation marks here perhaps indicate a critical questioning of this term
that we will return to later.

[35] Ibid., p. 25.

[36] Ibid., pp. 5, 63, 77.

[37] Wolfgang Schluchter, *Rationalism, Religion, and Domination: A Weberian Perspec-
tive* (Berkeley: University of California Press, 1989), pp. 140 ff. Cf. also Max Weber,
Economy and Society: An Outline of Interpretive Sociology, ed. Guenther Roth and
Claus Wittich (Berkeley: University of California Press, 1978), pp. 541–56.

life in the world untouched. Now it strode into the market-
place of life, slammed the door of the monastery behind it,
and undertook to penetrate just that daily routine of life with
its methodicalness, to fashion it into a life in the world, but
neither of nor for this world.[38]

Anti-traditionalism: The pursuit of profit regardless of traditional obstacles

If Weber's account of the spirit of capitalism as transcendental instrumental rationalism depends on its opposition to 'natural' lifestyles of
pleasure and leisure, to adventure capitalism, to any substantive concerns and value judgements, then it can also be said in all these respects
to be anti-traditional, to be not merely distinctively modern, but aggressively so. As Weber himself puts it: 'The most serious opponent with
which the spirit of capitalism...has had to struggle, was that type of
attitude and reaction to new situations which we may designate as
traditionalism.'[39]

In one sense this should come as little surprise, as this is not to say
much more than summarize the differences noted above: We have seen
how the elevation of the *vita activa* over the *vita contemplativa* was very
much part of an early modern rebellion against the values of antiquity
and the Christian Middle Ages. On a more economic level, we saw that
the rationally organized labour of modernity is portrayed by Weber as
breaking with the spontaneous disorganized idleness and adventurism of
traditional societies. Similarly the instrumental technological dimension
is represented as a departure from more obviously 'primitive' direct
subsistence forms of labour. The substantive values, like happiness,
which are excluded by the formalism of the spirit of capitalism are of
course *traditional* substantive values. Perhaps most significantly, the
'rationalism' of the spirit of capitalism is directly opposed to all things
traditional, which are registered by it merely as impediments to the
working out of its logic. Traditional ethics are seen as irrational 'inhibitions' or 'spiritual obstacles' from which the spirit of capitalism liberates us for ever more unlimited rational acquisition.[40] Here it is likely
Weber is thinking of such 'inhibitions' as the Scholastic restrictions on
usury and support of the 'just price', yet his usage is sufficiently general
that it is easy to conclude that *everything* other than the purely formal
rational spirit of capitalism is regarded as traditional and irrational, to
be swept away in its wake.

Weber repeatedly stresses the novelty of the modern capitalist spirit
and its discontinuity with all previous worldviews and forms of life. The
disjunction involved in the emergence of this spirit was so great that we

[38] Weber, p. 101.
[39] Ibid., p. 23; cf. *Economy and Society*, pp. 583–9.
[40] Weber, pp. 115, xxxix.

can speak of a complete reversal of values, because, as Weber indicates: 'a state of mind such as that expressed in the passages we have quoted from Franklin, and which called forth the applause of a whole people, would both in ancient times and in the Middle Ages have been proscribed as the lowest sort of avarice and as an attitude entirely lacking in self-respect.'[41] Weber cites the standard theological authorities to show that the very attitude that seems to be the spirit of capitalism was censured in the middle ages as *turpitudo* – unjust desire for gain.[42] He then goes on to show that even those moralists such as Anthony of Florence who sought to accommodate traditional views to new economic realities did not question the basic premise that such activities were ultimately shameful and at best to be tolerated and constrained as far as possible.[43] Weber even insists, crucially, that this view was not confined to the theologians and moralists, but was 'above all, the attitude of capitalistic circles themselves.'[44] This is maintained on the basis of evidence from charitable donations in the wills of rich people that indicate some desire to atone for their past activities. 'Here' Weber argues, 'the either non-moral or immoral character of their action in the opinion of the participants themselves comes clearly to light.'[45] At the heart of Weber's thesis is the attempt to explain the radical transformation that occurred when these values were replaced by the spirit of capitalism, the rational pursuit of profit purely for its own sake: an activity formerly 'at best ethically tolerated', and an attitude that it would have been 'unthinkable' to describe as ethical, becomes the 'essence of moral conduct'.[46] How was vice transformed into virtue? Here is a transvaluation and a break with tradition that soon turns aggressively on the surviving representatives of that tradition, whether it be the Protestant attacks on 'unproductive' monasticism, or Puritanical criticisms of the 'decadent' nobility, or bourgeois intolerance of the 'idle' poor.

RATIONALIZATION AND DISENCHANTMENT: THE SPIRIT OF CAPITALISM AS ANTI-THEOLOGICAL?

If Weber at times presents the emergence of the spirit of capitalism as something like the emancipation of reason from the fetters of irrational tradition, then it is also possible to see something else going on in his account of modernity. First, we can note that the tradition from which the spirit of capitalism emancipates itself is in fact one specific tradition – medieval Catholic Christianity – which then seems to be taken as

[41] Weber, p. 21.
[42] Ibid., p. 34.
[43] Ibid., pp. 34–5.
[44] Ibid., p. 35.
[45] Ibid.
[46] Ibid., pp. 35–6.

symptomatic of all pre-modern traditional cultures. Secondly, Weber more than once speaks of the sacramental economy of Catholic Christianity in terms that compare it to magic, so that the conflict between this tradition and capitalism seems to translate into a conflict between magic and modern reason. Here Weber's ideas about the emergence of the spirit of capitalism in modernity link in with his account of the disenchantment or 'de-magicification' of the world (*Entzauberung der Welt*), the removal of sacramental magic which is integral to the process of rationalization.[47] What is the evidence for such views in *The Protestant Ethic and the Spirit of Capitalism*?

These ideas certainly recur at various points in the essay. Thus in the description of the religious foundations of worldly asceticism, Catholicism is claimed to have made less progress in the 'rationalisation of the world, the elimination of magic as a means to salvation' than either the Puritans or even the Jews before them.[48] The Catholic priest is described as a 'magician who performed the miracle of transubstantiation, and who held the key to eternal life in his hand'.[49] In another beautiful, if awesome, passage which I quote here at length, Weber describes the existential situation of the puritan who, following the ruthlessly rational logic of the doctrine of predestination, turns his back on such 'magic' as superstition:

> In its extreme inhumanity this doctrine must above all have had one consequence for the life of a generation which surrendered to its magnificent consistency. That was a feeling of unprecedented inner loneliness of the single individual. In what was for the man of the age of the Reformation the most important thing in life, his eternal salvation, he was forced to follow his path alone to meet a destiny which had been decreed for him from eternity. No one could help him. No priest... No sacraments... No Church... Finally, even no God. For even Christ died only for the elect... This, the complete elimination of salvation through the Church and the sacraments (which was in Lutheranism by no means developed to its final conclusions), was what formed the absolutely decisive difference from Catholicism. *That great historic process in the development of religions, the elimination of magic from the world* which had begun with the old Hebrew prophets and, in conjunction with Hellenistic scientific thought, had repudiated all magical means to salvation as superstition and sin, *came here to its logical conclusion.*[50]

47 Cf. *Economy and Society*, pp. 477–80, 611–23.
48 Weber, p. 71.
49 Ibid.
50 Ibid., pp. 60–1. My italics.

Later Weber speaks of the Baptist and Quaker sects, whose total devaluing of sacraments 'accomplished the religious rationalisation of the world in its most extreme form', before indicating the connection that he believes this rationalizing disenchantment has with the spirit of capitalism: 'The radical elimination of magic from the world allowed no other psychological course than the practice of worldly asceticism.'[51] In all these passages Weber clearly links the spirit of capitalism, the rational pursuit of profit as an end in itself, with the disenchantment of the world, and the overcoming of magic and sacraments by reason. This is also seen as an integral part of the process of rationalization that characterizes modern Western history, which can nevertheless be traced back as far as the Hebrew prophets and Hellenistic scientists. This certainly sounds like a grand teleological narrative, not dissimilar to that of Hegel, telling of the emergence of Reason in modernity as the fulfilment of the destiny of the West. Likewise it has Comtean positivist tones of the successive overcoming of magic by religion and religion by reason. On this account, the emergence of the spirit of capitalism in modernity has striking similarities to the emergence of the 'secular' in political thought – a supposedly neutral, value-free space of pure utility, opposed to the traditional and theological. Yet we must be careful in speaking of the spirit of capitalism as 'anti-theological', for while this is true in so far as the spirit is linked with the disenchantment of the world and a hostility to sacramentalism, nevertheless it remains the case that, for Weber, this is emphatically not the spirit of pure Enlightenment reason, but rather the quite specifically and fundamentally *religious* rationalism of the Puritans.[52] We shall have to return to these contested questions later to see whether this is a fair characterization of Weber.

IS THE 'SPIRIT OF CAPITALISM' A PLAUSIBLE ACCOUNT OF MODERN WORK? THE CRITICAL DEBATE AROUND WEBER

Weber's thesis has been highly contested since its publication and continues to be one of the most debated texts in socio-economic history and theory. Many scholars have seen this thesis as one of the prime examples of an anti-Marxist historical method, which allows a proper agency to cultural-ideal factors relegated by Marxist historians to the merely reactive superstructure. Consequently Weber's thesis suffered attacks and equally unhelpful defences from those merely concerned with using it to make their methodological point. The text has been employed polemically again in the methodological debate between grand histories and local micro-histories. This need not have come as any surprise to Weber himself, given that, as noted above, Weber's own methodology

---

[51] Weber, pp. 95, 97.

[52] 'the spirit of hard work, of progress, or whatever else it may be called . . . must not be understood, as there is a tendency to do, as joy of living nor in any other sense as connected with the Enlightenment', Ibid., p. 11. This seems to me an overstatement, albeit understandable in context.

arose out of similar debates in nineteenth-century German academic life. We shall briefly consider here some of the critical questions that have been raised about Weber's account of the spirit of capitalism: First, whether he successfully demonstrates a solid causal connection between the ethos of Puritan society and capitalist economic practices; second whether he pays insufficient attention to empirical evidence and too much to literary 'superstructural' sources; third, following from this, whether his thesis is too imprecise actually to say anything about history, that is to say, whether the very category of 'spirit' is more typological than empirical, and, therefore, necessarily indemonstrable; finally whether all that Weber really offers is a dubious typological metanarrative of modernity as the triumph of reason over tradition.

The historical causes and uniqueness of the spirit of modern capitalism

The first of these objections concerns the heart of Weber's thesis: that the Protestant work ethic was one of the causes of the emergence of the spirit of capitalism. The issue at stake is one of causation. Implicit in this primary thesis is the secondary claim that changed attitudes to economic affairs were one of the causes (not just a consequence) of the emergence of modern capitalist economic relations. More specifically, it is claimed that this 'spirit of capitalism' was a necessary but not sufficient cause of the new economic situation. The conclusive demonstration of such a claim would obviously entail at the very least the isolation of two distinct phenomena – the Puritan Work Ethic and the spirit of capitalism – and then establishing that the latter never arises without the prior presence of the former. Beyond this, one might seek further evidence that this consecutive conjunction was more than just coincidence. Two sorts of historical example are brought forth against even the minimal first claim: illustrations of Puritan cultures where little significant capitalist development occurred (e.g., Scotland); and illustrations of non-Puritan cultures where it did (e.g., Antwerp and the Northern Italian Renaissance cities). The first set of illustrations seems to miss the modesty of Weber's claim. It is not that he believes that Puritanism will always and everywhere lead to advanced capitalist societies. Other factors will impinge upon the capacity of Puritanism to develop into capitalist economies, such as political stability, trading opportunities, material resources and so on, as Weber freely admits. The Protestant work ethic is not a *sufficient* cause of the spirit of capitalism, let alone capitalist economic relations. Rather it is one of a number of contributing factors in the emergence of the spirit and practice of modern capitalism. The second set of illustrations, of the emergence of capitalist economic relations in areas without Puritan influence, seems more damning at first. Brentano and other contemporary critics of Weber focus on the emergence of capitalistic economic practices in Northern Italy, and the corresponding appearance in the writings of Anthony of Florence, Bernhard of Sienna and Leon Battista Alberti of something very similar to the 'spirit of capitalism' which Weber highlights in the writings of Franklin. Weber's lengthy response to these criticisms is well worth close attention so as not to misconstrue his point.[53] Weber's reply is twofold: First he insists that he is concerned, as noted above, not with the forms of capitalist adventurism that are as old as history, but with what is distinctive about *modern* capitalism, which is to say the four characteristics listed above.[54] At times he seems to speak as if one of these characteristics were definitive alone – e.g. as if *rational* capitalism were unknown before modernity. Yet at other times he acknowledges the presence of analogous rationalized economic practices in Ancient Rome or China, for example, suggesting that it is more the particular combinations, and perhaps particularly the transcendental/moral sanction and valorizing that is distinctive. The second part of Weber's reply is to concede that when this particular combination of views does begin to make itself manifest in the Renaissance prior to Calvin, even if only in a confused way as in Alberti's concept of *industria*, then this is truly the partial emergence of something like the spirit of capitalism, although without the full consistency and particularly the intense theological sanction that it would develop under the influence of Puritanism. This key claim of Weber's should not be ignored: 'In the conception of *industria*, which comes from monastic asceticism and which was developed by monastic writers, lies the seed of an *ethos* which was fully developed later in the Protestant worldly asceticism.'[55] Crucially for Weber only these later developments could give this ethos the sort of popular sanction to enable it to take root in the emergent bourgeoisie, rather than remaining an economic philosophy for religious and a few learned progressive aristocrats. Nevertheless I would argue that passages such as this, along with other references to forerunners of modern rational-ascetic capitalism in the monasteries of St. Benedict, Cluny, the Cistercians and the Jesuits, indicate that Weber had a more careful account of the causal links between the Puritan work ethos and the spirit of capitalism than many commentators allow.[56] On this account, it seems that Puritanism proper is more responsible for the particular *success* of the spirit of capitalism in modernity, its breaking free of the monasteries and grasping a large section of society, than for the *invention* of this spirit. Protestantism contributed to the success of

---

[53] 'the spirit of hard work, of progress, or whatever else it may be called ... must not be understood, as there is a tendency to do, as joy of living nor in any other sense as connected with the Enlightenment', Ibid., p. 11. This seems to me an overstatement, albeit understandable in context, p. 141, n. 12.

[54] Weber claims Lujo Brentano, Simmel and Sombart all blur this distinction – Ibid., p. 128, n. 2.

[55] Ibid., pp. 143–4, n. 12 on Stoicism and Alberti, and p. 152, n. 29 on the Scotist economic ethics of Bernhard of Sienna and Anthony of Florence. N.B. The former footnote is a later edition to Weber's original essay, partly in response to the comments of his critics, and perhaps represents a slight softening of his rhetoric in the original essay, which can seem to suggest that rational-ascetic capitalism never existed before modernity.

[56] Ibid., pp. 72–4.

the rational-transcendental spirit of capitalism, but was not its *sine qua non*.[57] Thus the stress that Weber puts upon the specifically Calvinist ideas of predestination, proof and calling, might well have been somewhat overstated. His critics may well be right to think that Weber has made too much of these ideas, but they would be quite wrong to think this such a crushing blow to his argument, precisely because they are not necessary preconditions of the spirit of capitalism for Weber. Here it can be argued Weber had a more complex and 'weak' account of the causal relationship between Protestantism and Capitalism than is usually allowed for. Weber is not, for example, offering a crude inversion of the equally crude dialectical materialist account of history by arguing that ideas (the Protestant work ethic) are the cause of material realities (capitalism). Indeed when his critics argue for a more nuanced account of the relation between the two, 'dialectical' perhaps, or incorporating a 'feedback effect', that takes account of the impossibility of clearly isolating any chicken or egg moment in the complex interweaving of ideas and events, they are urging no more than Weber had originally intended and already insisted.[58] While it would be going too far to say that Weber is not interested in causality, it is *historical* causality he is interested in, not the simple causality of a controlled experiment where events can be endlessly repeated to isolate contributing factors.[59] Thus he writes: 'I would like to protest the statement...that some one factor, be it technology or economy, can be the "ultimate" or "true" cause of another. If we look at causal lines, we see them run, at one time, from technical to economic and political matters, at another from political to religious and economic ones, etc. There is no resting point.'[60] Similarly Weber denies in principle any accounts of *necessary* determinism in the social sphere.[61] So it seems in place of a simple necessary causal relation between Calvinism and Capitalism we are left with an account of their convergence and 'congruence' (Fischoff), their 'elective affinity' (Weber himself) which historically may have established a mutual 'resonance' whereby each contributed to the flourishing of the other.[62] Such a position enables us to escape the debates between debased Marxist materialism and a crudely idealist Hegelian reading of Weber, and to return to the insight that Weber and Marx share: that somehow Protestantism and Capitalism have a complex mutual affinity that enabled them historically to find allies in one another, without reducing either to mere functions of the other.[63] Furthermore, this account enables us here to employ Weber's

[57] Marshall denies this, apparently overlooking Weber's account of medieval monasticism and confusing the success of the spirit (which Weber does attribute to Protestantism) with its very possibility – Marshall, p. 153.
[58] Ibid., pp. 145–7.
[59] Cf. Ibid., p. 204, n. 61.
[60] Ibid., p. 151.
[61] Ibid., p. 155.
[62] Ibid., pp. 146, 149, 154. Cf. Giddens and Bendix.
[63] Marshall, pp. 141 f. Marshall himself dogmatically rejects the possibility of any reconciliation between the perspectives of Marx and Weber – p. 155.

account of the Spirit of Capitalism, while sitting rather more lightly to its relation to Protestantism.

The problem of evidence and circularity

My concern with Weber's account of the spirit of capitalism independent of the detail of his historical thesis about its causes and effects brings us to the second group of objections brought against Weber, which concern the lack of empirical historical evidence he provides for his thesis. Indeed it is sometimes claimed that this thesis about an 'ethic' and a 'spirit' is really an exercise in the history of ideas rather than socio-economic history. Famously the only 'empirical' data that Weber provides in his thesis is the study of differences between Catholics and Protestants in the tax returns for late nineteenth-century Baden, undertaken by one of his own students, Martin Offenbacher.[64] This is certainly not the most obviously helpful data for his thesis! The vast majority of the 'evidence' Weber offers in his account of the spirit of capitalism is in fact literary: whether it be Franklin, Baxter, Luther, Calvin or Milton, they are mainly sermons, treatises and similar texts. Weber's account of the spirit of capitalism seems too confined by its sources to the superstructure, in Marxist terms, and thus to be powerless to tell us about how this relates to the economic base, which seems to be his intention. Did matters of his eternal destiny and earthly vocation really cross the mind of the ordinary industrialist as he set about his work? Marshall sums up the criticisms of many here when he insists:

> Weber offers little or no independent evidence concerning the motives and world-view of either modern or medieval busi-nessmen and labourers. His evidence for the former...is drawn exclusively from Protestant teaching...His evidence for the latter is taken from casual observations of the forms of economic 'adventuring' in which medieval merchants partici-pated...But, of course, this is no proof at all.[65]

To look at accounts of business produced by literary elites, whether they be the medieval canonists and theologians or modern Protestant writers of sermons and manuals of godly living, tells us nothing, it is claimed, about the real motivations of the people engaged in these practices. Weber stands accused of presuming that the logical consequences of various doctrines were also real consequences, as if people simply prac-tised what was preached.[66] For Marshall and others the impossibility of interviewing fifteenth-century peasants or seventeenth-century business-men to discover their genuine motivations renders Weber's thesis

---

[64] Weber, p. 133.
[65] Marshall, pp. 67–8.
[66] Ibid., p. 121. See also Bendix, pp. 64–9.

'empirically unverified and possibly, in practice, unverifiable.'[67] Once again I reiterate that I am not concerned with defending Weber's causal historical thesis narrowly construed; nevertheless, it is worth making a few brief comments on this hyper-pious critique of Weber from the social historians: even if the direct connection between the literary-intellectual worldviews and the economic practices cannot be precisely established, it remains the case that Weber does succeed in showing significant shifts in both, roughly coincident and with certain affinities. More fundamentally, it is difficult to see how one could ever obtain completely 'independent' evidence for motives and behaviour, primarily because we have no access to motives other than as they express themselves in the public realm. It is far from obvious that interviewing fifteenth-century peasants would solve all the difficulties of hermeneutical understanding, as Marshall seems to suggest with a rather naïve empiricism. Alasdair MacIntyre makes exactly this point when he says 'an attitude can never be identified except in terms of the activities in which it is manifested.'[68] Marshall celebrates this comment as a critique of Weber's circularity, while chiding MacIntyre for eliding attitudes and activities, when he would do better to abandon his simplistic causal reading of Weber's thesis premised on precisely this debased Weberian empiricist distinction of facts and values.

Is Weber only concerned with history of ideas?

All this aside, it remains the case that my concern is with the plausibility of the description which Weber provides of the 'spirit of capitalism', not with any causal connection this may have to Protestantism. Therefore, the charges of tautological definition of each in relation to the other need not concern us here. Yet the other side of the problem remains: Is this 'spirit of capitalism' actually just confined to the 'superstructural' level of literature, culture and values? On these questions the work of the British economic historian R. H. Tawney can be of use. Tawney is often presented among the list of Weber's critics, yet he wrote from such a similar perspective that it might be better to regard him as one of Weber's greatest interpreters who rescues his thesis from some of its weaker points that critics had jumped upon. So while conceding the excessive emphasis Weber placed upon the particular significance of the doctrine of the calling, and his overstating the uniqueness and novelty of the Calvinist ideas, Tawney also dismisses the 'idealist' interpretation of Weber, pointing to his statements on the reciprocal relation of ideas and practices, religion and economics.[69] Even more crucially for us, Tawney makes more explicit than Weber the importance of the secularizing of social

---

[67] Marshall, pp. 129, 68.
[68] Ibid., p. 66.
[69] R. H. Tawney, *Religion and the Rise of Capitalism* (Harmondsworth: Penguin, 1990), p. ix.

and economic thought, and insists that Weber's thesis was one 'not of general economic history, but of religious thought on social issues.'[70] Tawney turns the criticism on its head: Weber is intending to write an intellectual history about the emergence of the *spirit* of capitalism, so it is neither accident nor deficiency that his sources are sermons and treatises rather than economic statistics or interviews with businessmen. On this account it is not so much that rational capitalism was somehow 'invented' by Puritans in the seventeenth century, rather it is that this practice came to be differently evaluated, and this novel interpretation of capitalism as moral came to a new dominance. Something like the spirit of capitalism is as old as history, as we argued above; the revolution in modernity is that the 'behaviour which had previously only been tolerated was now ideologically justified'; vice (adventure capitalism) or exceptional virtue for a minority (the rational asceticism of the religious orders) transvalued into general virtue for all.[71] Is this sympathetic interpretation of Weber a plausible one? We should be careful not to overstate the point; Weber is concerned, as he says, not just with ideas, but with 'their practical results', as in fact Tawney recognizes.[72] Nevertheless there are a number of passages in *The Protestant Ethic* that confirm Tawney's reading of the intellectual shift as the decisive innovation: First, we should note that Weber focuses our attention on the Puritans of Massachusetts precisely because here, he argues, the emergence of the spirit of capitalism *precedes* the emergence of capitalist economic practices. Obviously this serves to discount materialist reductions of the former to a function of the latter, but it also suggests that Weber's real concern is primarily with these shifts at the level of ethos. While at times he seems to paint these shifts in terms of the invention of an entirely new ethos, nevertheless, in the light of the comments on monasticism noted above, it could be suggested that the only real novelty is the explosion of this ethos to take over an entire society. Other passages in the chapter *The Spirit of Capitalism* make it evident that Weber's foremost concern was the shift at the theoretical level, the emergence of this new *ethos*: 'It is not mere business astuteness, that sort of thing is common enough, it is an ethos. *This* is the quality which interests us ... Capitalism existed in China, India, Babylon, in the classic world, and in the Middle Ages. But in all these cases, as we shall see, this particular ethos was lacking.'[73] Another crucial passage speaks of how contemporary capitalism 'once in the saddle' now has no trouble

[70] R. H. Tawney, *Religion and the Rise of Capitalism* (Harmondsworth: Penguin, 1990), p. xi.

[71] Marshall, p. 155. For a good critical anthology tracing attitudes to 'commercial life' throughout the history of the West see: Patrick Murray (ed.), *Reflections on Commercial Life: An Anthology of Classic Tests from Plato to the Present* (London: Routledge, 1997).

[72] Weber, p. 132, n. 1.

[73] Ibid., p. 17. Cf. p. 21: 'A state of mind such as that expressed in the passages we have quoted from Franklin, and which called forth the applause of a whole people, would both in ancient times and in the Middle Ages have been proscribed as the lowest sort

in recruiting a workforce which prefers profits to leisure.[74] Tawney not only enables us to see Weber's focus on cultural theoretical shifts to be no problem after all, he also provides considerable additional evidence for this shift in attitudes towards work and the unlimited pursuit of profit with documentary evidence from more prosaic sources than Weber, down to wills and court records.[75]

Spirit as 'ideal-type'

Beneath all these concerns lies the vexed question of what exactly Weber means by 'spirit' (*Geist*). The term has a Hegelian ring which has certainly encouraged the accusations of idealism – of naïvely presuming that ideas have their corresponding practices in which they are realized and worked out. Marshall draws attention to the various meanings 'spirit' seems to have in Weber's work: sometimes a motivating attitudinal complex that generates/encourages capitalistic practices, as when he writes of Franklin; and at other times the form of those practices themselves, as in the contrast with traditionalism (particularly in the 1920 introduction where the phrases 'economic form/system', *Wirtschaftsform/system*, seem to largely replace *Geist*).[76] Thus Marshall asks: 'Is the spirit of capitalism a worldview or the realisation of a worldview; an attitude or a pattern of conduct?'[77] While I have already indicated my unease with some of Marshall's dichotomies, there is a fair point here: if the 'spirit of capitalism' is *merely* a piece of intellectual history, it is not immediately obvious that it tells us anything about modern capitalism. It might well be little more than an unhelpful misinterpretation of that phenomenon. Again the question forces itself forward: Does this 'spirit of capitalism' really exist?

The spirit of capitalism in Weber is best understood according to the Rickertian theory of 'value relevance' (*Wertbeziehung*) which Weber absorbed during his breakdown of 1902 immediately prior to writing the original *Protestant Work Ethic* essay. This Neo-Kantian theory aims at a certain ideal, intersubjective, scientific objectivity in the humanities, by examining cultural artefacts according to the logical patterns of relevance these have to certain values. 'Value relevant descriptions' are neither purely empirical nor truly metaphysical, but rather, in typical

---

of avarice and as an attitude entirely lacking in self-respect.' Or p. 35: 'Now, how could activity [sic], which was at best ethically tolerated, turn into a calling in the sense of Benjamin Franklin?'

[74] Ibid., p. 25.

[75] Tawney's focus is on England; for a similarly detailed historical study of New England which supports Weber's thesis, see: Stephen Innes, *Creating the Commonwealth: The Economic Culture of Puritan New England* (New York: Norton, 1995).

[76] Marshall, pp. 18, 54, 55.

[77] Ibid., p. 65. Parsons, 1929, pp. 31–3, also argues that Weber is somewhat confused in using 'ideal types' for historically specific genetic arguments as well as universalizing comparative arguments.

Kantian fashion, logical, dealing in ideal types. As Marshall puts it, the spirit of modern capitalism is:

> an ideal-typical, one-sided accentuation of the mentality of modern capitalists. It is what the modern capitalist *Weltanschauung* would look like were it ruthlessly systematised in the direction of one underlying value, namely, that of seeing the accumulation of capital to be a duty and an end in itself.[78]

It is clear from this that it does not matter if this spirit never once occurs perfectly in reality. It remains a useful typological tool for making sense of the logic of a position. Tawney comments admirably on those whose excessive empiricist nominalism refuses all such terms: 'It would be paradoxical to dismiss Machiavelli and Locke and Smith and Bentham as irrelevant to the political practice of their age, merely on the ground that mankind has still to wait for the ideal Prince or Whig or Individualist or Utilitarian.'[79] With similar wisdom Tawney warns us on the other hand that, while he maintains that real shifts in the dominant cultural perspective did occur from the medieval to modern periods, nevertheless we should not succumb to using these ideal-types in an epochalist fashion, ignoring the diversity and complexity of actual cultures.[80]

The roots of Weber's spirit of capitalism in political economy

It has been argued by Marshall and others before him, that, while Weber's account of the connections between Protestantism and Capitalism had many features original to him, nevertheless the basic premise of some affinity between the two was not original, but was indeed so platitudinous over many generations as to be taken for granted by him.[81] Weber himself conceded as much in the frustrated footnotes he added in response to his critics:

> It is really inexcusable to contest so lightly, as some of my critics have done, facts which are quite beyond dispute, and have hitherto never been disputed by anyone... No one in the seventeenth century doubted the existence of these relationships... Besides the modern writers already noted, poets like Heine and Keats, as well as historians like Macaulay, Cunningham, Rogers, or an essayist such as Matthew Arnold, have assumed them as obvious.[82]

[78] Marshall, p. 51.
[79] Tawney, p. 25.
[80] Ibid..
[81] Marshall, p. 20.
[82] Weber, p. 256, n. 96. Elsewhere he also cites Lavelye (p. 137, n. 23) and Montesquieu (p. 11).

Tawney comments:

> the existence of a connexion between economic Radicalism
> and religious Radicalism was to those who saw both at first
> hand something not far from a platitude. Until some reason
> is produced for rejecting their testimony, it had better be
> assumed that they knew what they were talking about.[83]

It is not only the links between Puritanism and the spirit of capitalism
which Weber accepts from his predecessors, the very outlines of the
account of the spirit of capitalism itself were not original to Weber. It
is not so immediately obvious who were the first exponents of this spirit
from Weber's text – Franklin perhaps? Yet I would argue that it was
ultimately none other than the seventeenth-century theorists of mercan-
tilism and their successors in the eighteenth-century 'political arithmeti-
cians'. Such was the name given to the first advocates of the new science
of economics, supposedly purely rational and value-free, modelled on
the physical sciences.[84] *This* is the hidden intellectual provenance of the
idea of the 'spirit of capitalism', in what later generations would call
'political economy', represented by men such as Smith, Malthus,
Ricardo and Say. Marshall is helpful here in filling in the historical
gaps.[85] For, as he tells us, German academic life in the 30 years prior
to the First World War was divided by the methodological debates
known as the *Methodenstreit* including the exchange between the German Historical School of Economics and the Austrian marginal utility
theorists. The Historical School had begun as a reaction against the
overly formal, ahistorical and materialistic perspective of classical political economy, which they saw as seeking to justify the laissez faire
greed of '*Manchesterismus*' – the powerful new industrial capitalists.
When the Austrian utility theorist Carl Menger fought back in 1883, he
was in turn responded to by Gustav Schmoller, who is usually seen as
representing the 'Younger Historical School'. Weber's doctoral dissertation of 1889 and *Habilitationsschrift* of 1891 already indicate his sympathy for this latter, *historical* approach to economics, concerned with
the specificity of geographical and historical situation, against the tendency of classical political economy to regard eighteenth-century English
conditions as universally applicable. With all this taken into account, it
becomes evident that Weber's 'spirit of capitalism' is 'simply another
way of talking about *homo oeconomicus* – man and woman as dominated by considerations of self-interest and completely absorbed in the

---

[83]   Tawney, p. xii. Cf. also Michael Löwy and Robert Sayre, *Romanticism against the Tide of Modernity*, trans. C. Porter (London: Duke University Press, 2001), pp. 1–56 for more of this background to Weber's view of capitalism in the eighteenth and nineteenth centuries.

[84]   Cf. Tawney, p. 25.

[85]   Marshall, pp. 22–30.

pursuit of material gain'.[86] The key point of Weber's thesis is to take the standard account of the spirit of capitalism in political economy and to reject the traditional elements of self-interest, material greed and desire for leisure, which were all essential for such writers as Smith, offering instead an account that linked this spirit, at least at its point of origin, with an entirely different, ascetic spirit. As Marshall puts it: 'Weber is debating, not with the ghost of Marx, but – via German historical economics – with that of Adam Smith.'[87]

Rationalism as a particular 'religious' tradition rather than the goal of all history?

The final critical question concerning Weber's thesis, to which we return now, is the issue of the metanarrative of modernity as rationalization, touched upon earlier. Marshall refers to this as the 'Parsonian legacy' of teleological readings of Weber and has little time for what he sees as its dehistoricizing tendencies. Talcott Parsons, who was highly influential in publicizing Weber's views in Anglophone circles, claimed to have identified a fragmentary systematic theory of ideal types in Weber's work, which Parsons then sought to complete into a 'General Theory of Action'.[88] One of the primary examples of this attempt to find unifying themes in Weber's essayistic writings is the theme of the 'march of rationalization' which interprets progressive rationalization in every area of life, from religion, and law, to economy and politics, as the distinguishing feature of modernity and the destiny of the West.[89]

The issues at stake here are complex, but Weber seems, upon closer examination, to be somewhat more subtle than either group of his commentators in this respect. It is difficult to accept such a thorough refusal of this thesis of rationalization as Marshall would want.[90] Weber does seem to believe, even in the early writings, that the advance of modernity in the West is best characterized as increasing rationalization across many diverse areas of life. Yet, on the other hand, he does not seem to envisage this as the *necessary* outworking of a grand historical process in the manner of Hegel, the emergence of Reason in history. So Weber comments: 'the history of rationalism shows a development which by no means follows parallel lines in the various departments of life.'[91] Indeed there are a few tantalizing hints that when it comes to the

---

86 Marshall, pp. 22–3.
87 Ibid., p. 33.
88 Ibid., pp. 158 f.
89 Among those who have taken such a view of Weber's writings are Tenbruck, Schluchter, Luethy, Kolko and Eisenstadt, and, as Marshall notes disapprovingly, they are inclined to read Weber's earlier writings through the matrix of the *Religionssoziologie* of more than a decade later (Marshall, p. 21).
90 Cf. nn. 47–51 above.
91 Weber, p. 37.

nature of this 'rationalization' in the West, Weber is far more radically historicizing and anti-Positivist than even Marshall, viewing this 'reason' as, in a sense just another tradition, as ultimately incapable of rational self-foundation as any other.[92] The first evidence for this comes in his focus on the importance of religious views such as predestination and calling at the very foundation of the spirit of rational capitalism. While these doctrines are followed through with a ruthless rationality, the implication is that their very existence is a sort of brute pre-rational given, a charismatic authority standing outside the tradition of rationality which it generates. Thus Weber disagrees with Sombart: Capitalism is not just reducible to economic rationalization, nor is Protestantism reducible to the rationalization of religion, although rationalization is crucial to both.[93] On the contrary, it is precisely the ascetic, anti-eudaemonist denial of rational self-interest which is crucial for Weber: 'We are here particularly interested in the origin of precisely the *irrational* element which lies in this, as in every conception of a calling.'[94] Capitalist rationalism has at its very moment of origin a highly irrational 'religious' foundation. Although of course, Weber is also quite ready to admit that the spirit of capitalism rapidly outgrew its initial ally in religion and cast it aside, even turning against it. Beyond this Weber seems to be suggesting that *any* rationalism must have this initial irrational religious foundation, because rationalization can only be a secondary stance towards an initial position adopted for reasons exceeding that rationality. There is, on this line of argument, not one Reason opposed to religion and tradition, but just many rationalities, which are in fact traditions and faith positions, depending upon their point of departure: 'In fact, one may – this simple proposition, which is often forgotten should be placed at the beginning of every study which essays to deal with rationalism – rationalize life from fundamentally different basic points of view and in very different directions.'[95] This point is so important for a radical reading of Weber that it is worth including at length his later footnote when he makes the same point again:

[92] Here I am attempting to argue that Weber has at least moments of genuine insight which rescue him from succumbing completely to the Liberal Protestant historical metanarrative which John Milbank attributes to him, *Theology and Social Theory* (Oxford: Blackwell, 1990), pp. 92 f.

[93] Weber, pp. 36–7. Indeed the more radical rationalism of Voltaire and the Enlightenment, which Weber suggests might be more concerned with self-interest, was he claims (generalizing somewhat) more at home in the Latin Catholic countries than among the Puritan cultures.

[94] Ibid., p. 38. My italics.

[95] Ibid. In some senses then, Weber seems closer to the radical perspectivism of Nietzsche than most interpretations of his notions of rationalization allow; cf. Max Weber, 'Politics as a Vocation' (1918) in H. H. Gerth and C. Wright Mills (eds. and trans.), *From Max Weber: Essays in Sociology* (London: Routledge and Kegan Paul, 1970), p. 153, where he speaks of the contemporary situation as one where we must choose between many 'gods'.

Brentano . . . takes this remark as an occasion to criticise the later discussion of 'that rationalisation and discipline' to which worldly asceticism has subjected men. That, he says, is a rationalisation toward an irrational mode of life. He is, in fact, quite correct. *A thing is never irrational in itself, but only from a particular rational point of view.* For the unbeliever every religious way of life is irrational, for the hedonist every ascetic standard, no matter whether, measured with respect to its particular basic values, that opposing asceticism is a rationalisation. If this essay makes any contribution at all, may it be to bring out the complexity of the only superficially simple concept of the rational.[96]

CONCLUSION

We have introduced Weber at this early stage because his curious mixed methodology, combining history and philosophy, economics and literature, is particularly helpful to grasping something of what might be characteristic of modern work, even if he was neither the first person to articulate this, nor at times the most cautious in the detail of his claims. In his account of the spirit of capitalism, which we have summarized under the four characteristics of active-instrumentalism, transcendental-rational formalism, unnatural and anti-eudaemonist asceticism, and anti-traditionalism, he provides a helpful working definition of what other authors will term the spirit of utility. It is important to state at this early stage that this spirit of utility is neither a metaphysical idealist principle unrelated to reality, nor something purely empirical which can be simply pointed to, but rather a useful 'ideal-type' – the logical extrapolation of certain beliefs and attitudes.

We have sought to argue further that this description of the spirit of utility derives ultimately from the tradition of political economy with its concern for impersonal economic forces and value-free mathematical judgements, what we might call the first theoretical 'scientific' self-expression of the capitalist classes' approach to business. Yet Weber's account, indebted to the German Historical School of Economics, is crucially different from classical political economy, in a similar manner to Marx: it refuses the naturalization of specifically modern conditions into eternal, essentially true realities, offering instead a thoroughly *historical* account of their contingency. Thus, as we have shown here, Weber links the emergence of this spirit to dominance with particular classes and economic practices, and at the cultural-theoretical level to the revaluation of work in the Reformation and, more tentatively, to the advance of rationalization and disenchantment of the world.

Now, as indicated above, I have no interest in defending some of the detailed premises of Weber's historical account – the exact causal

[96] Weber, p. 140. n. 9, my italics.

relations of Protestantism to this spirit, the importance of the ideas of predestination, proof, and calling, and the uniqueness and novelty of modern rational-ascetic capitalism (which he seems to back down from in later comments on Medieval monasticism) – indeed I would happily concede inaccuracies here. Yet I would nevertheless maintain that the broader historical-theoretical picture is plausible in accounting for significant and undeniable shifts in thinking at the origins of modernity; intellectual-cultural shifts which in turn, seem not to have been without at the least a negative effect on socio-economic practices, by removing prior obstacles and thus opening new possibilities. Tawney's interpretation of Weber presents the thesis in a similar light, showing that the primary shift is at the level of social thought, downplaying the importance of specifically Calvinist ideas, and emphasizing the more general significance of secularization.

Weber's critical value comes precisely through this 'historicizing' of the political economists' ahistorical laws, into a spirit of utility, interrogating their 'natural inevitability'. Beyond this, as we have sought to show, he goes even further in the passages which hint towards a historicizing of reason itself, something that would expose the irrational and derivative origins of rationality and the 'mythic' nature of any formal rationality that seeks to go beyond and replace substantive traditional rationalities. These questions will emerge again later in our consideration of Adorno and Horkheimer in chapter 5.

Two questions remain: In his concern to stress the ascetic and religious-irrational origins of the spirit of capitalism against Smith's conception of self-interest does Weber overstate his case somewhat? In other words, first, is this spirit of utility really necessarily ascetic? According to Weber the pure spirit is at its origins and only later degenerates into hedonism. But would it not be more consistent to say that the spirit of utility in its transcendental formalism is utterly *indifferent* to the realm of nature, to self-interest or its absence (as in Kantian ethics)? Such indifference would then be equally compatible in practice with asceticism *and* hedonism, as subsequent history seems to have demonstrated. Second, is it not the case that the really significant break in modernity, if we must isolate one, is not between medieval rational capitalism and puritan rational capitalism, but between both of these and their successors in pure utilitarian secular rational capitalism;[97] not so much the emergence of an utterly new phenomenon, but the rise of a perennial phenomenon to a new cultural dominance? The real point of departure is not a change in field of action, for in a local sense the activity of the monastic orders was *innerweltliche* not *ausserweltliche* (directed into the world rather than other-worldly), while the Puritans' production remained as much constrained and ordered by greater, substantive accounts of human flourishing, such as rest, justice, charity and worship,

---

[97] Cf. Ibid., p. 125.

as that of the religious houses.[98] Rather the real break comes when the formal spirit of utility ceases to be subordinate to any such substantive traditions of rationality, sets itself against these traditions, and substitutes itself for them as a value-free, finally authoritative science of reality and action; formal rationality comes to replace substantive teleology.[99] That is why the fourth element in our account – the virus-like, promethean, iconoclastic hostility to traditions – is so important for understanding the role of this spirit in modernity, something which was already manifest in the anti-sacramentalism of the Puritans, but only later reached its logical conclusion in the political economists and utilitarians. Secularization is perhaps then more important to the spirit of capitalism than Weber would have us believe, not merely something that effects its later development, but an integral element in its unfolding logic and rise to cultural dominance. Both these critical questions to Weber's thesis are incorporated by Tawney in his retelling of the story in *Religion and the Rise of Capitalism*. Similarly some apocalyptic lines from the final pages of Weber's *Protestant Work Ethic* thesis look forward to these issues of how contemporary secular capitalism is darkly different from that of the Puritans:

> The Puritan wanted to work in a calling; we are forced to do so . . . In Baxter's view the care for external goods should only lie on the shoulders of the 'saint like a light cloak, which can be thrown aside at any moment'. But fate decreed that the cloak should become an iron cage . . . Today the spirit of religious asceticism – whether finally, who knows? – has escaped from the cage. But victorious capitalism, since it rests on mechanical foundations, needs its support no longer . . . In the field of its highest development, in the United States, the pursuit of wealth, stripped of its religious and ethical meaning, tends to become associated with purely mundane passions, which often actually gives it the character of sport . . . of the last stage of this cultural development, it might well be truly said: 'Specialists without spirit, sensualists without heart; this nullity imagines that it has attained a level of civilisation never before achieved.'[100]

With this in mind, we turn in the next chapter to perhaps the most famous critique of capitalism, in Karl Marx, asking what role the concept of utility plays here, and whether a materialist worldview can sustain the sort of critique Marx desires.

---

[98] See Innes for further evidence of this. I am grateful for conversations with Karl Hefty which made me realize the gap still separating Puritanism from Utilitarianism.
[99] Milbank, p. 90.
[100] Weber, pp. 123–4.

Is not life more than food, and the body more than clothing?

3

Labour, Excess and Utility in Karl Marx

The Problem of Materialism and the Aesthetic

In this chapter I shall attempt to explore some of the issues that have already been raised, as they occur in the work of Karl Marx. A discussion of the history of the concept of labour would hardly be complete without an engagement with this most influential of the 'philosophers of labour', yet his relation to questions of a theological aesthetics is less immediately obvious. I will argue that, despite his disclaimers, Marx's thought forms not so much an overcoming of philosophy and theology by science, but rather something resembling an anti-theology, with its own implicit metaphysics, ethics and aesthetics. Particularly through his engagements with other positions, more or less quasi-theological, his views on human labour and its specific situation under the conditions he terms 'capitalism' can be seen to have interesting parallels with the conflicting 'aesthetics of work' in twentieth-century theology outlined in chapter 1 and even more surprisingly with the interpretations of capitalism as *ethos* from Weber and Tawney which we considered in chapter 2.

This project, to use Marx to explore various philosophical questions about the nature of labour, is less startling today than would have been the case a hundred years ago, when Marx was almost universally regarded as a revolutionary and an economist, without direct interest for our concerns. At this time his philosophical decriers could simply dismiss him as too base for their attention, while his champions could look upon this same antipathy as Marx's thorough transcendence of the illusions of bourgeois ideology. Nevertheless the twentieth century did much to change this situation and the narrow portrayal of Marx upon which it was based. Partly in reaction to the increasingly limited and dogmatic appropriation of Marx by the Marxist-Leninist Soviet orthodoxy, alternative interpretations began to arise, particularly in the West, that stressed the humanist philosophical roots of Marx's thought, particularly (Korsch and Colletti) his massive indebtedness to Hegel. This process was stimulated and accelerated by the publication and translation of Marx's earlier, more philosophical writings: *The German Ideology* and the *Manuscripts* of 1844 in 1932, and gradually over subsequent years the

Grundrisse. These texts revealed a 'young Marx' who, while undoubtedly struggling to fledge his wings and break free from the German Idealist tradition, remained still in many ways within the language and thought patterns of that humanist philosophical tradition. These discoveries certainly did not end the discussion however, instead paving the way for debates over the relation of this 'young Marx' to his more established later writings such as *Capital*, and to that tradition that claimed his name, the dialectical materialism championed by Engels, Lenin and others. Were there, as Althusser argued, 'two Marxes', separated by a 'radical break': the early Young Hegelian social-democrat romantic philosopher, and the later properly 'scientific' dialectical materialist, who had shed the last vestiges of bourgeois illusions? Or, at the other end of the interpretative spectrum, Robert Tucker's argument that Marx was never really a serious social scientist or historian, but just another Romantic utopian dreamer, whose later efforts at 'science' were always at the service of this goal.

Unsurprisingly, it is generally the earlier writings of Marx that are more of interest to our intention of exploring the aesthetics of Marx's philosophy of work. Yet this is not to fall into the temptation common to English thinkers of wishfully ignoring the, to us more uncomfortable, materialist, determinist, 'scientific' anti-humanist elements of Marx, present not only in the later works, but from a very early stage. Indeed, any interpretation that sought to detect aesthetic and ethical elements of Marx's thought must address his critique of ideology and his apparent reductionism in viewing the 'superstructure' as simply determined by the economic-material 'base'. Thus we can neither accept the neat Marxist trick of writing off the 'early Marx' as the naïve uncritical reflections of youth, unconnected to the great master that emerged later; nor the anti-Marxist position that seems to have been popular among literary critics in the West, of dismissing Marx's moments of cruder materialism as the imposition of Engels and other lesser minds upon the otherwise coherent oeuvre of a great philosopher.[1] While there are undoubtedly differences in language (e.g., the gradual avoidance of the word 'alienation') and preoccupation, there exists also a more profound continuity of purpose and thinking from at least the 1844 *Manuscripts* right through to Marx's final works that belies any such divisions, themselves probably encouraged by Marx's tendency to disagree more violently with his intellectual friends than opponents, and hence to interpret his own development as a series of breaks.[2] It is in fact these very tensions and contradictions

---

[1] For the arguments against radical discontinuity between the early and later Marx see Leszek Kolakowski, E. P. Thompson, S. Morawski, Terrell Carver, David McLellan, Michel Henry, *Marx: A Philosophy of Human Reality*, trans. Kathleen McLaughlin (Bloomington: Indiana University Press, 1983), Ivan Mészáros, *Marx's Theory of Alienation* (London: Merlin, 1986), pp. 217–43, and Nicholas Lash, *A Matter of Hope* (London: Darton, Longman and Todd, 1981) pp. 10–23.

[2] Cf. Marx's own account in the 1859 *Contribution to the Critique of Political Economy*, in Terrell Carver (ed.), *Marx's Later Political Writings* (Cambridge: Cambridge University Press, 1996), pp. 159 f.

throughout Marx's thought that make him of particular interest in this debate. As has been observed by Engels, Lenin and others, Marx stands at the juncture of complex and contradictory traditions of European thought: German Idealist philosophy, French political philosophy and English political economy.[3] These traditions embody a wide range of views towards labour and to the aesthetical questions of the metaphysics of utility or excess that were discussed in chapter 1.

In this section we will explore these tensions through various topics in Marx's writings. The account will begin with the question of Labour and excess, and the fundamentally aesthetic anthropology and utopian hope that motivates Marx's entire project; then we will consider Marx's historicist critique of the concept of utility as used in bourgeois political economy; this will lead us to the return of utility under the guise of the 'use-value' which serves Marx as a materialist critique to the excesses of ideality which characterize not just the superstructure but even the base of capitalist society, through practices of reification, alienation and fetish; finally we will explore how these debates have been negotiated by Marxists considering questions of beauty and truth.

We will seek to show that Marx's original protest against capitalism was thoroughly aesthetic and that this was the mode in which the critique remained somehow suspended from transcendence, while simultaneously historically deconstructing all false abstractions and essentialisms. When, however, he tried to make this logic of critique itself into an absolute, puritanically purging himself of any residue of the aesthetic and transcendence, and grounding his critique purely in the immanent laws of conflictual 'natural' development, he merely made utility an end in itself, another naturalized false essence, restoring the very rational instrumentalism he had originally attacked, yet now restored without even serving any higher good, other than anarchic irrational desire.

LABOUR AND EXCESS: THE AESTHETIC
HEART OF MARX'S CRITIQUE

The entire socio-scientific and political project of Karl Marx, consistently present in all his adult writings, is founded upon and driven by a philosophy of labour with its own anthropology and quasi-eschatological hope. This philosophy of labour can be characterized as profoundly aesthetic, and as corresponding (despite certain cautious qualifications in later years) to the aesthetic of excess that we identified in the earlier discussion of twentieth-century theologies of work. Given that much of mainstream Marxism has denied that Marx had a 'philosophy' in any

---

[3] A third source in Epicurean 'materialism of freedom' (the subject of Marx's 1841 doctoral dissertation) has been identified by Constanzo Preve, who further specifies the other three as Hegel, Rousseau and Smith; see Etienne Balibar, *The Philosophy of Marx* (London: Verso, 1995), p. 7.

traditional sense, let alone an anthropology or – worst yet! – any utopian/ eschatological elements, this claim will require some substantiation.

The objections of Marxists, and behind them Marx himself, to such categories as 'anthropology' is that they imply a timeless account of the human essence which is typical of the illusions of philosophy, and hide the specific socio-political relations that any such account of human nature embodies and expresses. Thus, for example, the labour theory of the bourgeois political economists claims to show the 'essential' and, therefore, necessary relation of labour to property, when all that it really does is describe the contingent relation of labour to property under capitalist economic relations. This trick, whereby the contingent relations of a society are eternalized to seem necessary, is not unique to these political economists, but rather has been the fate of every culture prior to modernity. Only past or foreign cultures can be seen as products of their times and societies, while by a universal blind spot one's own seems necessary. Yet as we shall see later, it is in fact these same political economists, expressing the consciousness of bourgeois society as it begins to become aware of its economic contradictions, that make possible for the first time the transcending of this societal blindness to its own contingency. When this birth of self-consciousness happens in the writings of 'scientific' communists on the basis of analyses of the contradictions of capitalism and the seeds of its overcoming in the proletarian class utterly excluded from its benefits, we are not left utterly without anthropology of any sort. Marx's historicism draws back from radical nominalism, admitting the acceptability of generalizations, albeit now more modest ones that, unlike the abstractions of traditional philosophy, must arise from and be constantly checked by the hard realities of material production.[4] Marx's anthropology then is one such modest generalization, describing the nature of man under the specific historical conditions of capitalism, but also to a lesser degree indicating the nature of man as fundamentally historical that must lie behind all specific economic epochs, a sort of historicist anti-anthropological anthropology. This anthropology of labour is certainly more explicit and conventionally presented in the earlier writings, particularly the 1844 *Manuscripts*, yet it remains present, often negatively, but no less crucially, in the later more 'critical' writings.

Anthropology: Labour is the essence of man

Marx's anthropology of labour was in many ways an original synthesis of a diversity of traditions, but the decisive moment of its origins, the 'Archimedean point', should perhaps be fixed in his beginning to read the political economists Adam Smith, David Ricardo, Jean-Baptiste Say and James Mill as a result of his political and legal interests in 1843, and

---

[4]   See Marx's comments in the *Introduction to the Grundrisse* in Carver 1996, p. 146.

Engels's *Outlines of a Critique of Political Economy* in 1844.[5] These writers with their various 'labour theories', provided Marx with the key category of labour with which he was to rethink the Young Hegelian critical historicism of his teacher Bruno Bauer and others such as Feuerbach, transforming it from a philosophico-political critique into a socioeconomic critique *and* a political programme for action.

Marx's fundamental insight and presupposition for all his future work is that labour is the essence of humanity, 'man's essence in the act of proving itself . . . man's coming to be for himself.'[6] Mészáros goes so far as to say that, of all the various aspects of economy, labour is 'the one and only absolute factor in the whole complex . . . because the human mode of existence is inconceivable without the transformations of nature accomplished by productive activity.'[7] This account of labour as the essence of human nature first appears in the 1844 *Economic and Philosophical Manuscripts*, where it already marks a clear break from the German Idealist tradition of Hegel, Bauer, and even to a lesser degree the still 'idealist' materialism of Feuerbach. It appears first here in a rigorously historical mode as an analysis of human existence under capitalism, and negatively, through a phenomenological analysis of the alienation of labour inherent in rent, wages, capital and all other forms of private property, which in turn depend upon the division of labour. Under capitalism, Marx argues, the worker is confronted by his labour not as his own creation, or the extension of sensual body and power, but rather as someone else's property, a hostile alien force that competes with him, the tyrannous 'commodity', 'his own labour confronts him as another's property and . . . the means of his existence and his activity are increasingly concentrated in the hands of the capitalist.'[8] Given that labour is the essence of the worker's humanity, it follows that in the commodity the worker is alienated not only from his product, but also from his fellow human beings, human nature and his very self, becoming 'depressed spiritually and physically to the condition of a machine and from being a man becomes an abstract activity and a stomach'.[9] This language of 'alienation' or 'estrangement' (*Entaeussern, Entfremden*) reveals something of Marx's indebtedness to Hegel, whom he now interprets as a political economist (!) who is to be commended, along with them, for recognizing that '*labour* is the *essence* of man', while chided for only being able to see mental labour and thus only seeing the positive side of labour, not its alienated nature.[10] If Hegel is one of the key sources of Marx's conception of alienation, then it is the political economist Adam Smith who really gets the credit for

[5] Mészáros, p. 76.
[6] Karl Marx, *Economic and Philosophical Manuscripts of 1844*, trans. M Milligan (New York: Prometheus Books, 1988), p. 150.
[7] Mészáros, p. 79.
[8] Marx 1988, p. 22.
[9] Ibid., p. 23.
[10] Ibid., p. 150.

'discovering' the true significance of labour, something which he can only do under the conditions of modern capitalism: Marx follows Engels in calling him the 'Luther of political economy', who achieved a major breakthrough in discovering the subjective source of the value of things in the activity of human labour, against the '*idolaters, fetishists, Catholics*' who previously believed value to reside in things independent of human activity.[11]

While this account of labour carefully begins from the specific historical conditions of capitalism, which according to Marx have alone made it possible for us to attain to such knowledge, it is clear that the labour theory that emerges has a more general, anthropological significance, as Mészáros claimed above and as the approval of Hegel suggested. This is evident from a passage in the *Manuscripts* where Marx indicates that it is labour that sets human beings apart from animals: 'Conscious life-activity directly distinguishes man from animal life-activity... In creating an *objective world* by his practical activity, in *working-up* inorganic nature, man proves himself a conscious species being.'[12] Marx concedes that animals are also productive, citing the famous examples in political philosophy of bees, beavers and ants, but this leads him to more carefully elaborate what he means by labour: animals produce 'one-sidedly', while human beings produce 'universally'; whereas animals produce 'only under the domination of immediate physical need', man 'produces even when he is free from physical need and only truly produces in freedom therefrom'; 'an animal produces only itself, while man reproduces the whole of nature'.[13] Thus it becomes clear that it is not just any futile form of labour that Marx regards as the essence of humanity, but specifically *productive*, fruitful, transformative labour; we are *homo laborans*, but also makers, creators, *homo fabricans*.[14] More significantly it is not toil, nor labouring for the satisfaction of our basic needs that is distinctively human, but 'free' labour, production that is excessive, surpassing our needs, and creating something more than the mere reproduction of ourselves. If we remain in any doubt about the aesthetic nature of truly human work for Marx, he indicates this explicitly at the end of this passage: 'Man therefore also forms things in accordance with the laws of *beauty*.'[15] Human labour, for Marx, is excessive, creating things that exceed our basic needs and have value in themselves beyond their usefulness, things that are beautiful. This excess will take on the more economic form of 'surplus value' in Marx's later writings, yet with the same role: this excess is both the unique dignity of human labour, the human transcendence of animal subsistence, and the root of its potential for exploitation, as it is the surplus that

11   Marx 1988, p. 94.
12   Ibid., pp. 76–7.
13   Ibid., p. 77.
14   William Adams in Terrell Carver (ed.), *The Cambridge Companion to Marx* (Cambridge: Cambridge University Press, 1991), p. 249.
15   Marx 1988, p. 77 (my italics).

makes man into a worker whose labour is useful to someone else, as when under capitalism, it becomes the source of the capitalist's profits. Various other conclusions follow from Marx's anthropology of labour and excess: Humanity is irreducibly historical, because in transforming nature we also transform ourselves and the very conditions of our labour. Each generation stands upon and starts from the achievements, that is, the surplus labour of former generations. Through labour humanity makes not only things, but also the world and itself: 'man produces man – himself and the other man...*just as* society itself produces *man as man*, so is society *produced* by him'.[16] This is the basis of Marx's thoroughgoing historicism: because society and even human nature are human products, they can only be analysed historically, never as timeless essences, for, as he puts its: 'History is the true natural history of man'.[17] Hegel's radically promethean account of human nature as 'self-genesis' is transformed from a theory of intellectual history into economic and social history.[18]

This historicizing of human nature is repeatedly illustrated by Marx over the years using the powerful aesthetic illustration of the development of sensibility, an image which merits closer attention. We are told that the objects we create themselves create in us the senses to appreciate them, 'just as music alone awakens in man the sense of music, and just as the most beautiful music has *no* sense for the unmusical ear.'[19] Marx extends this not just to the formation of 'a musical ear, an eye for beauty of form', but also to the 'so-called mental senses (will, love, etc)' and concludes: 'The *forming* of the five senses is a labour of *humanised* nature. The *forming* of the five senses is a labour of the entire history of the world down to the present.'[20] In terms reminiscent of Romantic philosophy and likely to make an orthodox Marxist blush, Marx even speaks of nature as man's '*inorganic* body'[21] and society as the 'consummated oneness in substance of man and nature – the true resurrection of nature – the naturalism of man and the humanism of nature both brought to fulfilment.'[22] While Marx's language might cool in later years, the basic intuition remains, and continues to be expressed in aesthetic terms, whether it is in the *Communist Manifesto* of 1848, where he speaks of the creation of new needs, or the *Grundrisse* from 1857 where the power of art to create its own audience is used to illustrate the way that consumption shapes production.[23]

Yet there is a problem with this aesthetic account of human labour as free, excessive production of beauty comparable to art; it does not seem

[16]   Ibid., p. 104.
[17]   Ibid., p. 156.
[18]   Ibid., p. 161.
[19]   Ibid., p. 108.
[20]   Ibid., pp. 108–9.
[21]   Ibid., p. 76.
[22]   Ibid., p. 104.
[23]   Carver 1996, pp. 5, 137.

to be as 'empirical' as Marx protests his conclusions to be, since evidently much human labour is precisely not this sort of free artistic labour, but various forms of enslavement. As Marx comments when criticizing Hegel, this aesthetic account of labour must be only half the picture. Yet if this is so, we might well ask, where does Marx get his evidence that this is the 'true' nature of human labour, rather than the equally manifest elements of toil and alienation? Given his specific rejection of any accounts of a paradisal 'state of nature' such as those of the political economists, he cannot look to the past to distinguish the 'true' from the 'false', in the way narratives of Eden and the Fall operate within Christianity (although we should note that his later comments on the primitive Slav, Celtic and Peruvian communes seem very close to this). He is, therefore, forced to look to history as a complex progress of the developmental emergence of truth. This is significantly qualified from any naïve optimism by the darkly dialectical observation that the advancement of freedom is roughly proportionate to the advance of oppression, misery and enslavement. This is the key to Marx's ambiguity towards capitalism and the bourgeoisie that persists through his writings and so perplexes one at first encounter: capitalism is the absolutely *necessary* precursor to its own overcoming in the advent of communism; only capitalism could create the productive power and communicative technology that could make possible a truly socialist society. Likewise the bourgeoisie may usually be the objects of Marx's utter contempt, and yet their values of freedom and equality pave the way for their own undoing. The ground of this tragic vision lies at the heart of Marx's phenomenology of labour: in labour man not only asserts himself, transforming the world into an extension of his body, but at the same time becomes open to losing or alienating himself in the object of this self-assertion. This is not just incidental, but is an integral vulnerability in the history of man's labour: 'the assertion of his life is the alienation of his life.'[24] This seems to leave us with the same problem: if the history of human assertion is also the history of human alienation, how can one be claimed to be any more 'true' labour than the other? The answer to this problem is to be found in the fact that Marx's vision is not utterly tragic, because the dialectic does not oscillate in equilibrium, but does truly advance with what could be called a residue of assertion over alienation (although Marx does not make this explicit).[25] This is the only possible explanation for his confident expectation that the history of tragic dialectics is not eternal, but will come to an end, the end of 'pre-history' and the beginning of 'history' proper, when assertion will no longer necessarily entail alienation, but will be fully socialized and thus mutual and reciprocal. It is this vision of a communist society beyond the

---

[24] Marx 1988, p. 106.
[25] Cf. Lash's discussion (pp. 268–9) of the debate between George Steiner and Raymond Williams over whether Marx's account of history is best described as *commedia* or tragedy, respectively.

abolition of private property, which Marx claims to see beginning to emerge *from the immanent dialectics of history*, that forms the only possible basis for his otherwise groundless value judgement that free, artistic labour is truly human, while alienated labour is not (we will have to return to this later when considering Marx's metaphysics and 'scientism'). Once again while such explicit descriptions of this utopian state to come as we find in the 1844 *Manuscripts* are few and more tacit in Marx's later writings, it cannot be denied that some such value judgement and hope remains utterly integral, albeit implicitly, to everything Marx did and wrote, to the end of his life. We shall now turn to explore this expectation.

Eschatology: The emancipation of labour

Once again in seeking to explore Marx's 'eschatology' we are faced with the problem that confronted the investigation of his anthropology: the denial of the existence of any such thing from both his subsequent admirers and, to a lesser degree, from Marx himself. Mészáros illustrates this tendency well when he says that, with Marx 'there can be no place for a utopian golden age, neither "round the corner" nor astronomical distances away. Such a golden age would be an end of history, and thus the end of man himself.'[26] Those who claim to find such things in Marx are simply dismissed as 'vulgarizers' concentrating on isolated sentences. And yet as most commentators recognize, such a dismissal entails a wilful misreading of Marx's works which, admittedly in varying ways and with varying explicitness, consistently look for the advent of a new, utterly different society, brought in by the revolution that Marx continued to expect, albeit sometimes sooner, sometimes later.

Given that, as we have already shown, Marx's historicist critique of essentialism meant that he could not look to the past for the essence of true human nature with which to contrast its alienation, he insisted instead that this essence was being realized and must be realized in and through history; man's Being, in Feuerbach's terminology, must *be made to be* his essence, because they are not currently identical.[27] This creates one of the problems with Marx's eschatology: because this essence is yet to be realized there cannot be any direct experience of it. This opens questions as to the status of any accounts of this state: if they cannot be empirical, are they scientific predictions, moral imperatives, performative illocutions? This is something to which we shall return again. Yet as Lash notes, these qualifications are perhaps not so different from those pertaining to Christian hope and expectation, so that it can still be appropriate to speak of 'eschatology', and they certainly do not prevent Marx himself from speaking relatively frequently about what such a

---

[26] Mészáros, p. 241.
[27] Karl Marx, *The German Ideology* (New York: Prometheus Books, 1998), p. 66.

state might be like.[28] These comments are often more vague than might be hoped for, although such a reticence is perhaps what we should expect from someone claiming not to be a prophet, but just to envisage the overcoming of contradictions inherent in contemporary capitalism. This *Aufhebung* of alienated labour is presented in terms even more explicitly aesthetic than the basic anthropology considered above, upon which it is founded.

One of the earliest and most lyrical of such passages occurs in the 1844 *Manuscripts* and concerns the emancipation of sensibility under communism. Given the amount of discussion it has provoked and its particular relevance to our aims, it merits quotation in full:

> The transcendence of private property is therefore the complete *emancipation* of all human senses and attributes; but it is this emancipation precisely because these senses and attributes have become, subjectively and objectively, *human*. The eye has become a *human* eye, just as its *object* has become a social, *human* object – an object emanating from man and for man. The senses have therefore become directly in their practice *theoreticians*. They relate themselves to the *thing* for the sake of the thing, but the thing itself is an *objective human* relation to itself and to man, and vice versa. Need or enjoyment have consequently lost their *egoistical* nature, and nature has lost its mere *utility* by use becoming *human* use.[29]

It is clear from this that Marx follows his earlier recognition of the historicity of human sensibility by imagining and expecting its emancipation as a result of the emancipation of labour through the abolition of private property. This liberation is seen in terms of a reconciliation of human subjectivity with the objectivity of nature and technology, and a transcendence of egoism and utility through humanization, socialization, and, interestingly, a contemplation (*theoria*) appropriate to 'theoreticians'. This language of the liberation of man from the dehumanizing and objectifying effects of industrialism has much in common with the Romantic protests of Hegel and Schiller, although as Eagleton notes, Schiller's aesthetic liberation *from* sensuality into a Kantian idealist disinterestedness is now given a Feuerbachian materialist inversion to become the liberation *of* the senses.[30] Under socialism there will be no puritanical-ascetical restriction or withering of genuine needs, but a '*wealth* of human needs' and a 'new enrichment of *human* nature'.[31]

---

[28] Lash, p. 243.
[29] Marx 1988, p. 107.
[30] Terry Eagleton, *The Ideology of the Aesthetic* (Oxford: Blackwell, 1990), p. 203. See Friedrich Schiller, *On the Aesthetic Education of Man: In a Series of Letters*, trans. Elizabeth Wilkinson and L. A. Willoughby (Oxford: Oxford University Press, 1967).
[31] Marx 1988, p. 115.

Taken over from Schiller and Hegel unaltered is the sense of aesthetic contemplation or *delight* as the truly human relation to things, treating them as ends in themselves, instead of the instrumentalist logic of utility and pragmatism.[32] As Eagleton again puts it, Marx is 'most profoundly "aesthetic" in his belief that the exercise of human sense, powers and capacities is an absolute end in itself, without need of utilitarian justification', yet unlike the idealists, this overcoming of the alienation of subject and object does not happen merely ideally for Marx, but objectively and historically with real material preconditions.[33]

This aesthetic vision of a society beyond the alienation of labour is also, as the word communism suggests, one where individualism is transcended in a socialization that nevertheless does not destroy individuality but is its true fulfilment. Marx can, therefore, say that communism is 'the complete return of man to himself as a *social* (i.e. human) being'.[34] This follows from the abolition of private property so that the interests of people are no longer inherently opposed and conflicting, the gain of one no longer entails the loss of another, but rather their gain as well. Marx describes this as the humanization of need: 'the extent to which man's need has become a human need; the extent to which, therefore, the other person as a person has become for him a need – the extent to which he in his individual existence is at the same time a social being.'[35] The oppositions of subject and object, the individual and society are not the only ones that will be overcome by communism: 'it is the *genuine* resolution of the conflict between man and nature and between man and man – the true resolution of the strife between existence and essence, between objectification and self-confirmation, between freedom and necessity, between the individual and the species. Communism is the riddle of history solved, and it knows itself to be this solution.'[36] Much of this language of the resolution of conflict, the overcoming of oppositions in a higher unity, is clearly indebted to Rousseau and Hegel, and even more so to the Romantic materialism of Feuerbach, from whom Marx had yet sharply to distinguish himself when he wrote these passages in 1844. However even at this early stage in his intellectual development, Marx illustrates this overcoming of pragmatic utility by a delight in sociality as an end in itself in a striking passage, using a concrete example from his experience of the workers' movements in Paris, thereby giving his vision of transformation a historical and political edge that goes beyond Feuerbach, and would probably have seemed prosaic to the latter:

> When communist *workmen* associate with one another, theory, propaganda, etc., is their first end. But at the same

[32] Eagleton, p. 204; Carver 1991, p. 253.
[33] Eagleton, p. 202.
[34] Marx 1988, p. 102.
[35] Ibid.
[36] Ibid., pp. 102–3.

time, as a result of this association, they acquire a new need –
the need for society – and what appears as a means becomes an
end... Such things as smoking, drinking, eating, etc., are no
longer means of contact or means that bring together. Company, association, and conversation, which again has society
as its end, are enough for them; the brotherhood of man is no
mere phrase with them, but a fact of life, and the nobility of
man shines upon us from their work-hardened bodies.[37]

Means becoming ends, the aesthetic subversion of the instrumental logic
of modern technology and industry, is a key motif for Marx's account of
the emancipation of labour, for the *Aufhebung* of its estrangement, in
more philosophical terms. In the communist society things are done for
their own sake, for the sheer delight of sensuous activity, not for something else, whether survival, wages, or the increase of someone else's
profits. Another example Marx offers is the writer, whose works are 'an
end in themselves; so little are they "means", for himself and for others,
that he will, if necessary, sacrifice his own existence to their existence.'[38]
These various images of aesthetic delight are thus significant because 'art
figures for Marx as the ideal paradigm of material production precisely
because it is so evidently autotelic.'[39] Yet once again Marx seems to
differ from idealism in that this free artistic production is not just
opposed to the realm of the practical, but rather deconstructs the very
opposition of the practical and the aesthetic, in a materialist direction.
For Marx, art and work are no longer to be enemies, but under communism will become one, as he makes clear in his rejection of Stirner's
elitist conception of art as confined to the few who can attain to its
'uniqueness': 'The exclusive concentration of artistic talent in particular
individuals, and its suppression in the broad mass which is bound up
with this, is a consequence of the division of labour... in a communist
society there are no painters but only people who engage in painting
among other activities.'[40]

In his earlier writings Marx expects this socialization and humanization of labour under communism to entail the abolition of the division of
labour, which is integral to its estrangement, and its replacement by a
society of 'renaissance men', accomplished in all human arts and doing
each as they please, almost as if they were hobbies. Thus he writes in a
passage of the *German Ideology* in 1845, which has become famous as
one of his most concrete and explicit visions of life after the revolution:

in communist society, where nobody has one exclusive sphere
of activity but each can become accomplished in any branch

---

[37] Marx 1988, pp. 123–4.
[38] Quoted in Eagleton, p. 204.
[39] Ibid.
[40] Marx 1998, pp. 417–18.

he wishes, society regulates the general production and thus makes it possible for me to do one thing today and another tomorrow, to hunt in the morning, fish in the afternoon, rear cattle in the evening, criticise after dinner, just as I have a mind, without ever becoming hunter, fisherman, shepherd or critic.[41]

At this time Marx can even speak boldly of the abolition of labour as such, at least in any recognizable sense, as labour will be transformed into the 'self-activity' of 'complete individuals', 'casting off all natural limitations'(!).[42] This initial optimism of the mid-1840s seems to fade over the years as Marx develops his critique of utopianism (e.g., in criticisms of Owen, Fourier and Saint-Simon in the *Communist Manifesto* of 1848). Gradually he moves away from hoping for the abolition of the division of labour and a total transformation of labour into art, towards the more modest vision of the considerable reduction of working hours and the increase of free time, although he still hopes that this will itself transform the workers' consciousness as they develop their other powers in their leisure hours, and thus also indirectly transform the nature of their work.[43] 'Work cannot become a game', Marx now insists, against the more utopian Fourier.[44] Later still, in *Capital*, Marx makes it even more explicit that, while it may be improved, labour remains incapable of being completely liberated from toil to become the sort of free labour that he had envisaged 20 years earlier:

> The realm of freedom really begins only where labour determined by necessity and external expediency ends; it lies by its very nature *beyond the sphere of material production proper* ... [fully rational, socialized labour] always remains a realm of necessity. The true realm of freedom, the development of human powers as an end in itself, begins beyond it, though it can *only flourish with this realm of necessity as its basis*'.[45]

As Adams notes, it would be incorrect to interpret this as an abandonment of the aesthetic model of human flourishing. Instead he seems to have rejected the transformation of the very nature of work, in favour of a more 'realistic', limited account of the possible extent of this flourishing.[46] Nevertheless, from the *Communist Manifesto* through to *Capital*, the motivation of Marx's entire work remains the aesthetic vision of 'an

[41] Ibid., p. 53.
[42] Ibid., pp. 60, 97.
[43] David McLellan (ed.), *Marx's Grundrisse* (St Alban's: Paladin, 1973), pp. 165–6.
[44] Ibid., p. 171.
[45] Carver 1991, pp. 271–2.
[46] Ibid., p. 271.

association in which the free development of each is the condition for the free development of all.'[47]

The historicist critique of utility and political economy

We have already noted Marx's indebtedness to political economy for his central concept of labour, yet it would be mistaken to believe his attitude to this tradition to be purely positive. The third dimension of Marx's philosophy of labour that expresses an aesthetic of excess is his critique of utility which is directed largely against the political economists.

As has already been observed, Marx regards the logic of means and ends, of instrumentalism or usefulness, as part of the estrangement of capitalism and looks for its overcoming or at least restriction in favour of a more aesthetic immediate unity of means and ends. Under the rule of capitalism according to Marx, the triumph of utility is absolute and self-serving, entailing the 'complete subordination of all existing relations to the relation of utility, and its unconditional elevation to the sole content of all other relations'.[48] Even 'Life itself appears only as a *means to life*.'[49] People are reduced to the status of things, 'living capital', the '*commodity-man*...a *spiritually* and physically *dehumanised* being' to be bought and sold, so that slavery and prostitution are appropriate descriptions of the condition of most humans.[50] Political economy, which according to Marx is the 'real science of this theory of utility', is incapable of seeing people as truly human beings, but only as commodities in terms of their value.[51] Thus the only need that political economy can recognize in the worker is the need that the race of workers should not die out.[52] This is why such thought can be used to justify the absolute minimum in subsistence being given to the workers. Offensive though such an approach might seem, it was not merely invented by the political economists, but rather is nothing more than the true expression of the underlying logic of the practice of capitalism. Thus Marx praises Ricardo and Mill for being more honest than Smith or Say in facing up to this fundamental *indifference* of political economy towards the real conditions of specific workers.[53]

How does Marx account for the virtual total domination of the principle of utility? In the *German Ideology*, he undertakes to do so historically, linking utility with the rise of modern capitalism and thus enabling a complex evaluation of its significance, as at various times radical and conservative. Marx begins by following Hegel in identifying

[47] Carver 1996, p. 20; cf. Maynard Solomon, *Marxism and Art* (Brighton: The Harvester Press, 1979), p. 60.
[48] Marx 1998, p. 436.
[49] Marx 1988, p. 76.
[50] Ibid., pp. 86, 120.
[51] Marx 1998, p. 433.
[52] Marx 1988, p. 86.
[53] Ibid., p. 87

the original emergence of the theory of utility with the struggle of the forces of enlightenment against superstition, citing Hobbes, Locke, Helvétius and Holbach among its early exponents.[54] Yet he goes beyond Hegel in offering an economic explanation for this emergence: the principle of utility is merely the metaphysical expression of the fact that 'in modern bourgeois society all relations are subordinated in practice to the one abstract monetary-commercial relation.'[55] Thus the abstract principle of utility reducing everything to commodities corresponds to the practical effects of capital in modern society. As Marx had observed of the power of money, so it is also true of utility that in 'confounding and compounding' all things it utterly abolishes the specificity of things and thus any sense of their inherent worth or value in a destabilizing that tends through an infinite regress of means and ends towards nihilism.[56] So we are led to the discovery that the principle of utility is little more than the self-articulation of the bourgeoisie's exploitation of others to serve their own ends, and the destruction of the old system of values that was required to make this possible. Yet Marx acknowledges that the theory of utility was a 'kind of *enlightenment*' in its capacity to secularize and demystify this exploitation.[57] Utility served to sweep away the sentimental, religious justifications of exploitation revealing them as pure exploitation. This then is the radical element to the principle of utility: in the early days of the bourgeoisie's supercession of the feudal order it served to demystify and deconstruct traditional taboos that constituted, justified and enforced exploitation. The same interpretation is to be found in Marx's celebration of the 'revolutionary role' of the bourgeoisie in the *Communist Manifesto* for having profaned the sacred, 'drowned the ecstasies of religious fervour, of zealous chivalry, of philistine sentiment in the waters of egoistic calculation.'[58] One of the best examples of the bourgeoisie's use of the theory of utility to challenge the values of the old order is provided by the critique of the 'useless' monastic life in the early modern era. Even the family now seems an economic relation devoid of sentiment after this process of desacralizing: '[F]or exploitation cloaked by religious and political illusions, [utility] has substituted open, unashamed, direct, brutal exploitation.'[59] However this initial radical task of the theory of utility, best articulated by Bentham and Mill, in tearing down feudal illusions, soon degenerated along with the bourgeois class to whom it was indebted, to become a 'mere apologia for the existing state of affairs'.[60]

[54] Marx 1998, p. 433.
[55] Ibid.
[56] Marx 1988, p. 140; cf. Hannah Arendt, *The Human Condition* (Chicago: University of Chicago Press, 1998), pp. 154–7.
[57] Marx 1998, p. 434.
[58] Carver 1996, p. 3.
[59] Ibid.
[60] Marx 1998, p. 437.

Marx's thoroughgoing historicism is clearly evident again here. While he had earlier celebrated political economy for helping him to break away from the timeless abstractions of philosophy towards the more historical account based upon labour, he nevertheless believed political economy itself to be still too prone to such temptations of timeless essentializing. Political economists mistake the relations of capitalism for the eternal and necessary relations of human nature. This can be seen in their tendency to talk about labour using such timeless abstractions that sound reminiscent of some paradisal state in literature.[61] Marx sees the physiocrats as particularly symptomatic of this failing, in their turn away from the historicism of labour towards the essentialism of land, a move which seems to him like a return to fetish.[62] Against this Marx pushes his historicism still further, arguing, as with his earlier comments on sensibility, that use is historically constituted and so cannot be appealed to as an extra-temporal and extra-class category which alone can correct its mystical deceptions. In bold language Marx reminds his audience that utility is not an eternal given as Ricardo seems to suggest, but that only 'whim' determines production and only 'fashion' determines use.[63] In this move Marx reinforces his historicist critique of a naïve and essentialist account of utility – what is 'useful' is radically contingent upon history. The philosophy of Bentham and Mill, and political economy generally, interpreting everything in terms of utility, is exposed by Marx as the ideological expression of bourgeois capitalism masquerading as eternal necessities, and just as capable of hiding exploitation and oppression as the traditional mystical sentiments that it had assisted in deconstructing.

For Marx then, utilitarianism could be described as the 'spirit of capitalism'. Political economy, which articulates this spirit, is recognized by Marx as not a science after the model of the natural sciences as it claimed to be, but rather a 'moral science', more specifically, the 'science of *asceticism*', whose true ideal is the '*ascetic* but extortionate miser and the *ascetic* but *productive* slave'.[64] In characterizing capitalism as a form of asceticism that is nevertheless paradoxically bound up with luxury, Marx anticipates the account offered by Weber which we explored in chapter 2. The paradoxical identity of extravagance and thrift, wealth and poverty will require further consideration, but before this we must turn to Marx's more anti-aesthetical elements: his negative attitudes towards the excess of cultural production and his partial restoration of utility.[65]

[61]   Marx 1988, p. 122.
[62]   Ibid., p. 247.
[63]   Ibid., pp. 119–20.
[64]   Ibid., p. 118.
[65]   Ibid., p. 120.

THE LIMITING OF LABOUR BY UTILITY: MARX'S PERSISTING NATURALIST HOSTILITY TOWARDS AESTHETICS AND THE THEOLOGICAL

We have seen how Marx's critique of capitalism is based upon an aesthetical account of labour: labour as a radical creativity, fundamental to human nature; and, in its true, 'unalienated' form, delightful and autotelic like art. This, I would argue, is already a quasi-theological position, deriving from those quasi-theological traditions, German Romanticism and Idealism. How so? First, in Marx's case despite himself, in the non-empirical, metaphysical or ideal nature of its claims. Whether he recognizes it or not, Marx's theory of labour does entail an *a priori* account of human 'nature', albeit in the qualified sense we noted earlier. This is even more evident in his evaluative comments on 'alienated' and 'unalienated' labour: his ideal account of labour, his 'eschatology' as we termed it, cannot be empirically derived. As we might expect, like any critical strategy that wishes to oppose something, Marx is required to commit himself to some fundamental value judgements, that take him beyond the realm of positivism into a certain sort of *a priori*. Furthermore, I would claim that this aesthetic account of the true nature of labour is more explicitly theological, in that it must derive tacitly from the idea of Divine labour, or creation, not human labour. It is from the Romantic tradition primarily that we have received the conception of art as divine, a gift, granted to mystics and geniuses, an interpretation which remains powerful today.[66] Yet this ideal account of art as utterly spontaneous, non-instrumental, and so forth, is incoherent on purely human terms, without reference to its divine source and ideal. For us mortals, even art, like all labour, cannot completely rid itself of toil and alienation; it cannot achieve its perfect product, absolute autotely, total delight in the thing that is produced, free from any diminution of the labourer. Art, as the Romantics understood, may get closer to this ideal than other forms of labour, yet it remains necessarily finite, discursive, mediated; there remains a disjunction between the artist's mental ideal and the actualization of that form, between the production and the product. True art on this account, and thus Marx's ideal labour, can only be possible for God, for whom the idea and the creation of a thing are identical, who creates *ex nihilo* with no prior material to hinder his will, whose beatitude is his perfect delight in the goodness of his creation. This Romantic conceptuality of art and labour is predicated upon a certain transcendence.

---

[66] For the Romantic notion of art, see Raymond Williams, *Culture and Society 1780–1950* (London: Chatto and Windus, 1960), pp. 30–49. For the complex relationship between Marx and Romanticism see: Michael Löwy and Robert Sayre, *Romanticism against the Tide of Modernity*, trans. C. Porter (London: Duke University Press, 2001), pp. 88–99.

If Marx's aesthetic theory of labour is in some sense theological, then his other side, the anti-aesthetic utilitarian critique of excessive labour, is no less caught up in theological concerns. This time though, the utilitarian naturalist spirit is anti-theological. The reassertion of a form of utility begins under the influence of the Young Hegelian, Feuerbachian critique of the alienation of religion, and the extension of these categories of religious alienation to money, following Moses Hess. Following the break with Feuerbach and idealism, these elements in Marx's thought take a more materialist turn, developing into his innovative economic critique of all ideology and 'superstructural' phenomena, as such – phenomena which, for Marx, are clearly archetypically 'religious'. This critique is then turned back from culture to the economic 'base' to expose the ideality present even here, in 'exchange value'. This suspect 'exchange value' is also seen in specifically religious terms: as a form of superstition, fetish or idolatry. The excesses and injustices of this 'artificial' and socially constructed exchange value are then set against 'use value', which points towards a naturalist and ascetic limitation of the former, a reordering of value and production to serve human needs. It is this anti-theological and anti-aesthetical thread of the reassertion of utility, with its concomitant materialism and naturalism, that we shall now seek to trace in greater detail.

The alienating excess of intellectual production and its religious genesis

In the first half of this chapter we noted that it is the excessiveness of human labour, its capacity to produce beyond the mere satisfaction of need to create a surplus, that characterizes such labour as distinctively human for Marx. Yet we also indicated that it is this same excessive nature of labour and its surplus that is the source of the slavery of modern man under capitalism. Only someone who produces beyond self-sufficiency is useful to others, can be persuaded to surrender that surplus to someone else. Thus the excessive surplus under capitalism is turned against its maker, until, rather like the sorcerer's apprentice, the labourer is enslaved by his own creations. This of course is the alienation that lies at the heart of capitalism for Marx. Such an account of alienation has interesting implications when applied specifically to intellectual labour, which must be classed as *particularly* symptomatic of the excessiveness of human labour. It is in fact in this question of the ideal that Marx first 'discovers' alienation, and more precisely in the area of the religious.

Here we must return once again to Marx's roots in the German philosophical tradition. The Young Hegelian circles in which Marx moved during his early years of study had begun to synthesize Hegel's account of the history of *Geist* with a more French materialist positivism to offer a Comtean account of religion as primitive delusions to be transcended. The publication of Feuerbach's *Essence of Christianity* in 1841 arguing that not just the primitive religions, but even the God of

Christianity, could be understood in terms of the logic of reification, as an abstraction of human ideals, clearly had a great influence upon Marx. Three years later he wrote that Feuerbach's great achievement was the 'proof that philosophy is nothing else but religion...and that it has therefore likewise to be condemned as another form and manner of existence of the estrangement of the essence of man.'[67] Marx has here gone beyond his teacher Bruno Bauer who had tried to turn Hegel against religion in the name of 'Criticism'. Now Feuerbach has revealed that, despite the brief promise of the negative moment, Hegel's dialectic always reinstates religion and thus remains thoroughly theological throughout. This discovery means that the enemy is no longer just religion, but now also what had seemed its opponent but was only ever acting on its behalf: philosophy. And if philosophy suffers from alienation as much as religion, then it must be overthrown to be replaced by Feuerbach's 'establishment of *true materialism* and of *real science*'.[68] Philosophy as much as religion is founded upon an alienating reification, an abstraction that generates ideal fictions given a life of their own which then distracts and detracts from the sensual material reality of human existence. In the three years between *The Essence of Christianity* and Marx's Paris *Manuscripts*, when most of his own ideas seem to have taken shape, it is significant, as Margaret Rose has reminded us, that Marx was engaged in intense reading in the subjects of religion and aesthetics.[69] In 1842 Bauer had commissioned Marx to join his project of a radical reinterpretation of Hegel by writing an article that was to be entitled *Hegels Hass gegen die religioese und christliche Kunst* – Hegel's hatred of religious and Christian art – no mean task of reinterpretation given that Hegel seems to have exhibited admiration for both! While this was never completed and nothing remains of it, we know that Marx read widely for this task, including Constant, Barbeyrac and Meiners on religion, Debrosses on fetishes, Bottiger on Mythology and Grund on Greek Art.[70] The latter three authors all followed the Hellenism of Gibbon and others in attributing primitivism and fetish to Christian art, against the sensualism and realism of the Greeks, a position which would not have been popular with the Prussian Christian establishment and its patronage of Christian Gothic art. From this evidence and a few revealing asides in his articles in the *Rheinische Zeitung*, Lifshitz concludes that Marx's intended article would have sought to turn the Christian-Hegelian critique of fetishism as alienating objectivity and idolatry against Christianity itself.[71]

Marx's extension of these categories of fetish and alienation to economic relations can be seen already in the 1844 *Manuscripts*, where he

---

[67] Marx 1988, p. 144.
[68] Ibid.
[69] Margaret Rose, *Marx's Lost Aesthetic: Karl Marx and the Visual Arts* (Cambridge: Cambridge University Press, 1984), p. 60.
[70] Ibid., p. 62.
[71] Ibid., p. 63.

speaks of 'the spontaneous activity of the human imagination, of the human brain and the human heart, [which] operates on him as an alien, *divine* or diabolical activity';[72] and where he follows Shakespeare in calling money a 'visible divinity'.[73] We should note here that the apparently economic idea of 'commodity fetishism', the commodification that constitutes the alienation of labour for Marx, expounded in *Capital* volume 1 and variously hailed as 'the *basic* idea of the Marxian system' and 'one of the great theoretical constructs of modern philosophy', is at root a theologico-aesthetical concept, which Marx derived from his early studies in these areas.[74] This is evident in the constant use of religious illustrations of these phenomena, as when he says, in very Feuerbachian tones: 'It is the same in religion. The more man puts into God, the less he retains in himself. The worker puts his life into the object; but now his life no longer belongs to him but to the object.'[75] These illustrations persist right through to *Capital* and other later writings, so that we can agree with Lash that religion is not just another example of alienation for Marx, but rather is alienation *par excellence*.[76] Or more precisely as Milbank puts it, there is no contradiction for Marx in alienation being primarily economic, yet manifest first and foremost in philosophy and religion; rather this is expressive of Germany's backward situation where the national economic base is oddly lagging behind the cosmopolitan superstructure, hence the disjunction is greater there than in Britain or France where the two are more in pace with each other, with the result that alienation is less concealed and more obvious in Germany, particularly in that most abstract of discourses, German philosophy.[77]

From concluding that religion, as the most abstract of human activities, best discloses alienation, and from his Feuerbachian identification of Hegelian philosophy with religion, Marx then goes on to make one further step that marks his break with Feuerbach and departure from philosophy as such. This step is outlined in *The German Ideology* and the *Theses on Feuerbach* (1845) and it is important to our argument in that it seems to constitute an extension of the suspicion of the fetishized excess of religion to intellectual production generally. At this point the question arises with force: Is Marx hostile to thinking as such? Are all ideas nothing but 'ideology' for him?

The German Ideology is often seen as marking the beginning of Marx's 'critical' period and is a biting and often amusing piece of satire. Its central claim, that the Young Hegelians' critique of religion applies just as much to themselves, and that their supposedly 'critical'

---

72 Marx 1988, p. 74 (my italics).
73 Ibid., p. 138.
74 Mészáros, p. 93; Balibar, p. 56.
75 Marx 1988, p. 72.
76 Lash, p. 179. Cf. Karl Marx, *Capital: A Critical Analysis of Capitalist Production* (Moscow: Foreign Languages Publishing House, 1957–62), vol. I, pp. 71–83.
77 John Milbank, *Theology and Social Theory* (Oxford: Blackwell 1990), pp. 180–1.

philosophy is no more than religion, is made clear through the book's literary form. After an initial more gentle treatment of Feuerbach, Marx turns his undisguised contempt upon Max Stirner and his old tutor Bruno Bauer, who are presented as Church Fathers, 'Saint Max and Saint Bruno' at the 'Leipzig Council', a court of inquisition against the 'heretic Feuerbach'. This book represents an all out attack on the quasi-religion of Idealist philosophy, a 'revolt against this rule of concepts'.[78] 'Hitherto' Marx announces in the preface, 'men have always formed wrong ideas about themselves, about what they are and what they ought to be . . . The products of their brains have got out of their hands. They, the creators, have bowed down before their creations. Let us liberate them from the chimeras, the ideas, dogmas, imaginary beings under the yoke of which they are pining away.'[79] Those Young Hegelians who believe they have overcome the tyranny of such religious ideas by seeing through them to the philosophical truths beneath are compared by Marx to a man who thought people only drowned because of the idea of gravity and that by disbelieving in this superstition one could be free of gravity and its effects.[80]

Since his 1844 investigations into Hegelian legal philosophy Marx had become convinced that civil society, philosophy and culture should all be accounted for in terms of the economic material conditions of life rather than the other way round. In *The German Ideology* this intuition is beginning to take on the familiar Marxist vocabulary of economic 'base' and intellectual 'superstructure', the latter being characterized by 'ideology' or the distortion of truth. Thus we read that 'in all ideology men and their relations appear upside-down as in a *camera obscura*', while German philosophy is accused of descending 'from heaven to earth'.[81] More precisely Marx insists that art, politics and law, 'morality, religion, metaphysics, and all the rest of ideology . . . have no history, no development' because 'it is not consciousness that determines life, but life that determines consciousness.'[82] Again and again Marx hammers this point home: economic conditions are the 'real basis' of history, the formation of ideas must be explained from material practice not vice versa, we must not be fooled by the ideologist who 'takes every epoch at its word and believes everything it says and imagines about itself is true'.[83] The suspicion and unmasking of the 'phantoms' of religion now seem to have been extended, potentially at least, to the entirety of intellectual production, all ideas and culture.

We should note something here again: religion is not just one example among others of the alienation of ideology, the one through which Marx

---

[78] Marx 1998, p. 29.
[79] Ibid.
[80] Ibid., p. 30.
[81] Ibid., p. 42.
[82] Ibid., pp. 42, 101
[83] Ibid., pp. 61, 62, 71.

happened to come across the phenomenon, nor is it even simply the best example of this alienation as we indicated above; rather, *all* ideology *is* aboriginally religious for Marx. Here again he has radicalized the Young Hegelian and Feuerbachian position, towards a much more Comtean-positivist account of history and a thoroughly materialist rejection of any metaphysics. Thus Marx writes in *The German Ideology*: 'Division of labour only becomes truly such from the moment when a division of material from mental labour appears. From this moment onwards consciousness *can* really flatter itself that it is something other than consciousness of existing practice.' Next to this, Marx has added the revealing marginal note: 'The first form of ideologists, *priests*, is coincident.'[84] The implications of this are clear. For Marx, all ideology is at root religious, and thus the Young Hegelian critique of religion, the interrogation of who produces these ideas, whose interests they serve, what they hide, can now be extended to any and maybe even all intellectual productions, all culture. This suspicion towards any sense of the autonomy of intellectual production and subsequent reduction of ideas to expressions of class interest or other forms of power, has roots in Marx's pre-1845 writings and persists beyond *The German Ideology* as a consistent and powerful theme in his later works. Thus in the *Communist Manifesto* he commends the bourgeoisie's demystification of feudal ideas of monarchy and 'natural' hierarchy as covers for naked class interest, while then turning against the bourgeoisie and their own treasured values of liberty, justice and the family, which he argues are just as much an attempt to justify their own class position through naturalizing it to become part of an eternal order.[85] Likewise much later in *The Contribution to the Critique of Political Economy* (1859) he writes even more unequivocally: it is the economic structure of society that is 'the real basis from which rises a legal and political superstructure, and to which correspond specific forms of social consciousness. The mode of production of material life conditions the social, political and intellectual life-process generally. It is not the consciousness of men that specifies their being, but on the contrary their social being that specifies their consciousness.'[86]

Anti-aesthetics?

What does all this have to do with aesthetics? It is Marx's project of extending the unmasking of religion as power to all culture that has made him so fascinating to cultural and literary theorists, those interested in questions of aesthetics in the narrower sense.[87] Marx has

---

[84] Marx 1998, p. 50. Cf. Marx 1988, p. 80.
[85] Carver 1996, pp. 3–4, 16.
[86] Ibid., pp. 159–60.
[87] See Solomon, and Lee Baxandall and Stefan Morawski (eds.), *Marx Engels: On Literature and Art* (New York: International General, 1974).

become one of the 'masters of suspicion' along with Nietzsche and Freud who have been so important to twentieth-century criticism and its various projects of decoding and deconstructing cultural and aesthetic objects to reveal the power relations they express and embody. Such projects seek to be faithful to Marx's insight that 'the ideas of the ruling class are in every epoch the ruling ideas'.[88] Yet while this suspicion has been helpful in developing more sophisticated, contextual and even political criticism, it has also been problematic. This is because there seems to be something about literary and artistic objects, about the phenomenon of the aesthetic as such, that is opposed to this suspicion and analysis. Somehow the beautiful needs to transcend the merely political-pragmatic, partisan interests, instrumental projects. Even if all art, and all thought, is politically implicated and committed, this does not mean that it can be reduced to nothing more than this. If this were the case then beauty and philosophy would no longer exist in any recognizable sense, but the aesthetic would be reduced to propaganda and ideas to ideology. It seems we need some account of the freedom of thought and beauty; not the absolute immaterial freedom of the universal subject of idealism certainly, but also not the reductive materialism which sees all beauty and truth as modifications of immanent self-interest. This then constitutes the 'problem of aesthetics' for Marxism, a problem certainly present in Marx's own writings and then spawning an immense literature in the twentieth century: does the commitment to materialism and science make any aesthetics impossible? Can there be any meaningful sense in which a Marxist, believing in the priority of the economic, suspicious of all forms of bourgeois ideology, can still believe in the beautiful and true, beyond the merely instrumental? This then is the sense in which we must speak of an anti-aesthetic, utilitarian current to Marx's thought, alongside the aesthetic anti-utilitarian strand we discussed in the first half of this chapter. The aesthetic, the realm of the beautiful and the artistic, which was fundamental to Marx's account of human nature as naturally excessive, the basis of his critique of the instrumental and dehumanizing utility of capitalism, the intimation of transcendence in Marx's thought, has now become *suspect*, precisely because of its very excessiveness, its transcendent aspirations, its seeking after freedom beyond the instrumental manipulations of immanent power.

How are we to make sense of this contradiction of the aesthetic and the anti-aesthetic, the utilitarian and anti-utilitarian in Marx? Margaret Rose suggests that the aesthetic can be *both* the standard by which alienation is judged, and symptomatic of that alienation, which might explain Marx's ambivalence; art can be both passive-reflective (in a more realist, mirroring mode) and active-utopian (in a more imaginative, transformative role). Yet this is only coherent if Marx thinks that *some* aesthetic phenomena are expressions of alienation, rather than the

---

[88]   Marx 1998, p. 67.

aesthetic as such, or even just all aesthetic production to date. His language, while not precise, seems to lean towards the latter options, at the very least implying that the aesthetic is always vulnerable to such alienation. In this case, Marx must find some way that the active-utopian moment of the aesthetic can break through, arrive, without succumbing to the distortions, the vested interests and biases, that have characterized all artistic production to date. At the least, Marx must offer some criteria of discernment or judgement with which to distinguish the two, so that his own critique does not become subject to exactly the same objections he brought against the ideology of the bourgeoisie, only for that critique itself to endure the same fate, and so on, *ad infinitum*. Unless of course, as seems to be the case, Marx believes that the very criterion of such progressiveness is precisely its efficacious-ness – i.e., the progressive is known as such only in and after the event of its occurrence, not unlike Hegel's famous Owl of Minerva. In which case, once again we are faced with the residually Hegelian progressivist historicism, the unfounded confidence in being vindicated by the future where true beauty will emerge, that haunts Marx's thought.

Truth and science

Of the ancient transcendentals, it is not only Beauty that is problematic for Marx's materialist, utilitarian turn. Truth, which was also tradition-ally characterized as having a certain disinterested freedom, beyond power and self-interest, also requires radical reinterpretation for Marx, in order to be purged of transcendent pretensions; yet similarly it is arguable whether it can in any meaningful sense survive such a purgation.

From the very earliest days of unmasking the ideological pretensions of philosophy, and then political economy, to possess eternal truths, through to his more developed account of the dependence of the ideal superstructure upon the economic base, and his critique of intellectual production as such, Marx never completely abandons humanity's cap-acity to know things rightly. The suspicion, unmasking and humbling of ideas, the historicist and socio-genetic accounts of thinking, never drive Marx into scepticism. On the contrary, his rejections of ideology are always contrasted with another significant term, indicating true know-ledge: 'science'. In 1844 the breakthrough to this real knowledge is attributed to Feuerbach and variously described as 'positive, humanistic and naturalistic criticism', 'real science', and 'consistent naturalism' beyond idealism or materialism.[89] Already at this stage it is clear that this true science must be thoroughly *historical* in order to escape the delusions of the political economists or a merely ideal materialism (a return to Hegel here, to correct Feuerbach's anti-historical tendencies). Later he insists the methods and conclusions of his materialist science of history can be 'verified in a purely empirical way' and that his objects are

---

[89] Marx 1988, pp. 15, 144, 154.

necessarily natural historical.[90] This is a 'real, positive science, the expounding of the practical activity, of the practical processes of development of men'. Its aims will be more modest than traditional philosophy, confining itself to 'a summing-up of the most general results' and insisting that these conclusions will be of no value in themselves, but only insofar as they are useful in real history, in making sense of things and facilitating action.[91] This project is even clearer when in 1859 Marx is looking back on his intellectual development and speaks of his discovery of the need to describe the economic transformations of history, instead of their ideological manifestations, 'with the accuracy of physical science.'[92] A certain scientism of outlook characterizes Marx's work throughout, evident in his typically Enlightenment tendency to underestimate the cognitive character of less obviously theoretical modes of discourse, such as the symbolic or poetic, which always require theoretical supercession for Marx (resembling Hegel here).[93]

Yet Marx's thoroughgoing historicism saves him from too easy a naïveté about science and its conclusions. He is for example highly critical of the ahistorical 'scientism' of bourgeois political economy. As early as *The German Ideology* (1845), Marx insists that even '"pure" natural science is provided with an aim, as with its material, only through trade and industry, through the sensuous activity of men.'[94] Science is always already historical, economic, pragmatic. This in itself might seem unobjectionable, were it not for the fact that Marx's naturalism and denial of transcendence foreclose to him any accounts of how science and knowledge more generally, might, despite their unavoidable involvement with these things, nevertheless also point to something more. The radical nature of Marx's position, effectively identifying truth with power and action, can be seen explicitly in the *Theses on Feuerbach*, where he claims: 'Man must prove the truth, *i.e. the reality and power,* the this-worldliness of his thinking in practice.'[95] This assertion serves to explain his more famous eleventh and final thesis: 'The philosophers have only *interpreted* the world in various ways; the point is to *change* it.'[96] This is Marx's 'revolutionary' or 'practical-critical' theory of true knowledge as only known as real when *realized* in action. This is the positive reverse expression of his claim that ideology can be decoded as expressions of the interests and power relations of a class. In both cases knowledge is a form of power, and it seems the 'true' knowledge of the revolutionary is only distinguished from the false knowledge of the ideologists in that the former is critical and active to transform,

---

[90] Marx 1998, p. 37.
[91] Ibid., p. 43.
[92] Carver 1996, p. 160.
[93] Lash, p. 195.
[94] Marx 1998, p. 46.
[95] Ibid., p. 569 (my italics).
[96] Ibid., p. 571.

while the latter merely justifies and supports the current arrangement of power.

The problem once again arises however: can Marx's position escape his own suspicions? How can Marx's thinking confidently claim to have stepped outside the distortions of ideology in order to see clearly, without that very claim being contested on his own terms by someone else? As Lash puts it: 'If it really is the case that the phenomenon of idealist "inversion" arises *just as much* from a particular set of historical circumstances as does the inversion of the image on the retina...then Marx's own ability to "rectify" his vision becomes difficult to explain.'[97] If ideas are purely 'determined' by the economic base, then they are by definition incapable of genuine initiative, and are confined at most to manifesting socio-economic innovations. All of Marx's images for the problem with intellectual production, the *camera obscura*, the building image of foundations and constructions, and the image of a person whose self-representation is not the whole truth, suffer from an over-reaction to idealist philosophy, so that Marx merely inverts the dualism he was trying to transcend.[98] Marx has moved from denying transcendence and autonomy to ideas, to denying them any agency, and finally denying them any real existence as anything more than 'bubble-blowing'.[99] His new 'science' that emerges after the evacuation of any transcendence from truth is a purely pragmatic, instrumental knowledge to be used in action. While for Marx this is knowledge as revolutionary action, it seems difficult to deny that this instrumentalizing of Truth can leave nothing beyond relativist pragmatism and egoistic calculation. If revolutionary ideas, like those of the bourgeoisie can serve class interests, just as much as being critical of the illusions peddled by others, then it is unclear what is the ground for Marx's hope, truly utopian in being 'placeless', that such pure instrumentality will ever be transcended.

Truth, like its sister Beauty, under Marx, has not just rediscovered its material, historical mediation, which had been neglected by the idealists, but, through the dogmatic rejection of transcendence, has gone further and been reduced to nothing more than the historical-material, so that it is thoroughly instrumentalized as something 'useful', purely a form of power to be utilized. The materialist, naturalistic denial of transcendence reduces Beauty and Truth to mere tools, which crucially destroys their *critical* power. Both have become forms of utility.

The problem of morality, or, is all production good?

If Marx instrumentalizes Truth and Beauty so that they become mere manifestations of power, it should come as no surprise to discover that the third of the ancient transcendentals, the Good, also does not escape

[97] Lash, p. 113.
[98] Ibid., p. 120.
[99] Marx 1998, p. 64.

this fate. Once again this problem has been much discussed among Marxists: superficially, Marxism resembles an ethical system, it begins as a project critical of certain patterns of social organization and labour as inhuman and alienating. Yet, of course, Marx considered himself to be transcending the naïve and ideological categories of morality, of good and evil, with something more natural-historical, more scientific and value-free: 'communism abolishes eternal truths, it abolishes religion and morality.'[100] Consequently it is unclear what does form the real basis of his critique of capitalism: sometimes despite himself it seems to be unacknowledged residues of the transcendent which he is trying to abandon; at other times he turns to some uncritical formal or 'natural' criterion. The residually transcendent elements we have already discussed under anthropology and eschatology above. Yet we can now return to the problem noted there: these elements lack the discriminatory capacities of genuine mediations of transcendence. Marx fails to purge himself of values, and ends up investing value in production and historical development instead. Without any element of meaning beyond these activities, excessive to them, except perhaps the future, they become beyond judgement and discrimination. Here we can agree with Eagleton that Marx is at his most Romantic in having an expression/repression model of human capacities, 'in his apparent assumption that human capacities become morbid only by virtue of their alienation, repression, dissociation or one-sidedness.'[101] Yet is it enough simply to expect and act for the liberation of all human capacities and forms of production, when they are not all indiscriminately inherently positive as Marx seems to imply? Efficiency is not the same as welfare, and, therefore, the expansion of all productive forces cannot be a good or an end in itself, as Eagleton illustrates with the example of nuclear power.[102] The existence or emergence of human capacities does not generate the imperative that they be *actualized*. Labour does not have its own inherently positive meaning.

If then our powers 'supply us with no built-in criteria of selection'[103] and any appeal to transcendence has been foreclosed, what options are left for Marx? In the early writings the limiting check seems to be provided by a residually humanist account of human nature, which gradually fades away across his writings leaving only a more formalist concern with harmony and equilibrium. On this account good production can be known by the fact that it does not occur at the expense of

---

[100] Carver 1996, p. 18. On the question of morality and Marxism, see: David McLellan and Sean Sayers (eds.), *Socialism and Morality* (London: Macmillan, 1990); and Denys Turner, *Marxism and Christianity* (Oxford: Blackwell, 1983). While I am sympathetic to Turner's 'strong compatibility' thesis regarding Christianity and Marxism, and his 'identity thesis' regarding Marxism and morality, I suspect we are approaching these relationships from different angles.
[101] Eagleton, p. 221.
[102] Ibid., p. 222.
[103] Ibid., p. 223.

others and generates wealth in the widest sense to be enjoyed by every-one, not just the few. At times in Marx, this reads more like the Hegelian idea that human realization must occur in and through others, an overcoming of alienation that seems to belong to the superstructural realm of the voluntary, the moral and the cultural; while at other times this overcoming is located firmly in the natural historical base as an economic equilibrium of forces that will simply emerge through time. Once again we see how the rejection of transcendence leaves Marx attempting to sustain his critical project upon an unfounded confidence in the natural and the future as the loci of value. The problem of discrimination, or alternatively the *teleology* of human labour and pro-duction, remains. We turn now to consider how the base does still offer some criteria of discrimination for Marx, but only through an uncritical naturalism of utility, which is too suspicious of the 'cultural' and too trusting of the 'natural'.

Use-value and the reification of the natural-historical against cultural exchange

We have argued that one of the forms of the 'revenge of utility' in Marx, his curbing of the aesthetic, is to be found in his suspicion of intellectual production, which seems reactively to deny any proper initiative, agency and even reality to cultural productions, to symbols and ideas. It is as if the base-superstructure distinction serves to create an inverted Platonic cave where ideas are nothing more than shadows of realities, without any proper 'materiality', solidness of their own. Yet the other side of this dualism is equally significant for the 'revenge of utility': the economic base is rendered *too* solid, too positive and determined, without its proper ideality. Human economy, society and history are necessarily shot through with manifold symbolic, cultural determinations, that could always have been otherwise. A pure, pre-cultural, 'natural' econ-omy would not be human, as Marx should be the first to recognize. Yet, precisely because he is still seeking to establish a critical project, yet to do so immanently, without any reference to transcendence, he is forced to rehabilitate a certain reification of the natural historical, through the employment of the concept of 'use-value' as the only way he can offer a critique of 'exchange-values'.

How so? Marx seems to conceive of the position of use as one from which the excesses of exchange value can be criticized. The contradic-tions of capitalism become evident as the accumulation of luxury comes up against the basic animal needs of the starving. These needs, such as hunger, have something like a naturalistic, scientific objectivity to them for Marx, which he claims is ignored by the political economists for whom even the most basic demands seem luxurious.[104] It is the hard reality of these needs, the genuine 'use-value' of things, that will puncture

[104] Marx 1988, pp. 121, 154.

the ideal excess of social 'exchange value', which misses the true value of things, by over-valuing the luxurious. These are the 'natural' contradictions which will cause capitalism to implode, the disenfranchised proletarians to rise against their oppressors. The employment of 'use-value' by Marx corresponds to the tendency noticed above to regard the cultural superstructure as incidental and illusory and the economic base as the determinative truth breaking through. Yet this goes even further in 'naturalizing' the economic base, hardening it into a deterministic system purged of all elements of the symbolic, cultural or voluntary. Here we can say, following Milbank, that despite his attacks on Ricardian naturalism as ahistorical, Marx's progressivism is the form in which a residue of this naturalism remains.[105] This is because there is a sense in which capitalism is for Marx not just one era among others, but the most rational and the most truthful yet. Repeatedly the Comtean and Hegelian notions of historical transcendence of the symbolic emerge in Marx in the assumption that capitalism's deconstruction of cultural conventions opens the way for a more liberated and rational equilibrium that will emerge naturally, beyond the realm of the cultural-moral. To this we might respond with Milbank that Marx fails to recognize that there cannot be pure production/consumption behind or without cultural exchange, as the surplus of meaning is inherent in all human activity. So if use is not prior to exchange then production/consumption is as inescapably *conventional*, cultural and moral, as exchange, not the 'scientific reality' behind capitalism.[106] The naturalism in Marx's attitude to the economic base is also evident in his failure truly to get beyond the naïve faith of the political economists in equilibrium. Marx disagrees with them in insisting that it does not currently exist, because he believes (Romantically) that the true equilibrium must include *individual* fulfilment, not merely the best for society. Yet he still affirms that this equilibrium will emerge naturally, without specific human agency or moral ordering, albeit now in the future. The political economists' almost providentialist trust in a mechanistic equilibrium existing of itself despite the intentions of individuals, has simply been historicized into a more evolutionary biological model of an organism that balances itself with ever increasing complexity and rationality through time.

Immanence, the naturalism of utility and the problem of the ideal-material

We can conclude this account of the persistence of utility in Marx's thought, based upon his naturalist materialism, by saying that Marx ends up spiritualizing the cultural superstructure so that it becomes a mere reflection without initiative or agency, and naturalizing the economic base so that it becomes a mere self-harmonizing organism, again without initiative or agency. This dualism of base and superstructure, the

[105] Milbank, p. 190.
[106] Ibid., p. 191.

ideal and the material, leaves him with an uncritical fundamental suspicion of all cultural/intellectual production and an uncritical ultimate confidence in economic production.

This may seem an unfair caricature of Marx's views. The Frankfurt School in particular has sought to resist the more dualistic or crudely materialist interpretations of Marx's thought. A careful reading of his own writings also provides much that cannot be fitted into the crude systematizations of later official Marxist-Leninist orthodoxy. Thus we can find passages that give a more substantial account of the ideal and its capacity to shape as well as merely reflect, beyond any crude simplification: Marx insists the relation between the base and the superstructure is dialectical and even reciprocal.[107] He gives various examples of occasions when the superstructure might even be ahead of the base and thus seem to lead it: his own journey into socialism from German philosophy, and the famous comments on the art of the Greeks being among the most significant.[108] The illustration noted above against the idealists, of the futility of trying to overcome gravity by simply ignoring it, also suggests a certain substantiality of the ideas they were seeking to overcome. Likewise we can also find passages in Marx that do recognize the proper ideality, the conventional and culturally contingent nature of the economic base: he does repeatedly stress the historical contingency of perspectives, for example when he insists against Smith and others that the labour theory of value is not true universally but only under capitalism. Similarly he does expressly reject the biologism of prioritizing use over exchange in his later 'Notes on Adolph Wagner'.[109] Lash argues that we should not be seduced by a few misleading metaphors, such as that of reflection, or later misinterpretations, to construe the language of 'determination' in the relation between the base and the superstructure in too narrow a manner. He suggests that ideas are 'embedded in' but not strictly determined by material events, and that this in fact provides a better model for the sort of complex relations between the ideal and the material to which Marx himself draws attention in his historical writings such as *The Eighteenth Brumaire of Louis Bonaparte*. Lash also notes the very activist form of much of Marx's works, such as the *Manifesto* or the *Theses on Feuerbach*, which suggest less of a predetermined impersonal organism, and more of a call to act. Despite all these points however, a case like Lash's feels like special pleading, rescuing Marx not only from his zealous interpreters, but also from himself and his own mistakes. Even Lash admits Marx's hostility towards the cognitive capacity of non-scientific thought, and this along with his progressivist view of history means that it is difficult to completely release Marx from the dualistic and materialistic directions of his thinking.

---

[107] Marx 1998, p. 61.
[108] Ibid., p. 92, Carver 1996, p. 155.
[109] Ibid., pp. 241 ff.

I have traced two opposing currents in Marx's thought: the aesthetic and the utilitarian. I have also argued that these are not just different phases in his life's thought, despite shifts in emphasis, but rather competing tensions always present in his work. How then are we to make sense of their interaction? In looking at the three classical transcendentals, Beauty, Truth and Goodness, we saw how these elements persisted as residues of transcendence at the very heart of Marx's critical project, animating its life. Yet we also saw how, on his own terms Marx, because of his explicit exclusion of the transcendent, is unable fully to account for these three, so that they are reduced to mere modifications of utility, to become problematic for later generations of Marxists. If this account is correct, then the conflict between aesthetic and utilitarian elements in Marx's thought is no longer so difficult to resolve, for they are in fact two sides of the same coin: the denial of transcendence. It is because Marx's materialism requires him to think of beauty as no more than earthly, that his aestheticism, like many German Romantics, is almost too pure, too ideal and disinterested, like a Heaven on Earth. Marx's early utopian reflections downplay the inescapability of temporality and toil for even the most divine human labour. By attempting to make every activity and thing an end in itself, performed or existing for its own sake, Marx can have no account of the complex relations between things and their mutual relations to That which exceeds themselves and all other things.

Therefore, his pietistic refusal of even the most modest place to interest, to making use of things and even people, let alone offering oneself to be used in service of others, is unsustainable and collapses into that which it sought to refuse. Because all things are deprived of any end beyond themselves, it becomes possible to utilize them in such a way as to have absolutely no regard for these things themselves. Likewise because there is nothing beyond for which things are ultimately employed, no greater end to which all usage strives, use or mere utility becomes an end in itself. Thus immanent aestheticism must collapse into a crude naturalism where everything simply is for its own sake, for no reason beyond itself. Consumption and similar natural processes are now their own justification, without deeper meaning, or any higher purpose which might confer form on this consumption or discern when and what to consume. This then is the triumph of the *utile*, use as the self-grounding absolute end in itself, which, despite its appearance of rationality, is now revealed in all its crudely bestial self-interest. Without a transcendent Good to which things are ordered and from which they receive their own integrity and worth as themselves, utility can only be about usefulness for me, in the satisfaction of my supposedly 'natural' desires.[110] It seems Marx has succumbed to the same basic perspective as his original opponents, the champions of capitalism, the

---

[110] This descent of utilitarianism into naturalism and nihilism is well traced by Hannah Arendt, pp. 154–9.

political economists. Marx cannot see that utility and immanence are not incidental to capitalism, but rather as Zizek puts it: 'instrumental reason *as such* is capitalist', and so he tried to think beyond capitalism while retaining its essential spirit. Instead we might claim: capitalism and nature contain *no* immanent dialectical critique; a different practice of desire is needed.[111]

---

[111] Slavoj Zizek, *The Fragile Absolute – or, Why is the Christian Legacy Worth Fighting For?* (London: Verso, 2000), p. 19; cf. Milbank, p. 193.

There is nothing better for a man than that he should eat and drink and find enjoyment in his toil. This also, I saw, is from God; for apart from him who can eat or who can have enjoyment?

4

John Ruskin and William Morris

*An Alternative Tradition: Labour and the
Theo-aesthetic in English Romantic
Critiques of Capitalism*

In the last chapter we explored the theological and aesthetic ideas at the
root of Marx's critique of modern labour, and his partial suppression of
these roots in favour of more 'scientific', utilitarian ways of thinking. We
argued that this 'suppression' presents certain metaphysical problems in
Marx's thought concerning the impossibility of attributing an immanent,
naturalistic teleology to human labour when all reference to transcendent goals is disavowed. This in turn presents practical ethical problems
regarding the discernment of goods necessary for any moral ordering of
human production and consumption, leading to an impoverished account of emancipated labour and a tendency to oscillate between an
unfounded optimism or a sinister voluntarism regarding the attainment
of such a state. It is now time, therefore, to look elsewhere and turn to
another sister tradition of social criticism, much less well known, but in
its own way with considerable historical influence: that of the English
Romantics John Ruskin and William Morris. In the works of these two
authors the aesthetic and theological roots of their social critique and
vision of true labour are considerably more evident, and less subject to
self-censure. Their fondness for expressing themselves in popular essays
and even Romance has often led to them being regarded as intellectually
lightweight figures, yet I will argue that, at least at times, the florid and
fanciful tones hide insights more radical than those of Marx, capable of
correcting some of his problems, and of particular interest to our own
situation today.

In telling this story, we will begin with Ruskin's roots in the sympathies
of English Romanticism, before recounting his critique of political economy and its fiction of labour as serving some 'value-free' utility. This
critique has the same historicizing, denaturalizing conclusion as that of
Marx, but, particularly in the essay *Ad Valorem*, Ruskin makes more
explicit the necessity of *value-laden* alternative accounts of economy.
His famous definition of wealth as life might sound as immanently naturalistic a value as those of Marx's critique and hope, yet elsewhere he makes

clear the inescapably *moral* nature of his use of 'life' here, and hence the need to reconceive production and consumption in moral terms. This language of morality, which some have seen as a weakness in Ruskin, is actually, we shall argue, the basis of his advantage over Marx's materialism: for, in refusing to reduce cultural productions such as values to functions of our supposed sensual 'nature', Ruskin retains a sense of the transcendent goods to which labour and consumption must constantly be oriented in order for any transformation to take place, and avoids the contradictions of Marx's immanentist, naturalistic teleology. And it is surely no accident that, even though many of Ruskin's most important writings on society date from his self-professed 'years of doubt', yet nevertheless the references to these transcendent values are often made in quite explicitly theological terms. Ruskin goes on to point to specific practices and institutions in the past and present which embody such values as are capable of providing the basis for some resistance to the myth of utility. Here his Romantic inclinations are particularly evident, and, while there are definite dangers in some of these, such as authoritarian centralism in, for example, his militaristic examples, or a general conservative idealization of the past, yet many of these value-bearing practices are not without theological significance or relevance to contemporary discussion: monasteries, guilds, schools, the professions, the family. Finally we will concentrate on perhaps the most important of these resources for the resistance of utility, and the one that will be Ruskin's most important legacy to Morris: the idea of the artist as a vision for the qualitative transformation of labour, first elaborated in *The Nature of Gothic*. While, as we have seen, a certain Romantic vision of the artist was important for the early Marx, this idea of the artist as crucial to social transformation, and particularly the utopian vision of the overcoming of the opposition between art and labour, was first properly developed by Ruskin.

We will go on to see how Morris developed these ideas, both in his fiction and in his lectures. Morris was perhaps the first person in this tradition to be completely free of the reactionary dangers of his predecessors and, through his involvement with the beginnings of the Labour movement, provides the link between these ideas and the mainstream of twentieth-century British left-wing thought. Yet while he was more unambiguously forward-looking than Ruskin and others, his 'conversion' to Marxism meant that, as we shall see, he was more susceptible to the dangers of Marxist views of history, and more superficially hostile to the theological. In both cases however he is considerably more complex than he might at first appear. He certainly preserves the best of Ruskin's thought on the ideal of the emancipated labourer as artist, and clearly does not conceive of the transformation of society in the amoral deterministic ways of the cruder Marxists. Even if his teleology remains weak and quasi-naturalistic, his indebtedness to theological ideas is still evident, and he represents a full-blooded socialism that is centred on humanity's desire for beauty, avowedly 'environmentalist' and non-centralist, because it is fundamentally anti-utilitarian.

THE ROMANTIC BACKGROUND: FROM 'DARK SATANIC MILLS' TO MR GRADGRIND

The background to the aesthetic social criticism of Ruskin and Morris was the development in Britain in the latter eighteenth and early nineteenth centuries of a complex current of thought, spanning the arts, politics and philosophy, which was hostile to much of modernity and can be broadly termed 'Romantic'.[1] Beginning with figures as diverse as William Blake, Edmund Burke, Samuel Taylor Coleridge and William Wordsworth, this tradition was characterized by a general hostility towards the disenchantment, quantification, mechanization, artificiality and social-dissolution that they saw in the modern industrialized and urban world, the world of Blake's 'Dark Satanic Mills'. Their sympathies lay instead with the organic, the natural, the communal, the pastoral.[2] In these respects they have parallels with Rousseau in France or the *Sturm und Drang* movement in Germany. They rallied their opposition to the utilitarianism of Bentham and Mill around ideas such as 'tradition', 'culture' or the aesthetic, and frequently looked to an idealized mythic past for inspiration.[3] The French Revolution was an important event for many of these writers, and while, as we might expect, their loosely conservative sympathies were generally hostile to what they saw as Jacobin mob-rule, their perspectives were more complex than this. Indeed, Löwy and Sayre have argued that Romanticism cannot be simply politically aligned, but displays the full spectrum of political views from fascistic conservative to revolutionary utopian.[4] One of the resources of Romanticism in its critique of modernity was often an alliance with medievalism which became significant in architecture and the arts in this period, and which through Pugin and the Pre-Raphaelite Brotherhood was important for Ruskin and Morris, respectively. These Romantic sympathies had become very widespread by the 1840s, entering Church life through the influence of Keble and Newman and even finding expression in novels such as Walter Scott's *Ivanhoe* or somewhat later in Dickens's caricature of the modern industrialist in Mr Gradgrind of *Hard Times*. The most important influences on Ruskin and Morris were however Pugin and Thomas Carlyle, to whom we shall return later.

JOHN RUSKIN: A TORY COMMUNIST 'OF THE OLD SCHOOL'

Ruskin was one of the great literary figures arising out of this milieu, a prolific and often original writer on many topics, yet despite such

---

[1] See Michael Löwy and Robert Sayre, *Romanticism against the Tide of Modernity*, trans. C. Porter (London: Duke University Press, 2001), and Raymond Williams, *Culture and Society 1780–1950* (London: Chatto and Windus, 1960).

[2] Löwy, pp. 29–56.

[3] See Williams, pp. xiii–xx.

[4] Löwy, pp. 57–87.

important admirers as George Bernard Shaw, Proust, Gandhi and Clement Atlee, his reputation declined considerably for much of the twentieth century, when he was often dismissed as hopelessly contradictory and representative of the prejudices of his century.[5] More recent commentators have sought to free him from the exaggerated attention given to certain aspects of his biography and thought, and have rehabilitated his claim to be considered a 'radical', albeit one who resists much conventional classification.[6] It is sometimes suggested that the art critic and social critic are two unrelated parts of Ruskin's life; yet, despite the superficial shift in interest from the former to the latter which takes place around 1860, closer attention reveals how the two tasks were always integrated in Ruskin's thought, which is what makes him particularly interesting for a discussion of the role of the Aesthetic in critiques of modern Labour. The best illustration of this comes from Ruskin's 1853 *Stones of Venice*, where already in this book of art criticism the ideal standard of beauty in artworks forms a basis for the criticism of the injustices of the contemporary and ancient societies which produced these works. Here also, building on the ideas of Pugin and Carlyle, the medieval artisan is set forth as a vision of unalienated labour, beyond the modern oppositions of artist and worker, founded upon social cooperation and personal freedom and responsibility, rather than individualistic competition and mechanistic slavery. The unity of Ruskin's work is to be found then in his championing, against 'value-free' utility, of a 'true human value' that is 'simultaneously and indissolubly aesthetic and moral-and-social.'[7] However, before coming to these key ideas which were to have so much influence upon Morris, it is worth looking at Ruskin's critique of contemporary political economy where he shared much with Marx, then exploring how he goes beyond Marx in crucially recognizing the moral, and implicitly theological, nature of such critique.

The critique of political economy: The myths of necessary self-interest, exclusive possession, necessary conflict and neutral utility

> all political economy founded on self-interest [is] but the fulfilment of that which once brought schism into the Policy of angels and ruin into the Economy of Heaven.[8]

Ruskin was as scathing as Marx in his condemnation of the injustices of capitalist society. Like other figures before him in the Romantic tradition, he focused on the degradation of labour under industrialism and

---

[5]   Löwy, p. 146.
[6]   See ibid., pp. 132–3.
[7]   Ibid., p. 131.
[8]   John Ruskin, *Unto this Last and Munera Pulveris* – hereafter UTL – (London: George Allen and Sons, 1911), p. 109.

the destruction of the environment, both of which he saw as consequences of an economy and society that was nothing less than the idolatry of mammonism. The importance for Ruskin of political economy to this situation lies in its role as the official ideology of this mammonism, justifying its crimes through a purportedly value-free 'science' of labour and economic relations, which conceals what is actually an extraordinary reversal of values: the suppression of justice and charity and the exaltation of greed. Ruskin is quite clear that this new 'science' is actually the assertion of a new anti-Christian morality: 'I know no previous instance in history of a nation's establishing a systematic disobedience to the first principles of its professed religion.'[9] Ruskin develops this argument against political economy in four essays serialized in *The Commonwealth* in 1860, only a year after Marx's *Contribution to the Critique of Political Economy*, and later published as *Unto this Last* (a reference to the parable of the Vineyard, Matt. 20:14, which he takes as illustrating justice to the least in society). While he repeats many of these views elsewhere, this is his most systematic, and became his most famous, work of social criticism and so we shall concentrate on it here. In arguing primarily with J. S. Mill, but also with the ideas of Malthus and Ricardo, Ruskin rejects their purportedly timeless and value free account of human nature as *homo economicus*, which, he insists, makes vice more natural than virtue, reduces humans to machines and their actions to predictable motions, presumes necessarily antagonistic conflicts of interest on the basis of an uncritical account of possession, subordinates consumption to exchange and the acquisition of capital for their own sakes, and leaves consumption and usefulness sufficiently contentless and uncritical as to seem self-evident, natural and free of moral concerns.

The foundational delusion of political economy for Ruskin, is its attempt to establish a mechanical science of human behaviour, which is already an arbitrary decision in favour of crude materialism. In the wider terms that we have already established from Weber and Marx, this is the fiction of labour as utility. Because predictable regularity seems to belong more in this world to sin than the erratic business of virtue, this position must regard animal instincts of self-interest as more fundamental, natural, and constant to humans than moral or social affections which might appear to transcend self-interest, but which must for the materialist be decoded as 'really' just an ideological cover for more elaborate ruses of self-seeking. This is a familiar project throughout the materialist and naturalist traditions of modernity from Hobbes, through Hume, Mill, Nietzsche and today the Neo-Darwinians. While it can serve a radical agenda of exposing vested interests in supposedly innocent actions, if absolutized its nihilistic consequence is to render all virtue an impossibility. Thus the mother's love for her son is 'decoded' as just a narcissistic concern with the perpetuation of her genes (the

---

[9] Ibid. p. 79.

Darwinians); the idealist's concern with justice as merely an extrapolation from the fear that someone will harm him (Mill); and the saintly nun's rescuing of orphans is a psychological malfunction which seeks to compensate for her own barrenness (Nietzsche). The political economists belong to this tradition, but in its slightly more optimistic British strand, so that self-interest is seen as capable of forming the foundation of a just society (Hume, Adam Smith, Mill). Ruskin pours scorn on this modern idea that 'an advantageous code of social action may be determined irrespectively of the influence of social affection', i.e. that a state can be so ordered as to flourish on the basis of self-interest alone.[10] Against this view, in a powerful reassertion of the language of traditional Christian moral discourse on riches, Ruskin insists that the benign self-interest of the political economists is nothing more than 'avarice', which they falsely presume to be more 'constant' in human nature than the merely 'accidental' virtues.[11] Consequently they think of human nature 'merely as a covetous machine' about which laws can be discovered. Yet, Ruskin observes, people are not machines, their force is not calculable like 'steam, magnetism, gravitation', etc.[12] Rather a person is 'an engine whose motive power is a Soul', we are creatures with genuine agency, a fact which 'falsifies every one of their results'.[13] This appeal to the soul is, we might note, a common 'Platonic' feature of strategies of resistance to materialism and self-interest in modernity (the Cartesian Rationalists, the Cambridge Platonists, Kant and the German Romantics, and the English Coleridgeans), and its theological overtones are obvious. For Ruskin, modern political economy is founded upon this denial of the soul, and a true political economy would require a psychology that took account of this, thus becoming a much more imprecise science 'dependent on more than arithmetic'.[14] Such a psychology could no longer reduce all virtue to self-interest, and regard this as the fundamental essence of human nature. Against Ricardo, Ruskin asks why one should take one form of behaviour (selfishness) to be more 'natural' to our humanity than another.[15]

While some of the earlier anti-materialists weakened their case by advocating an all too pure idealism, seeing moral decisions as entirely rational and pure and independent of affections and desires, Ruskin has a more sophisticated account which allows for the mediation of transcendent values through material desires.[16] Thus, for example, he insists that justice includes affections: 'such affection as one man owes to another'.[17] Desires can have a role in ethics because they are not simply

[10]   John Ruskin, *Unto this Last and Munera Pulveris* – hereafter UTL – (London: George Allen and Sons, 1911), p. 19.
[11]   Ibid.
[12]   Ibid., p. 24.
[13]   Ibid.
[14]   Ibid., pp. 21, 91.
[15]   Ibid., pp. 113–14.
[16]   Contrast, e.g., Descartes and Kant.
[17]   UTL, p. 23.

inertly given as an immutable part of our nature, but are themselves cultural and thus always moral for Ruskin. Thus the business of being moral is not just about whether or not to obey one's desires, but actually what one is to learn to desire. Most of the world's demands are 'romantic' in the sense of being 'vision, idealisms, hopes, and affections', so that good economy for Ruskin begins in the 'regulation of the imagination and the heart.'[18] Nevertheless because virtuous desires point towards transcendent values and life, they are qualitatively different from vicious desires. Vices and virtues are, therefore, not just motions of a similar nature, as they might appear to the materialist who could at least admit the existence of the latter. Virtues, Ruskin tells us, 'alter the essence of the creature under examination the moment they are added; they operate not mathematically, but chemically, introducing conditions which render all our previous knowledge unavailable.'[19] This is a powerful psychological and metaphysical critique of the anthropology at the heart of political economy: it stands accused by Ruskin of falsely 'naturalizing' the cultural vices of the bourgeoisie into timeless truths of human nature, on the basis of a materialistic worldview which serves a mathematically predictive 'science'.

If the universality of self-interest is the most fundamental premise of political economy, another is the exclusive and inert nature of possession. Ruskin highlights this with his claim that 'possession, or "having," is not an absolute, but a gradated, power'.[20] Possession to be meaningful requires the ability to use something (a dead man cannot be said to have the treasures in his tomb in any meaningful sense), so that possession depends on things in the possessor and can be more or less. It is also possible for more than one person to have things (e.g., a family car, a library book, a civic playground). The denial of the latter truth leads to the political economists' belief in the original necessary conflict of interests. It is as naïve and generalizing to presume that different people's interests are always in conflict as it would be to presume that they are always in perfect agreement. As Solomon realized, it would be in neither woman's interest to chop the baby in half; and, as the true mother realised, her true 'interest' was better served by abandoning her immediate interest in the child. Even if people do have competing interests this does not mean they need compete over them, as Ruskin illustrates with the powerful example of a starving mother who gives her last crust to her starving child.[21] The belief in the necessity of competition leads to profiteering which is always seeking to take advantage of another's necessity or misfortune.[22] The power of the patron's money depends on the artist's poverty. If we were to follow the Schadenfreude of this

[18] Ibid., p. 97.
[19] Ibid., p. 20.
[20] Ibid., p. 90.
[21] Ibid., p. 22; cf. p. 60.
[22] Ibid., p. 60.

principle to its logical conclusions we would have to recognize that disasters and robbery provide the greatest opportunities for 'profit'.[23] Buying in the cheapest market and selling in the dearest, regardless of other concerns, is, for Ruskin, morally reprehensible. Yet we need not believe competition to be somehow more 'natural' to human nature than cooperation.[24]

The concern with profit brings us to another distortion of political economy: the focus on exchange and capital at the expense of consumption. Both of these in turn serve the fiction of 'wealth' and 'usefulness' as value-free terms. Here there are clear similarities with Marx's attack on the replacement of use-value by exchange-value under capitalism. The economists, according to Ruskin, are mistakenly fixed on 'money-gain' rather than 'mouth-gain'.[25] Mill's arguments only work if 'commodities are made to be sold, and not to be consumed.'[26] We would do better, according to Ruskin, to speak of 'advantage' in exchange, as opposed to 'profit' which would be better restricted to production, but because it is easier to gain more by exchange – a man with a hoard of gold can get his harvest done much quicker by *exchanging* the hoard for the labour of 20 men than doing it himself – this is considered more important by the capitalists.[27] Similarly, because the 'stored' labour value that is 'capital' can be realized more rapidly and in much larger quantities than through direct production itself, the production of *capital* for its own sake takes priority for the capitalist over the consumption which it ultimately should serve. The production of abstract exchangeable capital becomes the goal of economics, of production and exchange, rather than the production and exchange of real, useful goods for consumption. The European economy is too concerned with bulbs instead of tulips, as Ruskin puts it.[28] This inversion of means and ends, where the goal of economy becomes the creation of abstract exchangeable 'value' – monetary profit as an end in itself – in turn isolates this supposed 'value', 'usefulness' and 'wealth' from any meaningful human context, to become contentless and amoral. Yet this neutral utility is as much a nonsense as the pseudo-science of political economy which is founded upon it. All economy – production, exchange, consumption – consists of moral acts in which value-judgements are implicated; there can be no neutral labour. On buying for example, Ruskin claims, in a manner anticipating subsequent consumer-led campaigns for more justice in production and exchange: 'economists have never perceived that disposition to buy is a wholly *moral* element in demand'.[29] Hence he

23 UTL, p. 54.
24 For Ruskin's views on cooperation, see also: John Ruskin, *Time and Tide* (London: George Allen, 1904), Letters I and II.
25 UTL, p. 106.
26 Ibid., p. 81; cf. Ibid., p. 83.
27 Ibid., p. 93.
28 Ibid., p. 103.
29 Ibid., p. 84, n. 1.

insists that 'he that gathereth not, scattereth.'[30] All human labour and activity contains choices which turn it in one direction or another, so that it moves either towards life or death, with child-bearing and raising on the one hand, and murder on the other as the ideal types of all action.[31] Mill is, then, utterly mistaken in claiming that political economy has nothing to do with the 'comparative estimate of the moralist', as in fact his arguments inadvertently recognize.[32] What things are produced, and who they are sold to, and what they do with them, are all moral matters, as Ruskin points out with the pertinent example of bombs.[33] This brings us now to the question of the substantive values by which Ruskin seeks to redirect economy.

Ad Valorem: The inescapability of moral judgements and the rediscovery of transcendent values in economy.

Wealth, therefore, is 'THE POSSESSION OF THE VALUABLE BY THE VALIANT'[34]

Against the political economists' vision of a value-free science, Ruskin maintains that economy involves real objective values which are external to the subject and not reducible to its desires. Value is not ultimately the exchange-value or 'price' of the market: labour has a real worth independent of what people will pay for it. Just because this 'real' value is a very complex thing to calculate does not alter the fact that 'it *has* a worth, just as fixed and real as the specific gravity of a substance.'[35] Elsewhere he repeats this objectivity of value, independent of all questions of supply and demand, linking it already with intimations of a divine source to this value:

> The value of a thing, therefore, is independent of opinion, and of quantity... Think what you will of it, gain how much you may of it, the value of the thing itself is neither greater nor less. For ever it avails, or avails not; no estimate can raise, no disdain repress, the power which it holds from the Maker of things and men.'[36]

What is the nature of this value? To what does it 'avail'? Ruskin answers this question philologically: 'value' is derived from *valere* – to be well or strong, '*in* life (if a man), or valiant; *for* life (if a thing), or valuable.' So, he argues: 'To be "valuable," therefore is to "avail towards life". A truly

---

[30] Ibid., p. 101.
[31] Ibid.
[32] Ibid., p. 82.
[33] Ibid.
[34] Ibid., p. 91.
[35] Ibid., p. 70.
[36] Ibid., pp. 87–8.

valuable or availing thing is that which leads to life with its whole strength.'[37]

Here we can see a typically Romantic concern with 'vitalism', strongly indebted to Carlyle: the good is identified with flourishing and life; the bad with destruction and death. The service of life, is according to Ruskin, following Christ in the gospels, the law of the Sabbath.[38] In another famous line Ruskin boldly claims: 'There is no Wealth but Life. Life, including all its powers of love, of joy, and of admiration.'[39] This is not just life in some empty, abstract sense, but *human* life, so that the real meaning of J. S. Mill's apparently contentless usefulness should be understood as useful *to human flourishing* (in fairness, this is of course implicit in Mill, despite himself). This in turn restores the priority of consumption as the true goal of all production instead of exchange or abstract profit: 'all *essential* production is for the Mouth; and is finally measured by the mouth . . . consumption is the crown of production.'[40] It is because consumption – how things can be and are used – is the real test of production, that we can say that moral concerns cannot be bracketed out: the production of food and the production of bombs are not morally neutral matters. Ruskin here is refusing to separate actions from their goals, thus crucially reinstating teleological questions in economics: 'For as consumption is the *end and aim* of production, so life is the *end and aim* of consumption.'[41] All this sounds very similar to Marx's critique of exchange-value on the basis of use-value, and could be thought to suffer from a similarly uncritical, utilitarian account of natural human 'needs'.

The crucial difference comes however when Ruskin comes to define 'usefulness': if this is no longer an abstraction it must include the capacity for mis-use and ab-use. It is not the case, as Marx seems sometimes to imply with a residual optimism, that humans will follow their true good when all external impediments are removed. This we might add, elaborating on Ruskin, is what distinguishes us from animals: the highest good for humans is not natural and self-evident to us, in the way that eating, surviving and reproducing are for animals: 'It is the privilege of the fishes, as it is of rats and wolves, to live by the laws of demand and supply; but the distinction of humanity, to live by those of right.'[42] If we are naturally cultural animals, and our highest goods are to be realized culturally or spiritually, then these goods cannot be just natural to us, but must also be, in a certain sense, super-natural, cultural and moral. Ruskin points towards these conclusions when he argues that, because of this capacity for misuse, true usefulness – availing to

---

[37]   UTL, p. 87.
[38]   Ibid., p. 111.
[39]   Ibid., p. 109.
[40]   Ibid., pp. 105–6.
[41]   Ibid., p. 108 (my italics).
[42]   Ibid., p. 65, n. 1.

life – 'depends on the person, much more than on the article'. Usefulness requires moral characteristics in the person using something for it to be truly useful. While food, in itself, is more truly valuable than bombs, nevertheless food in the hands of a hoarder fails to realize its true value. Production, exchange and consumption are not absolute goods but require discrimination, *judgement*. The end of labour is not the arbitrary production of anything for anyone, but of the right things for the right people.[43] Some things should not be produced, some exchanges should not take place, some consumption should not happen. Ruskin moves cleverly from extreme, small scale examples to larger and more complex ones, showing how, to use contemporary examples, it is a moral decision and not a neutral matter determined by the 'laws' of supply and demand to sell weapons to tyrants, or charge extortionate amounts for anti-AIDS drugs to third world countries, in the same way as it would be to persuade a child to swap his sweets for a loaded gun. What is required is 'wise' production, wise distribution and wise consumption.[44] Usefulness, then, depends on the development of moral character in people, what Ruskin calls 'the valour' of the owner.[45] Thus true usefulness and wealth are 'value in the hands of the valiant.'[46] This moral element to wealth for Ruskin distinguishes him from Marx, and entails a call for a significant transvaluation of contemporary judgements: Much of what we think of as wealth is really for Ruskin 'illth', useless things that do not avail towards life; while what we see as comparatively worthless – natural resources such as water, air and light – we should regard as our true wealth.[47] Similarly many people and nations who are regarded as wealthy are seen by Ruskin as more like eddies and dams that obstruct the flow of wealth; whereas in reality, 'that country is the richest which nourishes the greatest number of noble and happy human beings; that man is the richest who, having perfected the functions of his own life to the utmost, has also the widest helpful influence.'[48]

It has been argued here that this moral teleological dimension to labour clearly distinguishes Ruskin from the problematic anti-theological and anti-aesthetic materialist agenda of Marx. For Ruskin, value – goodness and beauty – is intrinsic in things, in no way reducible to our subjective estimation. Yet it is also not just objective in a naïvely naturalistic sense, as if it could be simply 'read off' from the world; but in a real sense transcends our material happiness (while still being linked to the latter), and so must always be culturally mediated. This can be seen in his use of the language of justice, nobility and self-sacrifice. Thus when he speaks of the need for the discernment of goods, for *judgement*,

---

[43] Cf. ibid., p. 91.
[44] Cf. ibid., p. 102.
[45] Ibid., p. 92.
[46] Ibid., p. 91.
[47] Ibid., p. 88.
[48] Ibid., pp. 92, 109.

this is clearly linked to justice, which is then understood not as positivistic man-made legality, nor an immanent formal equality, but as approximation to a transcendent ideal, with evident theological roots (Coleridgean Platonism seems to be in the background here). He speaks of judgement as 'the royal character of all the saints' and refers to Dante's vision of the heavenly eagle of justice whose wings bear the scriptural inscription '*Diligite justitiam qui judicatis terram*' – those who judge the world must love justice.[49] This love of justice should lead us to order our economy not by paying as little as one can for anything and charging as much as one can, but rather by notions of 'just wage', 'just price', quality of products and fairness of exchange. When the political economists claim their science concerns how to get rich by any legal means, Ruskin calls upon them to concern themselves with justice rather than legality, so that 'our economy will no longer depend merely on prudence, but on jurisprudence – and that of divine, not human law.'[50] This justice is linked elsewhere with the divine as when Ruskin claims that human actions were 'intended by the Maker of men' to be guided by 'justice' not 'expediency', and even more explicitly with Christ, 'the sun of justice', whom the world rejected in favour of a murderer.[51]

Ruskin's language of 'nobility' also points beyond a purely materialistic construal of his ethics, and is in fact one of the ways that he at times distinguishes himself from other socialist groups. Thus he speaks as we have already seen of the need for valour in economics, and even of the need for the supposedly 'base' activities of commerce to become heroic and suitable for a 'gentleman'. A certain sort of dignity and virtue is required in labouring, exchange and production, because 'the maximum of life can only be reached by the maximum of virtue', for 'life is more than the meat', humans more than animals.[52] Ruskin is scornful towards those socialists whose concern for the material well-being of the poor does not extend to their dignity, and indeed is often premised on the belief in their incapacity for virtue. To the contrary, Ruskin says to the poor: 'Claim your crumbs from the table if you will; but claim them as children, not as dogs.'[53] Despite the undoubted patrician overtones, this 'heroic' concern with valour can be seen as resisting the miserly, base, *ressentiment*-driven spirit that Nietzsche detected in so much utilitarian socialism.[54] True communism is based on wisdom and liberality, not theft for Ruskin.[55] Similarly it issues from strength, not weakness,

[49] UTL, p. 64. Cf. Paradiso XIX and Wisdom 1:1.
[50] UTL, p. 64.
[51] Ibid., pp. 23, 61.
[52] Ibid., pp. 112.
[53] Ibid., p. 112.
[54] Cf. Löwy, p. 143, and, e.g., Friedrich Nietzsche, *Beyond Good and Evil* (Oxford: Oxford University Press, 1998), pp. 40–1.
[55] Cf. 'Fors Clavigera' (1871) in John D. Rosenberg (ed.), *The Genius of John Ruskin: Selections from His Writings* (London: George Allen and Unwin, 1963), p. 377.

because 'riches are a form of strength', and this strength is the precondition for being able to help others in need.[56]

The final piece of evidence of the transcendent orientation of ethics for Ruskin lies in his radical notion of self-sacrifice in economy, which he opposes to the political economists' self-interest. Thus when he wishes to illustrate noble, gentlemanly behaviour, he looks to the traditional liberal professions, the military, law, medicine and the Church, as a model for how producers and traders might transform economy.[57] All are defined by commitment to values beyond their own self-interest – defence of the nation, justice, health, salvation. More than this however, there is an implicit self-sacrificial heroism in this commitment: if the situation demanded it, the professional should be willing to sacrifice his or her own interests rather than sacrifice the principles of one's profession. This is most obvious in the military, where the sacrifice required might indeed be even unto death, but similarly we can see that we would expect judges to be so immune to intimidation, that, in the situation of a corrupt state, they should prefer their own suffering to the betrayal of justice, and likewise with the other professions; for, Ruskin maintains: 'the man who does not know when to die, does not know how to live.' There can be no doubt here that the value of life is being understood in more than a materialist sense, and that the roots of this conception are inescapably Christian: 'whosoever will save his life shall lose it, whosoever loses it shall find it.'[58]

The artisan as a foretaste of unalienated labour: The Nature of Gothic

> It is not that men are ill fed, but that they have no pleasure in
> the work by which they make their bread[59]

All that has been said up to this point has been to represent Ruskin as a powerful critic of the spirit of utility in modern political economy, and a more theoretically consistent and radical one than Marx because of his resistance of utilitarian materialism and explicit commitment to transcendent values. Nevertheless we have not demonstrated so far that this opposition to utility was in any sense 'aesthetic'. It is to this that we now turn.

We have already claimed that the linking of art and social criticism runs throughout Ruskin's work. As was pointed out by Northrop Frye, this can be seen even in one of his earliest works, written for his wife to be Effie while he was still an undergraduate at Oxford, the children's tale '*The King of the Golden River*' (1841) where the greed of two brothers

---

[56] UTL, p. 111, n. 1.
[57] A similar point is made by Mauss following Durkheim: Marcel Mauss, *The Gift* (London: Routledge, 2002), p. 89.
[58] UTL, p. 26.
[59] John Ruskin, 'The Nature of Gothic' (1853) – hereafter NG – in Rosenberg, p. 179.

destroys the natural beauty of a valley until it is redeemed by the simple virtue of the third brother.[60] It continues through most of the writings about art from the 1850s when Ruskin was teaching art in Working Men's College in London under the Christian Socialist F. D. Maurice, especially *The Political Economy of Art* (1857) and *The Two Paths* (1858–9). But its most famous expression occurs in the chapter on 'The Nature of Gothic', in *The Stones of Venice* (1853), a chapter that was to become the manifesto for the aesthetic critique of labour, and of which Morris was later to write: 'it is one of the most important things written by the author, and in future days will be considered as one of the very few necessary and inevitable utterances of the century.'[61] This chapter was published separately, first for the Working Men's College, and then again by Morris at the Kelmscott Press. Morris provides as good a commentator on what was so important about this text as any. For Morris, the key lesson that Ruskin taught a generation here was that 'art is the expression of man's pleasure in labour', and that 'it is possible for man to rejoice in his work, for, strange as it may seem to us to-day, there have been times when he did rejoice in it.'[62] The key sign of real change would, therefore, be the realization that 'beauty is once again a natural and necessary accompaniment of all productive labour'.[63] This was undoubtedly a Romantic revolution in notions of labour: work and art are no longer fundamentally to be opposed; indeed this very opposition is a mark of the false and partial reality of both. No longer can work be aligned simply with toil, necessity and subsistence, while the joy of art and the beautiful are relegated to a secondary, parasitic level, possible only for those whose leisure is bought at the cost of enslaving others to do their work for them. In so far as work and art *are* like this in the world, they are falling short of their *true* reality, where they are much more intimately intertwined. The aesthetic, ethical and metaphysical significances of this anti-dualistic move are radical: Beauty, for Ruskin, should be for everyone; but even more profoundly, the happiness of one need not be at the expense of others, the Good is not somehow ontologically secondary to and dependent upon a more fundamental and necessary agonistic reality of suffering.

Morris notes that this aesthetic vision of true labour was not entirely original to Ruskin. We have already traced elements of it in the works of Marx, while Morris also points to Robert Owen, for whom pleasure in labour is to be found in the fellowship of cooperation with others, or Charles Fourier's utopia, where a certain pleasure is to be found through

[60] Löwy, p. 131; cf. John Ruskin, *Sesames and Lilies, The Two Paths, and The King of the Golden River* (London: J. M. Dent and Sons, 1907).
[61] 'Preface to Ruskin's The Nature of Gothic' (1892) – hereafter PNG – in William Morris, *News from Nowhere and Other Writings*, ed. Clive Wilmer (London: Penguin, 1993), p. 367.
[62] Ibid.
[63] Ibid.

incitements to labour and the beauty of rational organization.[64] Yet unlike Marx, the latter two miss the key 'element of sensuous pleasure' in the work itself, which is for Morris the 'essence of all true art', as Ruskin grasps.[65] Morris neglects to mention the two authors who do not fit so easily into socialist canons, but were nevertheless the more immediate sources of these ideas for Ruskin: Pugin and Carlyle.

Ruskin probably first met Thomas Carlyle around 1850, when he had already been much influenced by the latter's *Heroes and Hero-Worship* (1841) and *Past and Present* (1843); subsequently he would describe him as the person 'to whom he owed more than any other English writer'.[66] Carlyle's detailed knowledge of German Romantics such as Schiller, Novalis and Goethe provides a distant connection between Ruskin's thought and some of the ideas we detected at the root of Marx's thought. In Carlyle's writings the dehumanizing mechanization and 'mammonism' of modern, industrial Britain is contrasted with an idealized medieval society, more 'organic', free, cooperative, and in harmony with nature, as for example in the characterization of Abbot Samson and his community in *Past and Present*.[67] Carlyle scathingly attacks the *laissez-faire* Liberal political economy which reduces human relations to self-interest and profit, and even links these developments with Europe's abandonment of Christianity, and the rise of utilitarian atheism.

Carlyle's medievalism was definitely in keeping with much of the dominant spirit in the late 1830s and 1840s, in the period when Ruskin was a student at Oxford and afterwards during his first major European travels, including the beginning of his love-affair with Venice. Unlike Ruskin however, Carlyle was not particularly seriously interested in the arts, despite the admiration he accords to the medieval artisan. It is Augustus Welby Pugin who first developed a similar social critique to that of Carlyle's into a fully fledged aesthetic philosophy for the Gothic revival in Victorian arts and architecture. For Pugin, Gothic architecture was *the* Christian architecture; while most modern architecture was thoroughly pagan and deplorable, as he had sought to illustrate in *Contrasts* (1836), and then argue in *True Principles of Pointed or Christian Architecture* (1841), and *An Apology for the Revival of Christian Architecture* (1843). The Gothic aesthetic here is at once the source of a social critique of industrial society and an alternative philosophy, albeit one that is unashamedly medievalist, reactionary, and, more problematically for many of his readers, Roman Catholic. While in some ways Pugin's developed aesthetic philosophy of the Gothic seems much closer to Ruskin's own than anything by Carlyle, it was the latter whom Ruskin always proudly acknowledged, while he took formal steps

---

[64] See Charles Fourier, *The Theory of the Four Movements* (Cambridge: Cambridge University Press, 1996).

[65] PNG, p. 368.

[66] Tim Hilton, *John Ruskin* (New Haven: Yale University Press, 2002) pp. 314 ff.

[67] Thomas Carlyle, *Past and Present* (London: Routledge, 1888).

to distance himself from the Romanism of the former by publishing *Notes on the Construction of Sheepfolds* three days after *The Stones of Venice*.[68] This was a pamphlet that expanded the anti-Roman views implicit in much of *The Stones* to make more explicit Ruskin's Protestant Medievalist alternative. So while both Carlyle and Pugin had genuine theological-social-aesthetic critiques of the injustices and dehumanization of modern industrial labour, it was only Ruskin who developed this into a broad-spirited, non-partisan socio-aesthetic philosophy, that could, for example, recognize the achievements of pagan art, and did not want to turn the clock back to the past.[69]

Ruskin was more interested in the forward looking vision of what true labour might be like, as he told his father in 1853: 'I shall show that the greatest distinctive character of Gothic is in the workman's heart and mind.'[70] If Gothic is for Ruskin an alternative 'work-ethic' to the modern one, in what does it consist? Ruskin elaborates six key features of 'Gothicness': savageness, changefulness, naturalism, grotesqueness, rigidity and redundance, which correspond to the characteristics of rudeness, love of change, love of nature, disturbed imagination, obstinacy and generosity in the worker.[71] Yet in elaborating these characteristics, other more crucial elements to the spirit of the Gothic emerge, namely: the overcoming of the division of labour, the free creativity of every workman, the subsequent reunification of labour and thought, function and ornamentation, work and play, utility and beauty.

In the section dealing with the 'savage' or 'rude' nature of Gothic, Ruskin protests against the 'degradation of the operative into a machine', arguing that the roughness of Gothic is the evidence of the absence of this dehumanizing degradation which results from the desire for tool-like precision. 'You must either make a tool of the creature, or a man of him' he tells us, for 'You cannot make both. Men were not intended to work with the accuracy of tools, to be precise and perfect in all their actions.'[72] The quirkiness, irregularity, wild details, flights of fancy, and rough finishes in Gothic art are not the mark of its primitiveness, but rather its humanity. They are the 'signs of the life and liberty of every workman' who is accorded the freedom to make his work his own, to exercise his own reason and imagination in his labour, which alone can provide true pleasure in this labour.[73] This approach to ornament is explicitly termed 'Christian' and contrasted with the 'servile' ornamentation of ancient Greece, Nineveh and Egypt, which prefers perfection, regularity, uniformity.[74] The Gothic artisan is a worker who is not enslaved to anyone else, and, therefore, is not alienated from his labour,

[68] Hilton, pp. 149 ff.
[69] Cf. Williams, p. 147.
[70] Hilton, p. 168.
[71] NG, p. 171.
[72] Ibid., p. 177.
[73] Ibid., p. 179.
[74] Ibid., p. 175.

but can truly express himself in it and take delight in this self-expression. For Ruskin, modern England is more like the servile arts of ancient Greece: obsessed with an artificial perfection and 'efficiency' at the expense of humanity. The spirit of Gothic for Ruskin is a 'work-ethic' of real freedom and creativity opposed to all imperialistic control. While order and regularity have their place, the love of order is not the love of art.[75] The Gothic is a spirit that recognizes its temporality and finitude while continuing to seek after eternity, unlike the pseudo timelessness and perfection of classicism. The modern world's desire for perfection is both too mediocre, in restricting our striving for true perfection, which will always exceed our capacity, and too unforgiving, in not tolerating this always falling-short. It rests content in the mediocre perfection of a finish, or a series of repeated patterns. The Gothic by contrast is more Christian in its wilder aspirations and greater humility and charity. It 'confesses its imperfection, in only bestowing dignity upon the acknow-ledgement of unworthiness.'[76] Yet its greatness is its 'strange disquiet-ude': 'that restlessness of the dreaming mind, that wanders hither and thither among the niches, and flickers feverishly around the pinnacles, and frets and fades in labyrinthine knots and shadows along wall and roof, and yet is not satisfied, nor shall be satisfied.'[77]

The role given to the individual worker's imagination entails the risk of constant failure, but this is not a problem. Ruskin's principle of redundancy which corresponds to the virtue of generosity expresses this well. The Gothic spirit commits workers to an 'uncalculating be-stowal' of the wealth of their labour. They are to be possessed by a 'magnificent enthusiasm' which leads them to an 'unselfishness of sacri-fice, which would rather cast fruitless labour before the altar than stand idle in the market.'[78] This liberality is also expressed in a cooperative spirit which carries the weaker workers, allowing their failures to be absorbed by the whole and to contribute to its richness.[79] In all these principles, the Gothic spirit reproduces the abundance of nature.

The Gothic spirit for Ruskin entails then the worker finding 'pleasure in the work by which they make their bread', and this pleasure consists primarily in their freedom from slavery, their freedom to use their own intellect and imagination to express themselves in their labour. These 'aesthetic' elements of unalienated labour – sensuous pleasure and au-tonomous creativity – correspond to the account we have already seen in Marx. It should be no surprise, therefore, that the hostility to the division of labour – that foundational principle of classical political economy – which we also saw in the early Marx at least, is shared by Ruskin. The division of labour is in reality for him the 'division of men'.[80] While he is

[75] Ibid., p. 185.
[76] Ibid., p. 176.
[77] Ibid., p. 190.
[78] Ibid., p. 195.
[79] Ibid.
[80] Ibid., p. 180.

not idealistically opposed to the implementation of one person's ideas by someone else, as if everyone should work entirely independently of any-one else, Ruskin insists nevertheless that there is a world of difference between blind obedience and cooperative inventiveness. Hence Ruskin, like the early Marx, is opposed to the foundational division of intellectual from manual labour, the liberal from the servile arts:

> We are always in these days endeavouring to separate the two; we want one man to be always thinking, and another to be always working, and we call one a gentleman, and the other an operative; whereas the workman ought often to be thinking, and the thinker often to be working, and both should be gentlemen in the best sense.'[81]

This separation of manual and intellectual labour is the root of all division of labour, and produces 'morbid thinkers and miserable work-ers'. Consequently, Ruskin insists: 'it is only by labour that thought can be made healthy, and only by thought that labour can be made happy, and the two cannot be separated with impunity...'[82]

It is not only the opposition between intellectual and manual labour that is overcome for Ruskin by the Gothic spirit. Clearly he envisages the true artisan as unifying serious work with a certain playfulness, as embodied by the gargoyles of the Gothic cathedrals. Similarly ornamen-tation, the business of making things look beautiful, is not for Ruskin, something supplementary to and separate from the more foundational utilitarian task of making a functional building. Just as work and play are mysteriously united in the Gothic artisan, so are beauty and utility, following Pugin here. This is an important counter to the charge of frivolous aestheticism that is often levelled against these Romantic philosophers. While their protest against the fiction of pure utility is indeed under the banner of beauty, this is not a beauty devoid of utility and thus dialectically determined by that which it opposes. Indeed so opposed to 'mere ornamentation' was Pugin, for example, that his writings were distant ancestors of twentieth-century functionalism (al-though this too can be regarded as a distortion of his synthesis). The two foundational principles of his 'pointed or Christian architecture' were: 'First, that there should be no features about a building which are not necessary for convenience, construction, or propriety; second, that all ornament should consist of enrichment of the essential construction of the building.'[83] This is illustrated by such features as the flying buttress, where a necessity of construction is made into a thing of beauty; in

---

[81]   NG, p. 182.
[82]   Ibid., p. 182.
[83]   Augustus Welby Pugin, *The True Principles of Pointed or Christian Architecture and An Apology for the Revival of Christian Architecture* (Leominster: Gracewing, 2003), p. 1.

contrast to the classicism of buildings such as St. Paul's cathedral, where utility is always hidden rather than celebrated.[84] Precisely because the Gothic spirit is unconcerned with artificial formal uniformity and symmetry, it can adapt itself unashamedly to real situations and needs, making them into occasions of beauty. Hence Ruskin writes of the Gothic builders: 'If they wanted a window, they opened one; a room, they added one'.[85] This is why Ruskin's love of beauty can be seen not so much as a repudiation of utility as its reconciliation with that beauty, and why he can speak of Gothic as 'not only the best, but also the *only rational* architecture', in the sense of being practicably serviceable, rather than rational in the formalistic, ideal sense.[86]

Lest it be thought that Ruskin's vision was purely theoretical, it should be noted that he sought to live out and propagate something of his alternative work-ethic in various ways, with it must be admitted varying degrees of success. In the interests of overcoming the division of manual and intellectual labour he took parties of Oxford undergraduates to engage in road-work projects in the Oxfordshire village of Hinksey in the 1870s, a project that is easily ridiculed, but which was intended to force first-hand involvement in the problems of land stewardship upon the upper classes.[87] More significantly he invested substantial money (one-tenth of his capital) and personal energy in setting up the 'Guild of St George', a society with the aim of purchasing land that it might then be cultivated justly and fairly in accordance with Ruskin's cooperative ideals.[88] The guild had its own constitution, published in *Fors Clavigera*, with explicitly theological foundations to its work-ethic, and Ruskin was its 'Master'.[89] While this Guild never reached great numbers, it proved influential upon the subsequent development of the cooperative movement, and upon so-called 'Guild Socialism'. Ruskin's greatest influence however was probably through his educational activities. His writings were frequently addressed to the 'workers of Britain' and central to his ideas of social renewal was the principle of free education for all, a principle which he embodied in his own involvement with the working men's educational movement.[90] Ruskin's hope for social transformation was based upon pedagogy. He also gave some concrete indications of what would be involved in his ideal society, including the professionalization of all workers, the replacement of wages with fixed salaries, the organization of trades into cooperative guilds, and the provision of pensions for those unable to work.[91] This might well

[84]   Pugin, p. 5.
[85]   NG, p. 189.
[86]   Ibid.
[87]   See Hilton, pp. 547–9, 566–7.
[88]   Ibid., pp. 495–7, 588–91. See also Ruskin's support for Octavia Hill's efforts to improve housing for the poor, Hilton, p. 392.
[89]   Rosenberg, pp. 415–16.
[90]   See *Time and Tide*, Letter XVI, UTL, pp. 15–16, or *Sesames and Lilies*.
[91]   See especially UTL, pp. 12 and 17, and *Time and Tide*.

sound like a politically ambiguous legacy, more 'High Tory Utopianism' than romantic socialism, as Hilton puts it.[92] Indeed, Ruskin encouraged this ambiguity of political labelling by being equally contemptuous of Disraeli and Gladstone, and describing himself variously as a Tory like his father, in the tradition of Scott and Homer, while also a Communist, 'reddest also of the red', in the tradition of Thomas More and Horace (!).[93] In both cases he regarded himself as belonging to the 'old school' rather than the present representatives of these traditions, and hence saw no contradiction. There is certainly a current of centralist authoritarian- ism in his patrician moral-pedagogical programme, yet perhaps in this hierarchicalism he partly recognizes the 'unavoidable non-reciprocity' inherent in education and transformation, which Liberalism had sought to deny.[94] Furthermore, as we have noted, his legacy was at least as radical as it was conservative. Equally, looking to the past for traces of resistance to political economy and another work ethic should not be automatically dismissed as reactionary, even if he, often knowingly, idealized this past in the process. Rather Ruskin rightly recognized that critical moral imagination must begin from the resources of counter- examples in the past and their survival in the present, however partial they may be. On the question of how these views related to Ruskin's complex religious position, more will be said at the end of this chapter.

WILLIAM MORRIS: ARTIST AND SOCIALIST

> Art . . . is not a mere adjunct of life which free and happy men can do without, but the necessary expression and indispensable instrument of human happiness.[95]

Morris, like Ruskin, was driven into social criticism by his love of beauty. In 1894, looking back on his life to write '*How I became a Socialist*', Morris describes his two great passions as: 'the desire to produce beautiful things' and 'hatred of modern civilisation', and insisted that the latter hatred was forced by his 'study of history and the love and practice of art'.[96] While still an undergraduate at Exeter

---

[92] Hilton, p. 495.

[93] Löwy, pp. 132–3; cf. *Fors Clavigera*, p. 374.

[94] This argument is made by John Milbank, *Theology and Social Theory* (Oxford: Blackwell, 1990), p. 199. For Ruskin's authoritarian and hierarchical instincts see e.g.: *Time and Tide*, Letters XII on dictatorship, XXII on masters, and XXV on rank. Nevertheless elites always exist to serve the whole of society for Ruskin – education, culture and wealth are not just for the rich – and are vehemently called to account on this point. I am grateful to Catherine Pickstock for reminding me of the unavoidable verticality of pedagogy; Matthew Bullimore's account of government by transcend- ence in the soul, city and cosmos (PhD Dissertation, University of Cambridge, 2005) explores this important political point at length through foundational texts of the Western philosophical and theological traditions.

[95] 'Looking Backward' (1889) in *News from Nowhere*, p. 357.

[96] 'How I became a Socialist' (1894) in *News from Nowhere*, pp. 381–2.

College, Oxford, Morris had read *The Stones of Venice* when it was published in 1853, and fallen in with the Pre-Raphaelite brotherhood which shared its medievalist vision of the artisan. During this period he toured the cathedrals of Northern France, began writing poetry, and was also influenced by the Christian Socialism of Charles Kingsley. He moved in 'Puseyite' High Church circles at first, and even briefly contemplated founding a monastery, but by the time he graduated he had abandoned this milieu and all his earlier plans of entering the Church.[97] Throughout the 1850s and 1860s he was primarily concerned with artistic matters, meeting Ruskin in 1857, experimenting with architecture and painting, and working with Edward Burne-Jones, Dante Gabriel Rossetti and the architect Philip Webb, before establishing his own design firm in 1861 with his inheritance, having already built himself a house in Bexley Heath according to the principles he espoused. In the later 1870s he became politicized over the 'Eastern Question', and began lecturing on art and society from 1877. It was not however until 1883 that Morris read any Marx, declared himself a socialist, and joined the Social-Democratic Federation. The following year he switched his allegiance to the splinter Socialist League and continued to write on political and artistic matters until his death in 1896.

Nevertheless, as with Ruskin, there was a clear continuity of thought linking the earlier aesthetic views to the latter explicit socialism, the romantic to the revolutionary, in E. P. Thompson's phrase. The hostility towards modern civilization was always, as with Carlyle and Ruskin, both aesthetic and socio-political: the poverty of art reflecting the ugliness of the workers' lives and the injustices that caused this. Morris joined Ruskin and the pre-Raphaelites in seeing the previous three hundred years of art as largely ones of decadence and decline; while in society, despite the increase in wealth, the modern world seemed to him only to have produced 'the mass of squalor and misery, the unhelped and apparently unhelpable hideousness, which forms the greater part of our big towns.'[98] While in his early days Morris had felt unable to clearly identify the causes and solutions of the problems of modern civilization, he nevertheless felt them just as acutely as he did in later life. Writing of this 'civilization', he is utterly scornful:

> What shall I say concerning its mastery of and its waste of mechanical power, its commonwealth so rich, its stupendous organisation – for the misery of life! Its contempt of simple pleasures which everyone could enjoy but for its folly? Its

[97]   E. P. Thompson, *William Morris: Romantic to Revolutionary* (London: The Merlin Press, 1955), p. 3. For a more recent biography of Morris see: Fiona MacCarthy, *William Morris: A Life for our Time* (London: Faber and Faber, 1995).

[98]   William Morris, *A Speech by Mr. W. Morris from the Cambridge Chronicle 23 February 1878* – hereafter 'Cambridge Speech' – (London: One Horse Press 1996), p. 4.

eyeless vulgarity which has destroyed art, the one certain solace of labour?[99]

He is equally scornful of the predominant utilitarian 'Whig frame of mind' which expresses the self-satisfaction of the prosperous English middle classes and is basically content with this 'civilization'. Only a very few, he tells us, rebelled against this 'measureless power of Whiggery', daring to criticize the status quo, most notably Carlyle and Ruskin, and these were those to whom Morris was drawn in seeking to express his dissatisfaction. Speaking of Ruskin, he writes in 1894:

> The latter, before my days of practical Socialism, was my master towards the ideal aforesaid, and, looking backward, I cannot help saying, by the way, how deadly dull the world would have been twenty years ago but for Ruskin! It was through him that I learned to give form to my discontent, which I must say was not by any means vague.[100]

In asking what was the substance of this influence of Ruskin upon the socio-aesthetic views of the young Morris, we shall see that he was in many ways the greatest expositor of the vision we traced above in 'The Nature of Gothic'.

Art and the redemption of work: The Ruskinian inheritance

> I am bidding you learn to be artists...and what is an artist but a workman who is determined that, whatever else happens, his work shall be excellent.[101]
>   The reward of labour is *life*. Is that not enough?...the reward of creation. The wages which God gets, as people might have said time agone.[102]

At the root of Morris's socialism is an aesthetic philosophy of labour which he derived from Ruskin, and which is manifest from his earliest public lecture on *The Lesser Arts* in 1877 and, beyond his conversion to Marx, in all his later writings, most notably in his famous utopian romance *News from Nowhere* (1890). *The Lesser Arts* is a manifesto against the separation of the 'lesser' decorative arts from the 'higher' arts of architecture, painting and sculpture. Speaking as one who had experimented with these higher arts, before settling for a life dedicated to the elevation of decorative art, Morris seeks to inspire his audience of the

---

[99] 'How I became a Socialist', p. 381.
[100] Ibid.
[101] 'The Lesser Arts', p. 250.
[102] 'News from Nowhere: or An Epoch of Rest' (1890) – hereafter NfN – in *News from Nowhere*, p. 122.

Trades Guild of Learning that their work is more true to the vocation of art than those artists courted by the galleries (there are echoes of Ruskin's contempt for Whistler here). The high art of the galleries is a dead reification divorced from the realities of life, which are left bare and ugly by the absence of art. The divorce of art and life, higher and lower arts, in the modern world has impoverished both:

> it is only in latter times, and under the most intricate condi-
> tions of life, that they have fallen apart from one another, and
> I hold that, when they are so parted, it is ill for the Arts
> altogether: the lesser ones become trivial, mechanical, unin-
> telligent, incapable of resisting the changes pressed upon them
> by fashion or dishonesty; while the greater, however they may
> be practised for a while by men of great minds and wonder-
> working hands, unhelped by the lesser, unhelped by each
> other, are sure to lose their dignity of popular arts, and
> become nothing but dull adjuncts to unmeaning pomp, or
> ingenious toys for a few rich and idle men.'[103]

The decorative arts have become servile, while the higher arts have become decadent and elitist, and the Romantic solution is the reconcili-ation of art with ordinary life. The true dignity of the decorative arts such as 'house-building, painting, joinery, and carpentry, smiths' work, potter and glass-making, weaving', etc, lies in their role as that by which people 'have at all times more or less striven to beautify the familiar matters of everyday life.'[104] The 'one great office' of decoration is to give people pleasure in the things they use and in the things they make, hence 'without these arts, our rest would be vacant and uninteresting, our labour mere endurance.'[105] Following Ruskin, art is simply the pleasure of creation that should accompany all labour; similarly decoration and ornamentation are not optional additions to production, but are essen-tial if it is to be truly human and not servile. The beautiful is not opposed to utility for Morris, but incorporates the latter within itself: 'nothing can be a work of art which is not useful; that is to say, which does not minister to the body when well under control of the mind, or which does not amuse, soothe, or elevate the mind in a healthy state.'[106] Much contemporary art is for Morris nothing but an opiate and escapism from the misery of life, and therefore 'weak, isolated, wanting in abun-dance and spontaneity', rather than transformative.[107] The current op-positions are founded upon the inequalities of society and the division of labour upon which they are based, and hence these too must be

---

[103] 'The Lesser Arts', p. 233; cf. Ruskin's *Time and Tide*, Letter XXI.
[104] 'The Lesser Arts', p. 234.
[105] Ibid., p. 235.
[106] Ibid., p. 251.
[107] Cambridge Speech, p. 6.

overcome. True work should involve the exercise of intellect and imagination, just as true art should be practical and popular. 'I do not want art for a few,' Morris insists, 'any more than education for a few, or freedom for a few.'[108] Culture is a radically democratic notion here. When people are no longer divided into the idle rich and the overworked poor, artists and workers, masters and slaves, 'men will assuredly be happy in their work, and that happiness will assuredly bring forth decorative, noble, *popular* art.'[109] This is not just a future hope for Morris, but has in fact existed at least to some degree in the past, specifically, following Ruskin, in the Gothic craftsman: 'Time was when the mystery and wonder of handicrafts were well acknowledged by the world, when imagination and fancy were mingled with all things made by man; and in those days all handicraftsmen were *artists*, as we should now call them.'[110]

Elsewhere Morris briefly summarizes the Gothic work-ethos as 'freedom of hand and mind subordinated to the cooperative harmony which made the freedom possible', and insists his celebration of this spirit is a contribution to the widespread 'revolt against utilitarianism' in the name of the arts.[111] Morris goes on, in the 1877 lecture, to call for a restoration of this ideal among the contemporary decorative arts, a revival of popular crafts by artists who would become almost a revolutionary vanguard to transform the nature of labour, learning to 'quicken with their art all makers of things into artists also'.[112] The first task in making workers into artists is the insistence upon excellence in working, instead of the 'sham work' and 'cheapness' generated by competition.[113] This cheapness has led to 'coarse food that does not nourish, with rotten raiment that does not shelter, with wretched houses which may well make a town-dweller in civilisation look back with regret to the tent of the nomad tribe, or the cave of the prehistoric savage.'[114] Here Morris is concerned with the beauty and morality that has been lacking in so much modern production. The second requirement is the resistance of vulgar 'love of luxury and show' which Morris believes affects all classes. This is the relative importance of utility and simplicity, and even appropriate sacrifices. Artists are called upon to make a moral stand, to resist the deception of satisfying supposedly 'natural' demand, and become those who shape fashion instead, leading the tastes of the people towards a more healthy society.[115] In this future society: 'all the works of man that we live amongst and handle will be in harmony with nature, will be reasonable and beautiful; yet all will be simple' without 'any

[108] 'The Lesser Arts', p. 253.
[109] Ibid., p. 254.
[110] Ibid., p. 238.
[111] 'Gothic Architecture' (1889) in *News from Nowhere*, pp. 332, 339.
[112] 'The Lesser Arts', p. 243.
[113] Ibid., pp. 249–50.
[114] 'Useful Work versus Useless Toil', p. 292.
[115] 'The Lesser Arts', pp. 249, 242.

signs of waste, pomp, or insolence, and every man will have his share of the *best*.'[116]

Morris envisages this transformation as extending to trade as well as manufacture and production, echoing Ruskin's call for just prices rather than the arbitrary bartering of the market. Thus he looks for a time when we would:

> adorn life with the pleasure of cheerfully *buying* goods at their due price; with the pleasure of *selling* goods that we could be proud of both for fair price and fair workmanship; with the pleasure of working soundly and without haste at *making* goods that we could be proud of'.[117]

While in later life Morris would abandon this optimistic view of how the transformation of labour can be achieved, replacing paternalistic education through an artistic elite with Marxist ideas of violent revolution as we shall see below, he never abandoned the Ruskinian ideal of the artisan as foreshadowing emancipated labour beyond the contradictions of contemporary work. In this he preserved the Romantic vision at the core of his social critique much more faithfully than Marx.

For example, the rather vague language of rich and poor, masters and slaves, of 1877 has been replaced by 1884 by more classically Marxist categories of class: there are, Morris tells us, 'a class which does not pretend to work, a class which pretends to work but which produces nothing, and a class which works, but is compelled by the other two classes to do work which is often unproductive.'[118] Similarly Morris no longer expects any transformation to be achieved by peaceful means.[119] Yet when he lists the three factors that can make work a blessing rather than a curse, as 'hope of rest, hope of product, hope of pleasure in the work itself', it is the last of the three that he regards as most important.[120] Whereas he believes most Socialists would agree on the first two, he acknowledges that he goes beyond them in the third when he insists: 'I yet demand compensation for the compulsion of Nature's necessity.'[121] The first task after a revolution would be to 'make all our labour, even the commonest and most necessary, pleasant to everybody'; a move which would go beyond the mere restriction of labour by leisure towards transforming it into something more pleasant, akin to leisure itself, beyond the dichotomies of work and play: 'But such a holiday our whole lives might be, if we were resolute to make all our labour reasonable and pleasant.'[122] The vision of the polymath, overcoming the

---

[116]   Ibid., p. 254.
[117]   Ibid., p. 250.
[118]   'Useful Work versus Useless Toil', p. 292.
[119]   Ibid., p. 306.
[120]   Ibid., p. 288.
[121]   Ibid., p. 295.
[122]   Ibid., p. 296. Cf. Cambridge Speech, p. 11: 'But with us every day is a holiday'.

division of labour by being skilled at many things himself, which we saw in the early Marx, is also found in Morris: 'A man might easily learn and practise at least three crafts, varying sedentary occupation with outdoor-occupation calling for the exercise of strong bodily energy for work in which the mind had more to do.'[123] Morris himself exceeded this modest estimate in his own life by practising 13 different self-taught crafts. The vision however remains that of Ruskin: that beauty will fill all of life, transforming necessity and utility into things of pleasure, just as in pre-industrial days, 'everything that was made by man was adorned by man'.[124]

The same vision of emancipated labour as art is central to Morris's famous utopian romance *News from Nowhere*, a vision of a communist Britain in 2003 after the revolution, which was serialized in 1890 in *The Commonweal*. Unlike much other proto-'Science-fiction' of this period, Morris does not foresee a world transformed by wild new technologies, where humanity is ever further removed from nature and labour, as one of the characters from the future tells us: 'this is not an age of inventions'.[125] Instead his utopia resembles an idealization of the best of fourteenth-century England: small communes without laws, money, and private property, where healthy and happy people work freely and cooperatively, producing only useful and beautiful things, enjoying the fruits of their labour and seeking at all times to create a beautiful environment with beautiful souls to occupy it. The contradictions of industrial modernity – masters and slaves, town and country, art and utility, work and play – are transcended in a 'life of repose amidst of energy; of work which is pleasure and pleasure which is work.'[126] For Morris, this is the foundation of the revolution upon which all other changes are based: 'Happiness without happy daily work is impossible.'[127] In the chapter 'On the lack of incentive to labour in a communist society' this ideal is elaborated further. While the nineteenth-century narrator cannot understand why people work if they are not paid, the people of the future cannot understand why people should *not* want to work. They respond:

> the reward of labour is *life*. Is that not enough? . . . the reward of creation. The wages which God gets, as people might have said time agone. If you are going to ask to be paid for the pleasure of creation, which is what excellence in work means, the next thing we shall hear of will be a bill sent in for the begetting of children.[128]

---

123 'Useful Work versus Useless Toil', p. 300.
124 Ibid., p. 301.
125 NfN, p. 192; cf. Morris's hostility to Edward Bellamy's techno-utopia in 'Looking Backwards'.
126 NfN, p. 222.
127 Ibid., p. 123.
128 Ibid., p. 122.

The activity of labouring is a necessity for all people: 'the race of man must either labour or perish. Nature does not give us our livelihood gratis; we must win it by toil of some sort or degree.'[129] Yet this does not mean that labour is a curse that everyone will seek to escape if they can – a position which had been foundational to the arguments of the political economists. Rather it can become a blessing, and indeed should naturally be accompanied by pleasure, like other natural necessities such as eating, sleeping or reproduction.[130] This pleasure consists in 'conscious sensuous pleasure in the work itself', like that of an artist.[131] The spirit of this new age will be a naturalistic sensualism, a 'delight in the life of the world; intense and overweening love of the very skin and surface of the earth on which man dwells, such as a lover has in the fair flesh of the woman he loves', rather than the 'unceasing criticism, the boundless curiosity' of the ancient Greeks, or the modern world.[132] Despite its superficial asceticism, Morris detects this sensualism in the spirit of the ordinary people in the middle ages, 'to whom heaven and the life of the next world was such a reality, that it became to them a part of the life upon the earth; which accordingly they loved and adorned'.[133]

In the chapter 'How the Change Came' in *News from Nowhere*, Morris provides an interesting account of how he expects the aesthetic instincts to be recovered. At first he imagines pleasure, art and rest emerging dialectically as alternatives opposed to work, before it is grasped that they are pointers to the true nature of work and its transformation. Thus the man from the future tells us:

> under the guise of pleasure that was not supposed to be work, work that was pleasure began to push out the mechanical toil, which they had once hoped at best to reduce to narrow limits indeed, but never to get rid of; and which, moreover, they found they could not limit as they hoped to do.[134]

Here Morris, in his openly Marxist phase, clearly holds onto the aesthetic hope of the transformation of labour rather than just its restriction, which we noted the later Marx had abandoned. Subsequently, art and pleasure cease to be in opposition to work, as that work is itself transformed into art, so that it can even be said that art 'has no name amongst us now, because it has become a necessary part of the labour of every man who produces.'[135] If Morris is interesting because he combines this Ruskinian

[129] 'Useful Work versus Useless Toil', p. 287.
[130] Cf. Ibid., pp. 287–8.
[131] NfN, p. 123.
[132] Ibid., p. 158.
[133] Ibid.
[134] Ibid., p. 201. We could compare here the recognition of the Frankfurt School that the Freudian 'pleasure principle' can be both an escapist opiate reinforcing the status quo, or a genuine source of critique and foretaste of redemption.
[135] NfN, p. 160.

vision of the redemption of labour with the 'practical socialism' of Marx, it is worth asking what tensions this creates.

Socialism or Marxism: Morality or historical determinism?

In 1894 Morris provides a definition of what he means by describing himself as a Socialist in order to avoid the vagueness that has attached itself to this term:

> what I mean by Socialism is a condition of society in which there should be neither rich nor poor, neither master nor master's man, neither idle nor overworked, neither brain-sick brain workers nor heart-sick hand workers, in a word, in which all men would be living in equality of condition, and would manage their affairs unwastefully, and with the full consciousness that harm to one would mean harm to all – the realisation of the meaning of the word COMMONWEALTH.[136]

Here, and in the communist utopia of *News from Nowhere*, Morris is much more unambiguous than Ruskin in his commitment to socialist ideals and to the working classes, a commitment that found concrete expression in his involvement with the nascent socialist political movements, in a manner quite different from the generally pedagogical activities of Ruskin. If Morris is more unequivocally 'progressive' and anti-authoritarian than Ruskin, he is not entirely free of the problems we detected earlier in Marxist socialism. While the above definition of socialism comes from his explicitly Marxist phase, there is nothing here that particularly distinguishes Morris's position from non-Marxist, moral forms of Socialism. There is not here the lapse back into utilitarianism, the historical optimism that harmony must emerge from the dialectic of history, the naturalism which sees an immanent teleology in labour itself and so does not seek to order it according to transcendent ideals; all of which we detected in the Marxist refusal of the theological.

Nevertheless, the most significant evidence of Marx's influence on the later Morris is his shift from a pedagogical view of the transformation of society by artists, towards an insistence that this transformation can only come about on the basis of a violent revolution. This shift is accompanied by the adoption of a classically Marxist view of the dialectic of historical progress, albeit one that preserves a certain Medievalism more suited to Carlyle or Ruskin than Marx. Thus in the lecture *The Hopes of Civilisation* (1885) the medieval period is celebrated, despite the naked robbery of the workers by feudalism, for its unenclosed common pasture and tillage, for its economic system that still spoke of just prices and unjust profits such as usury, and for its system of 96 obligatory holidays a year, which produced a common people 'bold'

[136] 'How I became a Socialist', p. 379.

rather than 'tame and sheep-like'.[137] Yet alongside this typically Ruski-nian medievalism, there are new emphases that are more critical of attempts to restore this ideal while avoiding violent revolution. Thus Morris writes, in comments that are just as much critical of his own earlier instincts as those of his more conservative predecessors:

> Many among the middle class who are sincerely grieved and shocked at the condition of the proletariat which civilisation has created, and even alarmed by the frightful inequalities which it fosters, do nevertheless shudder back from the idea of the class struggle, and strive to shut their eyes to the fact that it is going on.... They propose to themselves the impos-sible problem of raising the inferior or exploited classes into a position in which they will cease to struggle against the su-perior classes...This absurd position drives them into the concoction of schemes for bettering the condition of the working classes at their own expense, some of them futile, some merely fantastic.[138]

These schemes include false celebrations of 'involuntary asceticism', 'sham cooperation', and 'reactionary plans for importing the conditions of the production and life of the Middle Ages' into the modern world.[139] This certainly sounds like a damning indictment of exactly what Morris himself had proposed to his audience in those early lectures of the 1870s. The problem with these projects for the later Morris, following Marx here, was their avoidance of the reality of class conflict, and their naïve belief that the system could be transformed from within, rather than being overthrown by that conflict. Morris still believes that the Medieval workers 'lived in more comfort and self-respect than ours do', but now he draws more attention to their oppression by their feudal masters, and the impossibility of 'grafting' such a lifestyle onto modern capitalism. It is perhaps not too speculative to suggest that this pessimism was related to his own experience with his design firm, whose products had achieved success with the rich, but had failed to become anything like a truly popular art, because of their cost. Counter-cultural practices are always tamed by the logic of capital and turned to its own purposes; only a complete change will suffice now for Morris.

Crucially this new pessimism leads the later Morris to be scornful of any sense that the transformation required is a moral one, that it is possible to 'moralize' capital, as he puts it. Ruskin clearly believed that any transformation must begin with the soul, as we saw above, and Morris agrees with him that such moral ideas are theological in origin, but he appears now to disregard them for this reason: 'a sentiment

[137] 'The Hopes of Civilisation' (1885) in *News from Nowhere*, p. 310.
[138] 'The Hopes of Civilisation', p. 324.
[139] Ibid.

imported from a religion that looks upon another world as the true sphere of action for mankind [cannot] override the necessities of our daily life in this world.'[140] At times like this, necessary conflict and self-interest seem once again to be the inescapable only true realities; as with Marx; the foundational principles of political economy seem to have crept back in. Morris sees two possibilities for the future, although he is insistent that whichever comes about 'it must be produced by events...acting on our commercial system', rather than by 'artificial means'.[141] The new language of economic determinism learnt from Marxism is evident here. Indeed Morris himself makes explicit this shift in his thinking and Socialist thought generally that Marx achieved:

> the earlier Socialist writers and preachers based their hopes on man being taught to see the desirableness of co-operation, and adopting the change *voluntarily* and *consciously*...but the new school [i.e. Marxism], starting with an historical view of what had been, and seeing that a *law* of evolution swayed all events in it, was able to point out to us that the evolution was still going on, and that, whether Socialism be desirable or not, it is at least *inevitable*.[142]

The same ideas are operative when he claims that 'the logical outcome of the latter days of Capitalism will go step by step with its actual history' or when he speaks of the 'certainty' of the advent of socialism.[143] Perhaps this language should not be read according to a strict determinism, but the shift in emphasis away from moral judgement is obvious. Morris does insist that prophesying is 'no use', and he acknowledges the possibility that capitalism will continue to avoid its own ultimate crisis by always conceding enough at the last moment to ensure its survival, possibly through an ever expanding middle class (as perhaps has actually happened since Morris wrote). Nevertheless he can still describe it as 'unlikely to the last degree, or we will say impossible' that a 'moral sentiment' will be sufficient to bring about any change.[144] In *News from Nowhere* similar views are evident, in that the future utopia is imagined to be the result of a class war that arose through the failure of state socialism, and these changes are described as 'all a matter of course, like the rising and setting of the sun.'[145] One of the characters from the future tells us: 'the world was being brought to its second birth; how could that take place without a tragedy?'[146] Nevertheless despite these creeping views of historical determinism and the necessity of

---

140   'The Hopes of Civilisation', p. 326.
141   Ibid., pp. 326–7.
142   Ibid., p. 323, my italics.
143   Ibid., p. 328. Cf. ibid., p. 324.
144   Ibid., p. 328.
145   NfN, p. 133.
146   Ibid., p. 158.

revolution, Morris remains somewhat ambivalent; as, for example, when he recognizes the insecurity of his utopia, through the admission that however happy they might be, the people of the future could still choose to fall back into other ways.[147] Elsewhere, in his Marxist 'practical Socialist' phase, Morris still speaks of the need to 'use our wills', to make *voluntary judgements* which distinguish us from mere determined machines, in deciding to make good and useful things rather than anything or nothing.[148] The language of conscious moral discernment of the good, with its implicit transcendent teleology, has not entirely disappeared here. On another occasion he spoke as if necessity and morality were two parallel motive forces that must coincide for change to happen.[149] Furthermore, we have already noted that, unlike Marx, Morris always retained a sense of the *qualitative* transformation of human labour along with human nature itself in his utopia. He may now think that the change will only be accomplished on the basis of self-interest, but he retains the belief that this competitive self-interest will fade after the change, thus avoiding any false absolutizing of self-interest as inescapable. These mixed concerns return us to the questions of a naturalistic worldview and the attribution of an immanent teleology to labour, which we discussed in Marx above.

Naturalism?

Once again we are back at the central question that must face any social critique that hopes for the emancipation of labour: On what basis is this emancipation to come about? From where are we to 'get' the true labour by which the injustices of the present are criticized? Is it something that will simply emerge 'naturally' from labour itself? Or is labour somehow to be judged by an *ideal* beyond itself, although related to it? Is the true end, or *telos*, of labour immanent within labour itself, or is it somehow a transcendent ideal? In the former case it will simply emerge in the unfolding of its own logic; whereas in the latter it will require conscious, voluntary judgement in order for the ideal to be realized. Morris equivocates on this question, so that the standard by which he judges labour seems sometimes more transcendent than at other times. In *News from Nowhere* Morris speaks of the emergence of aesthetic labour, that is work for all that is accompanied by pleasure and beauty, as something spontaneous, as if, as we saw for Marx, the removal of the hindrance of the unjust distribution of property would somehow lead to true labour blossoming of its own accord, rather like a plant grows upwards as soon as any obstacles blocking the light have been removed. Thus the man from the future tells us:

---

147   Ibid., p. 214.
148   'Useful Work versus Useless Toil', p. 288. N.B. also his refusal of the language of 'necessity' or 'human nature' against the political economists: 'Useful Work versus Useless Toil', p. 302, NfN, p. 118.
149   E. P. Thompson, p. 724.

> The art or work-pleasure, as one ought to call it . . . sprung up almost spontaneously, it seems, from a kind of instinct amongst people, no longer driven desperately to painful and terrible overwork, to do the best they could with the work in hand – to make it excellent of its kind; and when that had gone on for a little, a craving for beauty seemed to awaken in men's minds . . . [150]

Morris imagines that the revolution will be followed by a brief period of utilitarianism, before people will become dissatisfied with this 'dull utilitarian' comfort and idleness, and will return to the 'superfluous' production of beauty.[151] Similarly, as early as 1877, Morris had insisted that 'men would wake up after a while' and, in a revealingly deterministic organic metaphor, 'the new seed must sprout'.[152] The key to this view of the 'natural' self-emancipation of labour is the importance of the controlling concept of 'Nature'. Nature is the most obvious candidate for a non-moral concept by which the injustices of current labour can be judged. As with Feuerbach's sensualism for Marx, this concept of Nature, inherited from Romanticism's opposition to industrialism, seems to provide an immanent, materialist teleology or criterion of judgement, which has no need of appeal to theology, or transcendence.

We noted earlier that Morris speaks of 'love of the very skin and surface of the earth' as the spirit of the new age in *News from Nowhere*, indicating the sensualist, naturalist materialism that seems to be the worldview upon which communism is to be based. His earlier more modest claim that Nature is 'ever bearing witness against man that he has deliberately chosen ugliness instead of beauty' reveals the roots of this appeal to Nature as criterion of judgement upon modern labour in Romanticism.[153] As we saw earlier, Naturalism was one of the key elements of the Gothic spirit for Ruskin and Pugin before him. From the earliest Romantic social critics onwards the ideas of the natural and organic were opposed to the artificiality and ugliness of modern industrial society. Beauty was manifest to humanity through nature, and beautiful labour would be in harmony with humanity's natural environment rather than destructive of it. However the crucial difference in Ruskin and Pugin's use of 'Nature' is that the natural was for them understood as *creation*, manifesting a divinely ordained order that nevertheless was excessive to it. In common with most of the earlier Romantics, they saw Nature in a more Platonic way, as imbued with spiritual forms that point beyond Nature itself to the spiritual and

[150] NfN, p. 160.
[151] Ibid., p. 159. Cf. 'Useful Work and Useless Toil', p. 299: 'Men who have just waded through a period of strife and revolution will be the last to put up with a life of mere utilitarianism, though Socialists are sometimes accused by ignorant persons of aiming at such a life.'
[152] 'The Lesser Arts', p. 240.
[153] Ibid.

divine. The problem with Morris's account of Nature, as with that of Marx, is that, in refusing all talk of 'Heaven', the theological, or transcendence, they seem to commit themselves to a materialist account of Nature which is incapable of delivering any teleology for labour beyond self-interest. Thus for example, we might well agree with Morris's typically Romantic, yet thoroughly radical recognition that it is the false presupposition that humanity is somehow not part of Nature that makes possible the subjugation of Nature, both in our environment, and ultimately in other people (an argument that anticipates that of the Frankfurt School, as we shall see in the next chapter).[154] Nevertheless, it does not follow from this that humanity is *just* a part of Nature like any other animal. For animals, crucially, do not appear to have anything that truly corresponds to the gratuitous production of art. Nor do they seem to be capable of making the sort of conscious judgements for goods beyond their 'natural' self-interest, which seem necessary in distinguishing good labour from bad. Indeed the Romantic tradition had always recognized that, as a *cultural* animal, humanity is crucially different from all the others in not having a fixed nature. Humanity is that creature which can make and choose its own nature, and indeed has done through history – a radically historicist perspective that, as we saw earlier, was used by Marx to deconstruct the false essentialism of the political economists' account of human nature. In more theological terms, we might say that humanity is a *spiritual* animal, or that our nature seems to be oriented towards some sort of end beyond itself, or even towards a *super*natural end. Thus it is impossible just to 'read-off' an account of the end-of-labour, let alone the good-for-humanity, from looking at how people actually behave. This would correspond to the 'naturalistic fallacy', emptying normative language of its ideality and reducing it to description. The political economists may well be right to observe that humans mostly operate according to selfishness, but this is in no sense a necessary law, let alone the key to some ahistorical 'human nature'; indeed this *homo economicus* is as much a cultural-historical product as any other pattern of human behaviour, as we argued above in chapter 2. Human 'nature', in the sense of how we generally behave, provides no criteria with which one could judge human behaviour.

Therefore, while Morris might be right to see a naïvety in attempts to transform labour consciously and voluntarily, his is surely the more unfounded optimism when he thinks that, when freed from coercion, everyone will be able to discern what is best for themselves and their neighbours and to work according to this criteria.[155] From where exactly is this knowledge of our genuine collective needs, let alone the will to provide for them, supposed to emerge? It is sadly very far from obvious that, as Morris believes, when 'people freed from the daily terror of starvation found out what they really wanted, being no longer

[154] NfN, p. 200.
[155] Ibid., pp. 123–7.

compelled by anything but their own needs, they would refuse to produce the mere inanities which are now called luxuries, or the poison and
trash now called cheap wares.'[156] The same ahistorical naturalism is
evident in this uncritical language of our 'needs' as that we saw in
Marx's notion of use-value in the previous chapter. Elsewhere Morris
is very critical of much language of 'human nature', but here it seems to
have crept back in, despite himself, just as this 'nature' by which he
judges contemporary labour and society, is clearly still full of theological
residues and not the neutral, naturalistic 'morality' beyond all socio-
historical conventions which he intends it to be.[157] Human labour
requires some ideal standard excessive to itself if it is to be judged and
ordered.

RUSKIN, MORRIS, AND THE THEOLOGICAL

In this chapter we have sought to illustrate something of an English
Romantic tradition of social criticism, of opposition to industrial capitalism and its justification through political economy that was as much
founded upon an aesthetic vision of the true nature of human labour as
we argued Marx's was in chapter 3. However whereas in Marx this
vision has to be detected and drawn out from a few key passages,
particularly in his earlier writings, and, we argued, was partially suppressed by contrary materialist, utilitarian currents to his thought, in
Ruskin and Morris it is much more obviously centrally articulated, and
more or less persists throughout their writings without suppression. In
this respect we have claimed that these apparently marginal, essayistic
and rather idiosyncratic figures have a certain surprising consistency to
their aesthetic critique of capitalism which is lacking in Marx. Both
Ruskin and Morris look to the aesthetic figure of the artisan to argue
for the transformation of labour from toil into something pleasurable,
overcoming the oppositions of intellectual and manual labour, liberal
and servile arts, masters and slaves, beauty and utility, work and play,
which are all enshrined in the foundational injustice of the division of
labour. Morris perhaps articulates this idea at greater length than
Ruskin, although it is Ruskin who more properly recognizes its truly
ideal nature. While we might look to historical examples (such as the
medieval craftsman), or nature, or other illustrations of what this ideal
might be like (e.g. thought, or childhood play), it will never be found in
its fullness in any of these things. These can only ever be imperfect
intimations. There has never been any human labour which is not in
some sense 'alienated', involving toil, a falling-short of the product from
the intended plan, some dissatisfaction in the work done. As Ruskin
recognized, *only God* can delight perfectly in his work, create without

---

[156] 'Useful Work versus Useless Toil', p. 304.
[157] Cf. NfN, pp. 93, 118, 'Useful Work versus Useless Toil', p. 299.

loss to himself, without any failure to achieve his plan.[158] This does not mean that this is not an ideal at which we should seek to aim, and to order human labour, but rather just that, because it is *ideal* it is not an immanent teleology which will emerge of its own accord, but rather it will require us to exercise our conscious judgement, it is a *moral* matter. Ruskin makes this very clear at various points, and Morris does not entirely forget this lesson of his master, but he does somewhat drift from this position in his later years under the influence of Marxist materialism and historical determinism. Nevertheless his aesthetic instincts always prevent him from seeing Socialism in purely utilitarian terms, or succumbing to the scientism that was so influential upon mainstream Marxism. Likewise Morris's utopia is profoundly opposed to the centralist dangers that have beset that tradition; while Ruskin's conservative, paternalistic instincts, combined with his voluntarism, do seem to leave the door open to dangerously authoritarian interpretations of his message, even if he is right to stress a certain necessary 'verticality' to transformation. If Morris's later inclination towards the naïvely Marxist belief that labour will resolve its own contradictions and realize its true immanent end is utterly implausible, Ruskin's pedagogical belief that society can be transformed through moral education seems at best idealistic and impractical. Despite this we have glimpsed areas where Ruskin's ideas did have significant, if modest, effects: in the provision of education to the working classes, in the cooperative movement, upon the early British Labour party and upon Indian Socialism via Gandhi. We might also go so far as to see later movements such as the environmentalist tradition or ongoing campaigns for fair wages and fair prices as in keeping with his vision. Most crucially perhaps, Ruskin realized that any lasting change would have to *depend upon* as well as engender a reordering of desire; the cart could not be put before the horse. Ruskin and Morris should be of interest to any social critique that seeks to resist the myth of the neutral 'market' and instead to encourage the ordering of society towards human flourishing, starting with the very nature of labour itself.

It might still not be clear how this aesthetic critique of labour under capitalism has anything to do with theology. Indeed while neither Ruskin nor Morris are as explicitly anti-theological as Marx, they are not without serious ambivalences towards theology, and especially Christianity. Both were brought up in typical middle class Victorian Evangelical families; both were influenced by Catholic leanings during their university years in Oxford. From here they took differing journeys: Morris had lost his faith by the time he left university, and, while he generally avoided the attacks on religion of other radicals, remained a non-believer for the rest of his life.[159] Hence his admiration for the middle ages is always combined with a criticism, albeit surprisingly sympathetic, for

---

158 NG, p. 190.
159 Thompson, pp. 710–11.

its otherworldly hopes.[160] Likewise religion is a thing of the past that has been left behind in his utopia in *News from Nowhere*. The people of the future have no belief in Heaven, and refer to belief in God as something confined to history, while the Bible is for them 'the old Jewish proverb book'.[161] Occasionally Morris uses the language of a 'new religion' or a 'new morality' to speak of the philosophy of the communist society of the future, but unlike others he did not attempt to spell out what this might look like, let alone invent rites for it. Ruskin is more complex in relation to religion. His entire oeuvre is saturated with biblical and theological language and imagery as we have seen.[162] However, judging from his correspondence and comments in his autobiography *Praeterita*, he seems to have experienced a growing crisis of faith, like many of his generation, which climaxed in Turin in 1858 with what he later spoke of as an 'unconversion'.[163] It is unclear whether this should be understood as an unconversion from church-going, evangelical orthodoxy, or traditional Christianity.[164] Whatever the case, Ruskin remained interested in 'spiritual' matters over subsequent years when he wrote most of his political writings. Some of the correspondence suggests that his continued use of heavily Biblical language during this period was nothing but a cynical ploy to appeal to a predominantly Christian readership, but even if this were Ruskin's intention, it would seem to underestimate the extent this language was part of the very fabric of his thought, whether he intended it to be or not. In 1874 he seems to have undergone some sort of 'reconversion' stimulated by meditating on the life of St Francis in Assisi, and by a spiritualist experience he had, but this was hardly to the evangelicalism of his childhood.[165]

Given this complex relation to Christianity and theology, it might seem disingenuous to speak of Ruskin and Morris's critique of labour as theological as well as aesthetic. Nevertheless, this claim is made more

---

160   Cf. his medieval political romance 'A Dream of John Ball' (1886) in *News from Nowhere*.
161   NfN, p. 84.
162   See Mary and Ellen Gibbs, *The Bible References in the Works of John Ruskin* (London: George Allen, 1906).
163   John Ruskin, 'Praeterita' (1885–9) in Rosenberg, pp. 426, 541–2; cf. Hilton, pp. 254–6.
164   Hilton (p. 452) argues persuasively that Ruskin 'never ceased to believe that the Christian God was his maker and that Jesus Christ was his saviour.' Ruskin had more difficulty with Evangelical views of Scriptural inerrancy (see *Time and Tide*, Letter VIII), and with the institutional churches (see Rosenberg pp. 428, 539, for his more 'catholic' sympathies in later years, p. 536 for his dissatisfaction with the 'Liberal' Christianity of Maurice, and pp. 250–1 for his sense of the entire world as God's temple). Michael Wheeler's *Ruskin's God* (Cambridge: Cambridge University Press, 1999) provides an excellent account linking Ruskin's aesthetic and political views with a coherent Scriptural theological framework grounded in ideas of Wisdom.
165   Cf. Hilton, pp. 559–61, 607–12, Rosenberg, p. 428.

in terms of the logic of their arguments than the detail of their professed faiths. Thus it is no accident that the things they look to as intimations of true aesthetic labour are all things that have often been aligned by modernity with theology as cultural enclaves resisting the onslaught of rational utility: art, morality, the family, nature, and all things medieval. The latter example is particularly significant: as we saw above, the Gothic revival was a return to explicitly *Christian* values against the 'pagan' modern world, just as Carlyle had seen atheism as the root of modern 'mammonism'. Both Ruskin and Morris are clearly aware of this in their discussion of Gothic, or just 'Christian' architecture, as they sometimes call it, and its work ethos. It is surely not insignificant that even Morris's future post-Christian utopia climaxes with a sort of agape feast in a church; just as it is not insignificant that Ruskin's manifesto against political economy was named after one of Christ's parables. Even more crucially, the vision of emancipated labour as art that they offer can only make sense as ultimately God's labour, as one of Morris's men from the future hints: 'The reward of labour is . . . the reward of creation. The wages which God gets, as people might have said time agone.'[166] Why 'only'? Because as was argued above, the ideal is not actually fully realized in any of the practices pointed to: even the Gothic craftsman or the child's play does not perfectly unify beauty and utility, work and rest, or achieve perfect pleasure in the work done, without toil, loss, or failure. Only God's labour truly fulfils these conditions, and only by seeing these other activities in relation to this ideal can they be read this way. Only because we know that true labour would include a perfect delight in the work made, seeing it as 'very good', do we know our own labour as falling short of this ideal. As we saw above, the foundations of this critique do not make sense on materialistic, immanent terms, but require the ideals, the teleology to be transcendent. As Raymond Williams argues, Beauty for Ruskin is also the True and the Good, and it is Divine.[167] Nevertheless this theological nature of the aesthetic in Ruskin and Morris is not made completely explicit by them. We will have to look elsewhere for those who will directly name the theological as a source of resistance.

---

[166] NfN, p. 122.
[167] Raymond Williams, pp. 135, 138. Cf. also *Time and Tide*, Letters IX and XI, where Ruskin suggests that dancing, music, and festivity might be aboriginally religious.

Without vision the people perish.

5

The Frankfurt School

The Critique of Instrumental Reason and Hints of Return to the Theo-Aesthetic within Marxism

In the last chapter we traced a British romantic socialist tradition of thinking about labour in the nineteenth century. This tradition, as we have seen, developed in alternative ways from Marxist thinking but was rooted in similar aesthetic and theological ideas, which we claimed in chapter 3 lie at the heart of Marx's critique of labour, but which were largely suppressed by other more utilitarian, anti-aesthetical and anti-theological currents in Marx's thought. However, it is not the case that the entire Marxist tradition continued to ignore these aesthetic and theological currents. At various points in the history of Marxism they have resurfaced with more or less force, and perhaps the most significant of such rediscoveries of theology and aesthetics is that of the Frankfurt School, which we will consider here.[1]

While standing within the Marxist tradition, the Frankfurt School – most famously Max Horkheimer and Theodor W. Adorno – repudiated the reductionist analysis of cultural phenomena which characterized the crudely materialist currents in Marxism. Members of the Frankfurt School wrote extensively on cultural and aesthetic questions, and their

---

[1] The *Institut für Sozialforschung* was established as an affiliated institute of the University of Frankfurt in 1923. In 1931 Horkheimer succeeded Grünberg as the director, a post he held until his retirement in 1958. Although Adorno did not formerly join the *Institut* until 1938 he had been friends with Horkheimer since the 1920s, and had worked alongside him throughout his directorship. In 1933 the *Institut* went into exile in Switzerland, before settling in New York and affiliating to Columbia University in 1934. It finally returned to Germany in 1949. Throughout Horkheimer's directorship the *Institut's* official journal was the *Zeitschrift für Sozialforschung*. See Martin Jay, *The Dialectical Imagination* (Berkeley: University of California Press, 1996) and Zoltán Tar, *The Frankfurt School: The Critical Theories of Max Horkheimer and Theodor W Adorno* (New York: John Wiley and Sons, 1977). I have chosen to concentrate on the most influential figures from the Frankfurt School rather than the more obviously theological, marginal figures such as Bloch and Fromm, to indicate how these concerns were not just peripheral to the project of the Frankfurt School.

interests in art, religion and philosophy can be seen as a recovery of a Marxism with stronger affinities to Hegel's concerns. Inasmuch as the Marxist polemic against culture began as a critique of theology, which was then extended to all ideology as 'priestly' deception, as was noted in chapter 3, so the Frankfurt's School's rehabilitation of the cultural can be seen as a return to the theological. If this is the case, the authors in question certainly did not make it completely explicit, and continued to show a suspicion towards many forms of religion.[2] Nevertheless such a return can be clearly detected across their work as we shall seek to show. The first evidence we shall present for this claim is the restoration of a certain autonomy to the aesthetic, which, as we noted in chapter 3, was reduced by cruder versions of Marxism to something purely practical and instrumental. Having regained something of its transcendence, art becomes once again a locus for utopian political hope and resistance to the status quo. Through the discussion of Adorno's aesthetic theory we can see that for him this political force lies not in its content but in its form and how this contradicts rather than reflects reality. This then will lead into a discussion of what reality exactly art protests against, namely the world of instrumental reason. The description and critique of instrumental reason that Horkheimer and Adorno provide develops the account of the spirit of utility as the nature of modern work under capitalism, discussed in chapter 2. Here we start from how Adorno's critique of Popper's positivism resembles his account of art as more than reflective and only truthful in its contradictoriness, restoring some sense of transcendence to truth against its scientific instrumentalisation by cruder Marxists. Then we shall recount the genealogy and critique of this scientistic positivism, which Horkheimer and Adorno offer in *Dialectic of Enlightenment*. Here they supplement Weber's account of the spirit of utility, by showing how 'modern', enlightened, instrumental reason is actually as old as history, something we noted Weber's ambivalence about. They also make other elements more explicit than Weber: the links between enlightened philosophy such as that of Kant and bourgeois economic rationalization; the roots of this instrumental reason in domination; the hostility of utility towards traditional substantive teleology; and the mythic irrational side to this 'rationalism'. While we found hints of all these things in Weber in chapter 2, Adorno and Horkheimer make them much more evident, indicating here their indebtedness to Nietzsche and Freud.

These additions to the account of utility as the spirit of modern work, which we traced in Weber, are matched by equally significant

---

2   See, for example, Adorno's firm censuring of attempts to reunite art with religion, in 'Theses upon Art and Religion Today' – hereafter 'Theses' – in *The Kenyon Review* VII: 4, 1945, pp. 678–9; or his description of religion as socialized paranoia, in Theodor W. Adorno and Max Horkheimer, *Dialectic of Enlightenment* - hereafter D of E - (London: Verso, 1997), p. 197; or Horkheimer's dismissal of the Neo-Thomists, in Max Horkheimer, *Eclipse of Reason* (New York: Continuum, 1974), pp. 62–91.

developments and modifications of Marx's account of the redemption of work. In having a more critical focus on the problem of utility and its genealogy, Adorno and Horkheimer escape Marx's naïve optimism about reason and historical progress. Whereas we noted above their re-Hegelianizing of Marx, in this respect they move further *away* from Hegel than Marx, in a pessimistic direction more indebted to Schopenhauer, Kierkegaard and Nietzsche. Here Adorno and Horkheimer explicitly note how Marx (and Hegel before him) fails to escape the 'optimism' of the bourgeois political economists. Adorno and Horkheimer recognize, where Marx seems not to have done so, that human labour does not contain its own naturalistic positive teleology that will simply work itself out when all other obstacles are removed. To make labour an end in itself in this way only perpetuates the empty formalism and universal pretensions of bourgeois labour. To work is neither the essence of being human nor an absolute end in itself. *Dialectic of Enlightenment* is particularly helpful in describing the curious way that this hyper-rationalist, disinterested approach to work, because of its very formal emptiness, transforms itself into its opposite: irrational, bestial pure self-interest; Kant becomes Sade. This dialectical relationship of asceticism and hedonism in modern work was something which Weber hinted at and which we sought to argue for in the discussion of Marx. In all these ways, the Frankfurt School moves our discussion of work forward. However, despite the tantalizing hints that art and theology might not only point out the problems of modern work but also offer resources for resisting these dangers, of imagining how it might be otherwise, Adorno and Horkheimer stubbornly reject any positive account of this. They are, for example, highly dismissive of proposals such as those of the romantics we considered in the last chapter. Therefore, at the end of this chapter we shall interrogate the adequacy of their 'negativity', a negativity which they frequently present as a Jewish critique of Christianity.

THE 'AUTONOMY' OF AESTHETICS

'Art since it became autonomous, has preserved the utopia
that evaporated from religion.'[3]

The Frankfurt School's interest in aesthetics goes back before its foundation. Horkheimer studied philosophy of art under Hans Cornelius in Frankfurt, writing his thesis on Kant's *Critique of Judgement*, while Adorno studied music in Vienna under Berg. It is unsurprising then, that they did not follow the 'orthodox' Soviet Marxist aesthetic tradition of Zhdanov and Stalin, which rejected the claims of modernist aesthetics. Against the 'bourgeois' idea of 'disinterestedness' in art, the Soviet tradition had encouraged the political commitment of *Tendenzliteratur*,

---

[3] Horkheimer's Art and Mass Culture, p. 292, cited in Jay p. 179.

of 'realistic' art, which accurately described the social relations of the people, against the 'subjectivism' of modernist art from Dostoevsky through to Joyce and Kafka. The Frankfurt School's break with even the more moderate sympathizers of this Soviet tradition can be seen in Adorno's discussions of Lukács and Brecht. Both writers were far from simple ideologues of the Soviet system. Indeed the Lukács of *History and Class Consciousness* was virtually the progenitor of the tradition of re-Hegelianized Marxism to which the Frankfurt School belonged. Yet Adorno berates him for his later submission to 'official optimism' in *The Meaning of Contemporary Realism* with its 'unrelieved sterility of Soviet claptrap.'[4] Against Lukács' complaints of modernist subjectivism, Adorno responds that his 'reflection theory' (*Abbildtheorie*) is a 'vulgar materialist shibboleth'.[5] The truthfulness of art resides not in its reflection of empirical reality, but in its autonomy or distance, which is constituted by form rather than content. Art should have nothing to do with a 'message', with 'stating something', and art that seeks to do this, like the *Tendenzliteratur*, will fail both as art and truth.[6]

While Adorno is hostile towards didactic works of art, this does not mean that art should be apolitical; on the contrary, it is more that art has become *the* locus of the political. Thus Adorno claims that today works of art bear 'the burden of wordlessly asserting what is barred to politics . . . This is not a time for political art, but politics has migrated into autonomous art'.[7] Across the writings of the Frankfurt School there is a consistent sense that art has partially held out against the advance of disenchantment and rationalization in modernity which has subjected the rest of our world to the utilitarian, dominating logic of instrumental reason. In so far as it is autonomous, art is a refuge where something is preserved from the spirit of Enlightenment. Artworks still have 'something in common with enchantment'; they are 'neutralised epiphanies'.[8] Not only the political and the sacred have taken refuge in art, but also metaphysics: 'For art is . . . what metaphysics . . . always wanted to be.'[9] Indeed it is 'spiritual' in the Hegelian sense, even if not pure or absolute spirit.[10] Even more basically, 'art causes people to wonder, just as Plato

---

4   Ed. Ronald Taylor, *Aesthetics and Politics* – hereafter A & P – (London: Verso, 1980), p. 168; see also Andrew Bowie, *From Romanticism to Critical Theory: The Philosophy of German Literary Theory* (London: Routledge, 1997), pp. 193–281, and Simon Jarvis, *Adorno: A Critical Introduction* (Cambridge: Polity Press, 1998), pp. 90–123.

5   A & P, p. 172.

6   Ibid., p. 168.

7   Ibid., p. 194.

8   D of E, p. 19; Theodor W. Adorno, *Aesthetic Theory* (London: Athlone Press, 1997), p. 80; cf. Theses, p. 680. This sense of art as vestigially connected to magic, ritual and the sacred resembles Walter Benjamin's account of the 'aura' of an artwork in his essay 'The Work of Art in the Age of Mechanical Reproduction', in Walter Benjamin, *Illuminations* (London: Pimlico, 1999), pp. 214–18.

9   Aesthetic Theory, p. 344.

10   Ibid., pp. 86 f.

once demanded that philosophy do, which, however, decided for the opposite.'[11]

The real surprise here is not this association of art with the magical, spiritual and metaphysical which would be common to most Marxists; but rather the subsequent refusal to dismiss the political value of these cultural realms. Instead, art, for Adorno, is in essence radical; both critical of the status quo and the basis of utopian hope for something different. 'Even in the most sublimated work of art' Adorno insists, 'there is a hidden "it should be otherwise".'[12] The truth that art speaks is the untruth of the status quo, it is the 'antithesis of that which is the case'.[13] Art breaks the spell of actuality and enables us to see that things could be different. This longing for a better world, *'une promesse du bonheur'*, is linked by Horkheimer with the residually *theological* in the aesthetic.[14] Adorno agrees that works of art 'point to a practice from which they abstain: the creation of a just life.'[15] In this they also resemble the purposelessness of childish play, another 'autotelic' activity which resists instrumentalization. Play is possible, according to Adorno, because the child's vision sees the world as an array of colours and qualities that exist simply for the joy of doing so, rather than the grey vision of the adult which reduces all to quantities and utility. In an extraordinary passage in *Minima Moralia* Adorno argues this aesthetic relation to the world is not a childish blindness but a refusal of resignation:

> Play is their defence.... In his purposeless activity the child, by a subterfuge, sides with the use-value against the exchange value. Just because he deprives the things with which he plays of their mediated usefulness, he seeks to rescue in them what is benign towards men and not what subserves the exchange relation that equally deforms men and things. The little trucks travel nowhere and the tiny barrels on them are empty... The unreality of games gives notice that reality is not yet real. Unconsciously they rehearse the right life.[16]

It is important however to note here that, despite this favourable account of the political power of the aesthetic, its utopian elements are, particularly for Adorno, only ever negative. There can be no positive account of this utopia, or how it should be attained, let alone the recognition of anything as the positive advent of these utopian realities.[17] This is Adorno's problem with Lukács and Brecht's uncritical celebration of Soviet society: it presumes 'the reconciliation has been

---

[11] Ibid., p. 126.
[12] A & P, p. 194; cf. Theses, p. 678.
[13] A & P, pp. 159.
[14] Jay, p. 179.
[15] A & P, p. 194.
[16] Theodor W. Adorno, *Minima Moralia* (London: Verso, 1996), p. 228.
[17] Cf. *Minima Moralia*, pp. 155–7.

accomplished, that all is well with society, that the individual has come into his own and feels at home in his world.'[18] Whereas the truth, Adorno insists, is that 'the antagonism persists, and it is a sheer lie to assert that it has been "overcome", as they call it, in the states of the Eastern bloc.'[19] The 'official optimism' that compels Lukács and Brecht to see positive counter-forces and trends in the officially 'socialist' countries and in the workers' movements ignores the principle, which Adorno champions, that 'the negation of the negation – the "distortion of the distortion" *is* the positive.'[20] Art may offer a hope of reconciliation of form and content, of subject and object, yet this utopia is properly unrepresentable because it nowhere exists, and any imaginings of it are inescapably implicated in the negative realities that produce these fantasies. Art cannot attain any genuine autonomy, because it is only produced out of the contradictions of what already is; its transcendence is a 'fractured' one: art has no other transcendence or autonomy than its contradiction of reality. Hence any art which seeks to anticipate these realities through abolishing the contradictions and dissonance is doomed to fail. Here Adorno is referring not just to the 'socialist realists', but also to the Romantic, primitivist and moralist traditions, which would seek a way out of the contradictions of instrumental reason either in a return to a pre-civilized natural state, or in a subjective overcoming of these contradictions.[21] These include the 'heavily-bearded naturalists of the 'nineties, who were out to have a good time' with their naïve utopian visions of the 'fulfilment of human possibilities'.[22] Adorno brings out, by contrast, the unspeakability of the utopian in a simple parable:

> The relation to the new is modelled on a child at the piano searching for a chord never previously heard. This chord, however, was always there; the possible combinations are limited and actually everything that can be played on it is implicitly given in the keyboard.... What takes itself to be utopia remains the negation of what exists and is obedient to it. At the centre of contemporary antinomies is that art must be and wants to be utopia ... yet at the same time art may not be utopia in order not to betray it by providing semblance and consolation.... Art is no more able than theory to concretise utopia, not even negatively.... only by virtue of the absolute negativity of collapse does art enunciate the unspeakable: utopia.[23]

18   A & P, p. 176.
19   Ibid.
20   Ibid., p. 168.
21   Cf. Theses, p. 677.
22   *Minima Moralia*, pp. 156, 155; Could Adorno be thinking of Morris here?
23   Aesthetic Theory, p. 32; cf. Horkheimer, in Seyla Benhabib, Wolfgang Bonss and John McCole (eds), *On Max Horkheimer: New Perspectives* (Cambridge: MIT Press, 1993), p. 61: 'the heaven to which one can show the way is no heaven at all.'

The pessimism of this perspective is inescapable: nothing is pure; not even the most simple 'natural' joys such as eating or play are free of complicity through escapism in the evils of the whole: 'Because all happiness found in the status quo is an ersatz and false [!], art must break its promise in order to remain true to it.'[24] The utopian Good, the emancipation of human labour, is entirely without positive mediation here; there are no signs or foretastes of its advent.

The importance of dialectics to Adorno's thinking, and, to a lesser degree, to the other members of the Frankfurt School, should now be clear.[25] Art's character is twofold: it is *both* 'autonomous' *and* a '*fait social*'; something which seeks to rise above utility to eternal truths, yet is also unavoidably something produced, an artefact.[26] Modern art's very autonomy is a product and expression of bourgeois society, of the separation of art from other concerns such as ritual and its reduction to a commodity for exchange. All human activity and expression, for Adorno, has always entailed some degree of reification, yet this 'false-hood' is also the very condition of possibility of its protest and truthful-ness. Thus Adorno could say: 'it is not ideology in itself which is untrue but rather its pretension to correspond to reality.'[27] Because art can never escape the circumstances of its production, as the vulgar Soviet aestheticians had recognized, its *only* autonomy, its only artistic and political worth, consists in its contradiction of reality, its truthful neg-ation of the untruthfulness of the status quo, its negative utopianism.

THE CRITIQUE OF POSITIVISM AND THE GENEALOGY OF INSTRUMENTAL REASON

as [theological ideas] fade, the world of numbers is becoming the only valid one.[28]

I have argued that the rehabilitation of the aesthetic by the Frankfurt School represented a turn away from the crude materialism of Soviet Marxists and a partial return to the repressed theological interests at the roots of Marxism, although at least in Adorno it is only at the most what Benjamin, speaking of Mallarmé's philosophy of art, called a 'negative theology'.[29] The crude Marxist deprecation of the aesthetic is however part of a larger restriction of truth to 'scientific' knowledge, understood

---

[24] Aesthetic Theory, p. 311. Cf. D of E, p. 130 and Benjamin's famous phrase: 'There is no document of civilisation which is not at the same time a document of barbarism.' Illuminations, p. 248.

[25] See especially: Theodor Wiesengrund Adorno, *Negative Dialectics*, trans. E. B. Ashton (New York: The Seabury Press, 1973).

[26] *Aesthetic Theory*, p. 229; cf. *Minima Moralia*, pp. 225–6.

[27] Cited in Jay, p. 179.

[28] Max Horkheimer, *Critique of Instrumental Reason* – hereafter C of IR – (New York: Seabury Press, 1974), p. 157.

[29] *Illuminations*, p. 218.

according to the example of the natural sciences and economics. Theology is accorded the same fate as other symbolic forms of cultural expression of being denied any cognitive or truth-bearing capacity; indeed all symbolic production is regarded as aboriginally a theological deception, founded in the reification of nature through animism. Hence the other side to the Frankfurt School's 'return to the theological' is its more critical stance towards positivism and scientific rationality. It is to this that we will now turn, noting as we proceed the advances over Weber's account of utility and over Marx's account of the emancipation of labour.

The distance between the Frankfurt School and a naïve scientistic positivism can be seen in Adorno's debate with the critical philosophy of Karl Popper.[30] Here Adorno claims that the priority of formal logic is 'the core of the positivistic ... view of any science'. Positivism believes in the truthfulness of this method, yet this method – formal logic – is too simple to account for the complexity of reality, which is forced into its restrictive categorizations. Logic is incapable of grasping the contradictions of reality and is determined to reconcile everything into one harmonious system, as evident in the *una scientia* or *mathesis universalis* of Bacon, Descartes and Leibniz.[31] As *Dialectic of Enlightenment* puts it: 'For the Enlightenment, whatever does not conform to the rule of computation and utility is suspect ... Unity is the slogan from Parmenides to Russell. The destruction of gods and qualities alike is insisted upon.'[32]

This destructive unity corresponds to the logic of exchangeability. By quantifying everything on one scale, bourgeois society falsely makes everything appear exchangeable and destroys its distinctiveness and reality. Thus positivism misses the disjunction between appearances and reality, concerning itself purely with reality as empirically given and as capable of being categorized by logic. In mistaking appearances for reality it has no sense of the negativity of reality; it affirms current realities, as they appear, to be the truth. Thus positivism is reactionary in consolidating the status quo and making alternative visions impossible.

The Positivist delusion of a tidy, non-contradictory reality is linked with the idea of science as absolutely objective, free of the contradictions of the socio-historical contexts that produced it, an ideal of autonomy that is then made definitive for all knowledge. Positivism represses the truth that knowledge, like art, is always inescapably marked by the complex circumstances of its production. Knowledge, like art, has a

[30] This controversy over the methods appropriate to the human and social sciences became a full public debate following the Tübingen meeting of the German Sociological Association in 1961 and Adorno's contributions to this debate which will be used here appeared in a volume with those of his opponents in 1969 as '*Der Positivismusstreit in der deutschen Soziologie*', trans. G. Adey and D. Frisby, *The Positivist Dispute in German Sociology* – hereafter PD – (London: Heinemann, 1976).

[31] D of E, p. 7.

[32] Ibid., pp. 6 and 8.

contradictory 'dual nature': it is *both* 'independent and dependent'.[33] Adorno claims, following Horkheimer, that positivism, despite its pretensions to objectivity, is historically an expression of *subjective* reason.[34] This subjectivity can be seen both in the way that such rationality imposes categorical schemata upon the material, which is then classified according to these subjective structures rather than according to its own inherent logic.[35] More profoundly this subjectivism can be seen in the 'genealogy' of modern reason, which elaborates in interesting ways the account of utility as the spirit of work under capitalism that we discussed in chapter 2.

This genealogy of Enlightenment rationality was a central concern of the Frankfurt School and the subject of their most famous work, the '*Dialectic of Enlightenment*'.[36] Written during the height of the Nazi domination of Europe, this work sets itself the task of asking 'why mankind, instead of entering into a truly human condition, is sinking into a new kind of barbarism.'[37] Whereas most commentators saw totalitarianism and anti-Semitism as a departure from Liberal Enlightened reason, Adorno and Horkheimer argued that the truth is more dialectical: while they still affirmed that 'social freedom is inseparable from enlightened thought', they also concluded that the recent descent of modernity into mythology and destruction was not just an aberration but implicit in the very logic of Enlightenment itself.[38] The same technology that had made possible rises in living standards had also driven the vast military operation of Nazi Germany and the most organized, efficient project of genocide in human history. At the heart of scientific reason lies the self-assertion of a dominating subject mythically separated from nature. Enlightened reason cannot simply be opposed to the mythologies from which it claimed to bring emancipation; the relation is more dialectical: 'myth is already Enlightenment; and Enlightenment reverts to mythology'.[39] This by no means leads Adorno and Horkheimer to reject the Enlightenment wholesale and embrace irrationalism; rather they argue that Enlightenment must become more self-critical and endeavour to liberate itself from 'blind domination'.[40]

The critique of Enlightenment Adorno and Horkheimer provide is offered from four perspectives. First, a reading of Homer's *Odyssey* presents Odysseus as the first bourgeois individual, the wandering adventurer who embodies '*homo oeconomicus*'.[41] He typifies the subject's self-assertion against the objectified world through rational

[33]   PD, p. 4.
[34]   Ibid., p. 5.
[35]   Ibid., p. 7.
[36]   See also Jarvis, pp. 20–43.
[37]   D of E, p. xi.
[38]   Ibid., p. xiii.
[39]   Ibid., p. xvi.
[40]   Ibid., pp. xv–xvi.
[41]   Ibid., p. 61.

risk, renunciation and sacrifice, which serve to justify the oppression and domination necessary in his quest.[42] This quest is the only goal that matters, an end-in-itself which supersedes all other ends. Here it achieves a 'secularization' of the world by abolishing all qualities and substantive teleology, as can be seen from the shadowy, unheroic, role given to the gods.[43] This secularizing destruction of qualities and gods corresponds to the way utility drains all colour from the world making play impossible, as noted earlier under the discussion of aesthetics. Self-preservation, is the 'true maxim of Western civilisation', as Spinoza realized.[44] Thus, Adorno and Horkheimer argue, the foundational European sagas were already myths of Enlightenment. Whereas Weber had generally argued that the spirit of risk, 'adventure capitalism', is as old as history, but that rational, 'ascetic' capitalism was distinctively modern, Adorno and Horkheimer employ Freudian psychological insights to insist that the two types are not so easily distinguished. Risk and rational planning, self-assertion and self-restraint are in practice not tidily opposed as in Weber's typology but are two sides of the same coin, dialectically related. If the distinction cannot be maintained, then it follows that 'ancient' and 'modern' capitalism cannot be so neatly separated, and, as we argued in chapter 2, Calvinism is not so significant a point of origin; rather the 'modern' bourgeois spirit is already evident in Homer. Likewise Adorno and Horkheimer are quite clear about the secularization inherent in this spirit and at the same time, its mythic, non-rational foundation, both of which we argued for in chapter 2.

The second element of the critique, a Nietzschean reading of Kant, reveals the archetypal enlightened philosopher's surprising affinities with the Marquis de Sade, in that his critical reason is the dominating spirit of science, ruthlessly rational and amoral, mythically opposing subject and object in order that the former may dominate the latter. Kant's categorical imperative, the bourgeois ideal of a man who is a law unto himself, is the forerunner of Nietzsche's superman, pure will to power.[45] Yet even Nietzsche recoils from the full horror of realizing that this ideal can be fulfilled as much by the common criminal as by some noble hero.[46] Whereas Sade, in his character Juliette, is more ruthless in carrying the Enlightenment critique of reason through to its nihilistic conclusion. Here the domination of nature by the autocratic subject returns back on itself when the subject is transformed by domination into the image it projects: nature has its revenge when the rational subject is itself reduced to a blind object, bestial irrationality. The domination of nature only vindicates nature through a 'mimesis unto

[42] D of E, p. 62.
[43] Cf. Ibid., pp. 55, 46, 89 and 49.
[44] Ibid., p. 29.
[45] Ibid., p. 114.
[46] Ibid., p. 100.

death': 'the subjective spirit which cancels the animation of nature can master a despiritualised nature only by imitating its rigidity and despiritualizing itself in turn.'[47] Rational scepticism can no longer be held at the door to preserve the status quo, as Kant had done.[48] The onslaught of demythologization is relentless: in Sade's zoological sadism love is transformed into lust, pity is exposed as weakness, knowledge as violence.[49] Reason itself cannot escape this demythologizing; the Enlightenment's quest for demystification becomes *self*-destructive, exposing its own nature as just another myth. While we found hints in Weber in chapter 2 of the affinities between the bourgeois spirit of utility in economic life and the bourgeois transcendental philosophy of Kant, there was nothing of the explicitness of Adorno and Horkheimer's identification of the two in the claim that 'the unleashed market economy was…the actual form of reason'.[50] Similarly we also noted in Weber and Marx the ambiguous mixture of asceticism and hedonism in the spirit of capitalism, the tendency for thrift, planning, and modesty to transform into extravagance, hyper-consumption, and 'sport', yet in neither is the relation made so clear as in the coupling of Kant and Sade in *Dialectic of Enlightenment*. Finally neither Weber nor Marx point out the dominating and dehumanizing nature of utility with the force of Adorno and Horkheimer.

This transformation of reason into its opposite is illustrated in the final two sections of the book, through more empirical accounts of the 'culture industry' and anti-Semitism. The description of the culture industry shows how the potential enemies of capital can be deceptively enlisted in its service, so that the public are made to believe that they have ever more freedom and pleasure through the commodification of life as entertainment, while all the time life is secretly more homogenous and more administered than ever. This subterfuge serves a 'Tantalus' ritual of the stimulation of retroactive 'needs' which produces the endless 'compulsion to buy' and a subsequent resignation towards the status quo.[51] The final section on anti-Semitism is a socio-psychological analysis of the mutual constitution of the identity of persecutor and victim, so that anti-Semitism conforms to the logic of Hegel's master–slave dialectic and demonstrates how Fascism 'uses the rebellion of nature against domination as part of that domination'.[52] This in turn conforms to the very logic of civilization itself, which is 'the victory of society over nature which changes everything into pure nature'.[53]

[47] Ibid., p. 57.
[48] Ibid., p. 92.
[49] Ibid., pp. 101 and 108.
[50] Ibid., p. 90.
[51] Ibid., pp. 140 and 167
[52] Ibid., p. 185.
[53] Ibid., p. 186.

THEOLOGY AGAINST UTILITY?

What however does this grand critique of Enlightenment instrumental reason, the spirit of utility, have to do with the theological? At the most basic level, theology and the Frankfurt School share a common enemy in positivism, and the critique that Adorno, Horkheimer and others offer can be helpful to theology in questioning the hegemony of scientific knowledge which excludes theology. More profoundly the Frankfurt School's critique of Enlightenment represents an internal correction of the Marxist tradition's alignment with a naïve positivist account of the hegemony of scientific knowledge, an alignment that led to an equally crude dismissal of theology alongside the aesthetic and other cultural realms. Yet it would be misleading to present the Frankfurt School simply as champions of theology against Enlightenment.[54] First, the critique of Enlightenment is, as with the rehabilitation of the aesthetic, dialectical rather than entirely hostile. Equally theology, along with art, myth and other forms of symbolic expression, is not simply opposed to Enlightenment; rather they are dialectically related. Thus explicit references to the theological in Adorno and Horkheimer are mixed. Enlightenment certainly has an anti-theological secularizing effect, always seeking to banish the gods.[55] Yet equally they insist that both the Homeric gods of ancient Greece and the God of Israel are already representatives of Enlightenment: the Homeric deities because they have dethroned the older gods and are no longer directly identified with things but only signify them, as Apollo is the god of the sun but not the sun itself; while the God of Israel in his creation *ex nihilo* rather than in an endless cycle and his banishing of all the nature deities is equally an expression of Enlightenment.[56] Similarly, while the theological, like art, is certainly capable, as the Soviet Marxists had argued, of serving the status quo through a mystification that brings false reconciliation with the contradictions of reality, yet crucially it is equally capable of providing resources for resistance and hope. Horkheimer brings out this radical element to the theological in his essays in the *Critique of Instrumental Reason.*[57] Discussing threats to freedom, after what appears to be a startling profession of Jewish faith in an aside, Horkheimer makes the following extraordinary claim: 'The ideas which can relativise such experience are, in the last analysis, inseparable from theology, and as they fade, the world of numbers is becoming the only

[54] See also n. 2 above.
[55] D of E, pp. 90 and 92.
[56] Ibid., p. 8.
[57] For the possible influences on Horkheimer's post-war interest in religion, see: Peter Stirk, *Max Horkheimer: A New Interpretation* (Hemel Hempstead: Harvester Wheatsheaf, 1992), pp. 196–202. Clearly many of his friends and disciples saw this move at the time and since as an apostasy, while others have simply denied any such shift (Benhabib, pp. 60–1, 276, and 70 ff.).

valid one.'[58] Transcendence itself is the necessary foundation for the hope that things might be otherwise: 'Does not Christianity... stand in utter opposition to conformism, however much secular authority may have been indebted to religion in this respect? Non-conformity, freedom, self-determined obedience to Someone Other than the status quo may be regarded as typically Christian realities.'[59] Elsewhere, Horkheimer insists that theology does not share the indeterminacy of existentialist talk of 'authenticity', so that what is needed to cure this vagueness is 'a knowledge of the theological tradition, for our grasp of the inextricable meshing of human freedom and its conditionings, as well as the Kantian hope, have their historical roots in that tradition.'[60]

More specifically, while rejecting Cartesian dualism or a cheap psychologism, both of which ignore the objective material aspects of oppression, Horkheimer believes that traditional theological anthropology can preserve a radical sense of freedom neglected by the deterministic Soviet materialists, while also avoiding the former dangers of 'spiritualism'. Aquinas is cited with approval: 'the old principle that man is a rational animal, "a compound of soul and body," and with it the whole of traditional anthropology have not lost their validity.'[61] More explicitly:

> 'Soul' is becoming, in retrospect as it were, a pregnant concept, expressing all that is opposed to the indifference of the subject who is ruled by technology and destined to be a mere client. Reason divorced from feeling is now becoming the opposite of *Anima* or soul.[62]

Adorno is not entirely without similar claims, as when he asserts that the resurrection of the dead takes seriously the inseparability of the spiritual and physical.[63] Or when he insists:

> The self should not be spoken of as the ontological ground, but at the most theologically, in the name of its likeness to God. He who holds fast the self and does away with theological concepts helps to justify the diabolical positive, naked interest.'[64]

Anthropology is not the only contribution theology can make to resistance; it is also implicated in the 'eschatological' questions of hope for the

[58] C of IR, p. 157.
[59] Ibid., p. 149; cf. Ibid., *p.* 50.
[60] Ibid., p. 7.
[61] Ibid., p. 14.
[62] Ibid., p. 60.
[63] *Minima Moralia*, p. 242; cf. Tar, p. xi, on parallels in Schelling's notion of the 'resurrection of the natural subject' and Bloch's *Naturphilosophie*.
[64] *Minima Moralia*, p. 154; cf. D of E, p. 198.

future and the 'ethical' question of what praxis might contribute to that hope. Thus Horkheimer links this hope with Judaism's messianism, which persists in a weaker form in Christianity's hope for the Messiah's return and the consummation of the kingdom of Heaven, the 'expectation that against all probability and despite the previous course of history paradise would one day come'.[65] As noted above, this theological hope was, according to Horkheimer, the root of Kant's utopianism, and his ideas of justice and freedom only make sense in the context of this transcendent foundation.[66] The social progressivism of Holbach and Condorcet is merely a secularized version of the old theological philosophy of history.[67]

The praxis that points towards this hope is none other than charity, love of neighbour.[68] This is the theological virtue which in secularized form remains the basis of the ideals of the French Revolution as well as Marx's philosophy.[69] The Christian 'pity' and 'compassion' that Sade had condemned as pure weakness is another form of the same awareness of the connection between the particular and the universal, between oneself and everyone else. Adorno and Horkheimer regard such pity as 'humanity in a direct form' and affirm that it is utterly opposed to that Roman *virtus* which, from the Medicis to the Fords, has been the 'only truly bourgeois virtue', Stoical *apatheia*, self-assertion unmoved by the sufferings of others.[70] That the idea of brotherly love is also found among secular radicals, and at times such as the eighteenth century seemed more alive among them than with the 'natural theologians' whose God was little more than a guarantor of the laws of nature, still does not detract from its theological origins:

> Such selflessness, such a sublimation of self-love into love of others had its origin in Europe in the Judaeo-Christian idea that truth, love and justice were one … The necessary connection between the theistic tradition and the overcoming of self-seeking becomes very much clearer to a reflective thinker of our time than it was to the critics of religion in by-gone days.[71]

Horkheimer concludes this 1963 essay on theism and atheism with the claim that the situation of the last century has been turned on its head:

---

[65] C of IR, p. 150. Here he was developing the ideas on the messianic that Benjamin set forward in the Theses on the Philosophy of History; the influence of Bloch can also be detected.

[66] C of IR, p. 71; the work of the Jewish Neo-Kantian Hermann Cohen was probably influential here (Tar, p. 58).

[67] C of IR, p. 72.

[68] Ibid., p. 150.

[69] Ibid., p. 151.

[70] D of E, p. 101.

[71] C of IR, p. 50.

the atheists now are those who are simply obedient to the status quo, while it is the believers, who cling to the 'thought of something other than the world, something over which the fixed rules of nature, the perennial source of doom, have no dominion', who might actually offer some resistance to the world of 'docile masses governed by clocks'.[72]

THE 'JEWISH' CRITIQUE OF 'CHRISTIAN' POSITIVE MYTHIC RECONCILIATION: PROBLEMS WITH THE 'OPTIMISM' OF HEGEL AND MARX

Such comments as the above indicate the extraordinary reappraisal of the theological that the Frankfurt School stood for within the Marxist tradition. Far from theology being simply deception complicit with the status quo, Adorno and Horkheimer bring out the historical indebtedness of Marxist resistance and hope to theology, which we argued for in chapter 3, and the contribution that theology might still make to such practices. However as noted earlier it would be a mistake to present the Frankfurt School as simply 'pro-theology'. The dangers of theology are, for them, essentially the same as those of art discussed above, indeed they are the generic dangers of the mythical-symbolic: of providing a false premature reconciliation of the contradictions of reality. Theology then becomes consolation, ideology, justification of the status quo. The most interesting way of exploring this negative critique in the works of Adorno and Horkheimer is to see how they set up Judaism in order to criticize such tendencies in Christianity.[73]

We have already seen that the faith of Israel represents for Adorno and Horkheimer an advance of Enlightenment compared with its neighbouring nature religions. The world of Judaism is a 'disenchanted' one, where 'the idea of the patriarchate culminates in the destruction of myth'.[74] Yet, agreeing here with Weber, the Frankfurt School saw Christianity, particularly in its Catholic form, as a return to magic, a lapse from Jewish Enlightenment. The cult of angels and saints, the restoration of the feminine in the cult of the Virgin, and the belief in the *analogia entis*, amount to a certain re-enchantment of the world, so that Enlightenment

---

[72]   Ibid., pp. 50 and 49.

[73]   It is worth noting that almost all of those involved with the Frankfurt School were from assimilated upper-middle class Jewish families. This was not something most of them chose to make much of, and in some cases it seems to have had minimal influence. Yet while there was no formal involvement with Jewish concerns such as Zionism, members of the Institute did undertake studies of anti-Semitism as we have seen that developed the work of Marx on the 'Jewish question'. More explicitly, two members of the Institute, Leo Lowenthal and Erich Fromm had been involved in the Frankfurt Lehrhaus and the circle around Rabbi Nobel which included Martin Buber and Franz Rosenzweig, while Benjamin's account of the messianic was clearly indebted to his reading of the Kabbalah. See Jay pp. 29, 31–5, 56, 200, and Tar, pp. 182–9.

[74]   D of E, p. 23.

when it reasserts itself in Calvinism is as opposed to the Catholic *ordo* as ancient Israel was to paganism.[75] Christianity cannot be classed purely as regression from Judaism in that both its universalizing of a national religion and its stress on grace and love beyond law are an advance on Judaism (albeit latent in the latter).[76] Nevertheless the regression to magic is not merely accidental to Christianity but goes to its very heart: the belief in Christ and his cross. The belief in the incarnation absolutizes the finite, Christ is 'the deified sorcerer', and this 'intellectualization of magic' is the 'root of evil'.[77] The crucified god is, for Adorno and Horkheimer, a prematurely contrived reconciliation of civilization and nature which is equally alien to Judaism and the Enlightenment.[78] The confession of the crucified saviour supposedly introduced torments into the Godhead itself, thus deifying suffering, with the consequence that the 'acceptance of destiny became a religion'.[79] The contrast with the Jews is made again: the Jews are 'not ascetical people as the first Christians were, they have never glorified or worshipped or sought or praised suffering but only experienced it. . . . According to the Jewish law men cannot become saints through suffering, as in Christianity.'[80] The 'deception' of Christianity lies in giving a positive meaning to suffering and self-denial.[81] Reconciliation is falsely declared to have arrived, so theology is transformed into theodicy, the justification of God, which is actually the justification of the status quo with all its injustices and oppression. This leads to a gross falsification of history: because the claim is made that the secret truth of history is that it is 'all to the good', the horrors of reality are redescribed as necessary sacrifices.[82]

Christianity is not unique in this crime; indeed it has supposedly bequeathed it to its children, Hegelian idealism and the Soviet Marxists. Thus Adorno and Horkheimer conclude: 'Christianity, idealism, and materialism, which in themselves contain truth, are therefore also responsible for the barbaric acts perpetrated in their name.'[83] The betrayal is most evident when these philosophies align themselves with political power. Thus the pre-Constantinian Christianity of the martyrs is more attractive to Horkheimer than Bernard of Clairvaux. Christendom is described as a betrayal of Christ and Kierkegaard is celebrated for his

---

[75] D of E, p. 90.
[76] Ibid., pp. 176–7.
[77] Ibid., p. 177.
[78] Ibid., p. 114.
[79] Ibid., p. 122.
[80] Ibid., p. 123.
[81] Ibid., p. 178.
[82] Benjamin made the same point against historicism in his biting ninth thesis on the Philosophy of History: 'There is no document of civilisation which is not at the same time a document of barbarism, *Illuminations*, p. 249.
[83] D of E, p. 224.

insistence that a Christian culture was a contradiction in terms.[84] Other theologians belonging to a more negative tradition are also approved of, including Luther, Pascal and Barth, but not, perhaps surprisingly, the modern demythologisers, whom Horkheimer accuses of emptying faith of any content.[85]

These paradoxical or negative theologians are regarded as preserving more faithfully the negativity of Judaism into Christian faith. This Jewish negativity is marked in a number of ways: 'The Jews seem to have succeeded where Christianity failed: they defused magic by its own power – turned against itself as ritual service of God.'[86] Taboos were transformed into rational civilizing principles, laws kept without any civic power to enforce them. Hope is founded on the experience of suffering without ever transforming this into a justification of the same, let alone a philosophy of world history: 'Jewish religion allows no word that would alleviate the despair of all that is mortal. It associates hope only with the prohibition against calling on what is false as God, against invoking the finite as the infinite, lies as truth.'[87] The Jews hold on to reconciliation only through the negative dimension of messianic 'expectation'. Jews have been so hated in Europe because they embody the forbidden that everyone desires: 'happiness without power, wages without work, a home without frontiers, religion without myth'.[88] The Jewish prohibition on idolatry and marginal political status has prevented them from becoming compromised by power, and has preserved an authentic negativity against all false consolations and idealizations of suffering.[89] Horkheimer concludes: 'This element of contradiction is inherent in the Jewish tradition as it is in dialectical philosophy.'[90] The dialectical belief that transcendence and truth are *only* encountered in discrepancy and failure rather than in the false consolations of harmony is exactly as was noted earlier in Adorno's aesthetics.[91]

[84] C of IR, pp. 36–7; cf. *Critical Theory*, p. 129: 'Christianity lost its function of expressing the ideal, to the extent that it became the bed-fellow of the state.'
[85] D of E, p. 179; C of IR, pp. 46–8. Among the demythologizers, Horkheimer mentions Bishop John Robinson whose book *Honest to God* popularized the ideas of Paul Tillich. The latter was for many years a friend of Horkheimer and other members of the school. As a professor at Frankfurt he had helped in obtaining Horkheimer a chair, and earlier had supervised Adorno's *Habilitation* on Kierkegaard. See Jay, pp. 24, 25, 29, 31.
[86] D of E, p. 186.
[87] Ibid., p. 23.
[88] Ibid., p. 199.
[89] Cf. Horkeimer: 'for me the main thing is the ban on images' (Tar, p. 185), and Adorno (*Negative Dialectics*, p. 207): 'The materialist longing to grasp the thing aims at the opposite: it is only in the absence of images that the full object could be conceived. Such absence concurs with the theological ban on images. Materialism brought the ban in to secular form by not permitting utopia to be positively pictured; this is the substance of its negativity.'
[90] C of IR, p. 113.
[91] Cf. D of E, p. 131, and *Negative Dialectics*, *passim*.

It should be clear by now that the negative dialectics which are distinctive to the Frankfurt School and its project of critical theory are aimed not so much at Christianity but at Soviet Marxism and the Hegelianism from which this derives.[92] More critically, we can question the justice of this projection of Hegel back into Christianity and the Frankfurt School's account of the Cross as theodicy, of Christianity's glorification of suffering as necessary. While there are certainly currents of Christian thought that incline in this direction, it was not until Hegel that this previously unusual interpretation of the Cross and the Fall, associated with Gnostics and particular mystical traditions, became mainstream, perhaps because of its affinities with secular modern notions of history. Thus in one curious passage Horkheimer casually speaks of St Augustine as an ancestor of modern ideas of progress, whereas in fact the Bishop of Hippo's philosophy of history was exactly the opposite, much closer to the dialectical pessimism of the Frankfurt School.[93] Similarly Augustine's Platonic view of evil as a privation of being can be understood as insisting upon exactly the opposite of the necessity of suffering: evil is totally arbitrary and utterly unnecessary. It is Hegel, who turns the Fall, the Cross, and resurrection into logic and then into the form of world history, so that the kingdom seems to have arrived in nineteenth-century Prussia, who is responsible for the sins of historicist theodicy.[94] Authentically Christian hope must remind itself that the Cross was the work of sinful men, and that the Kingdom is still 'not yet', the scroll of world history can only be unsealed by the Lamb, not even by the philosophers. In many ways the Frankfurt School's more pessimistic view of history and progress, in contrast to Marx and Hegel, corresponds to their 'theological' critique of utility above, and anticipates the critical comments we put to Marx at the conclusion of chapter 3. There is no evidence that labour contains within itself the solution to its own problems, which will thus simply resolve themselves

---

[92] See Theodor Wiesengrund Adorno, *Hegel: Three Studies*, trans. Shierry Weber Nicholsen (Cambridge, MA.: MIT Press, 1993) for Adorno's complex critical indebtedness to Hegel, and also Benhabib, pp. 270–2, where the possible Kierkegaardian roots of this critique of Hegel are noted. Adorno's early work (1933) on Kierkegaard is complex, but in many ways anticipates much of his later thought and reveals how foundational questions of theo-aesthetics are to his thought: he is at once here interested in the post-idealist critique of idealism offered by Kierkegaard, while simultaneously accusing this critique (and, later, those of existentialism and phenomenology as well) of its own idealism through undialectical and abstract notions of 'inwardness', 'subjectivity', and 'existence'. In this latter sense, Adorno is interested in rehabilitating Hegel as more mediating and dialectical than the detractors of idealism had realized. See Theodor Wiesengrund Adorno, *Kierkegaard: Construction of the Aesthetic*, trans. Robert Hullot-Kentor (Minneapolis: University of Minneapolis Press, 1989).
[93] C of IR, p. 72.
[94] Cf. Oliver O'Donovan, *Resurrection and Moral Order* (Leicester: Inter-Varsity Press, 1986), pp. 58–75, and John Milbank, *Theology and Social Theory* (Oxford: Blackwell, 1990), pp. 147–73.

through the advance of history. Adorno even suggests, as we argued concerning Marx, that this 'vulgar materialism' retains a 'dubious affinity' with political economy.[95] Because labour does not contain its own positive end immanently within itself, judgement and teleology are required rather than just the realization of productive forces. Moral decisions are required about what is to be produced and even whether to produce or not. Adorno insists:

> The naïve supposition of an unambiguous development towards increased production is itself a piece of that bourgeois outlook which permits development in only one direction because, integrated into a totality, dominated by quantification, it is hostile to qualitative difference.[96]

It is not the case that every power must be realized; indeed, Adorno argues, against the implicit activism at the heart of so much socialist thought, that to think of labour as the essence of humanity and emancipation as even more activity is to remain entrapped within bourgeois patterns of thought indebted to political economy. 'Perhaps' he suggests 'the true society will grow tired of development and, out of freedom, leave possibilities unused, instead of storming under a confused compulsion to the conquest of strange stars.'[97] The true utopia might well look a lot more like 'eternal peace' than an ant nest.[98] We shall return to this question in the next chapter.

ONLY NEGATIVE HOPE? THE PROBLEM OF MEDIATION AND AUFHEBUNG

A final more difficult question remains however. We can accept the Frankfurt School's critique of Marx's 'Hegelian optimism': labour is not inherently positive. Yet is the opposite necessarily the case? Is human activity and production, material and symbolic, necessarily tainted, negative, violent? Does any gain necessarily require loss? This appears to be the position of Adorno and Horkheimer, and we must ask whether they are in danger here of mythically absolutizing negativity and so ignoring the ethical dangers of such a move.[99] If dialectic *only* produces negation then it remains completely determined by what it negates, because it is itself an empty method, the tool of the sophists, as Adorno himself recognizes.[100] It is difficult to see how this is anything other than a pseudo-transcendence that could never truly bring anything

[95] *Minima Moralia*, p. 44.
[96] Ibid., p. 156.
[97] Ibid.
[98] Ibid., p. 157.
[99] Cf. 'Happiness itself is negative', C of IR, p. 76.
[100] *Minima Moralia*, pp. 244–5.

new. If everything is *so* soiled that there has *never* been any virtue breaking through, then it seems resistance is as futile as if there were nothing wrong. Negation has no immanent teleology, any more than labour does. It is far from clear that ethical and redemptive practice can be founded upon purely negative experience, whether it be Adorno's 'new categorical imperative' to prevent the Holocaust from recurring, or Horkheimer's Schopenhaurian pity.[101] In both cases we seem to have an entirely fictional, noumenal ethical realm, an accidental 'spontaneous growth of ideas', an evolutionary hiccup which bears no relation to the phenomenal realm where the law of self-interest is absolute.[102]

The dangers of making the dialectic into a metaphysical theory of negativity are half acknowledged by Adorno and Horkheimer.[103] Indeed we have already seen their critique of absolute demystification in Sade, and elsewhere they reject absolute negativity, the scepticism which sees the world as pure vanity, as equally mythic and apathetic as its pantheistic opposite.[104] However they argue that Judaism stops short of this total demystification, instead it 'conciliates magic by negating it in the idea of God', a move which seems to escape their censuring of Christian 'magic' or instrumental Enlightened reason.[105] It seems then one can still believe in something, just not anything in this world. Yet it is hard to see how this differs from Kant's arbitrary restraining of reason to make room for an equally unmediated, transcendental faith. Indeed, the vague talk of Enlightenment rescuing itself from myth seems often to look a little like Kant's utopian hope for the truly rational society, without the instrumental reason which characterizes his epistemology and ethics.[106] It seems ultimately that any sympathy Adorno and Horkheimer have for religion is only at most that of Kant: religion becomes necessary transcendental ethical utopian postulates, empty of content, devoid of mediation and thus never to 'arrive', unable to account for the absurd necessity of such beliefs removed from their historical mediation, nor for their ultimate ontological *untruth* which transforms them into instruments of domination, as *Dialectic of Enlightenment* describes so

---

[101] See J. M. Bernstein, *Adorno: Disenchantment and Ethics* (Cambridge: Cambridge University Press, 2001), especially pp. 385 ff. on ethics after Auschwitz, although notice even here the necessity of bringing in positive mediations of hope, in the form of the dog's tail wagging (p. 440) or the vulnerability and dependence of children (p. 455). For Horkheimer's later Schopenhauerianism see C of IR, pp. 63 ff., and Stirk, ch. 8, and especially his comments on this notion of 'pity' as too abstract and expansive: p. 214.

[102] *Critical Theory*, p. 130; cf. C of IR, p. 74: the ultimate reality is not the good, but 'unappeasable will'.

[103] Cf., e.g., *Negative Dialectics*, pp. 5 and 406. See Jarvis, pp. 211–16, for a discussion of the relationship of negativity in Adorno to nihilism.

[104] D of E, p. 23.

[105] Ibid.

[106] This is the neo-Kantian direction Habermas takes the Frankfurt School agenda. See Jarvis, pp. 217–31 for a good discussion of Habermas's relation to Adorno, and of the ineliminability of the utopian for Adorno.

well. If religion is retained only as an 'impossible' hope, a necessary 'illusion', a 'projection' which is an 'impotent revolt against reality', then is it not necessarily deceptive, arbitrary and violent?[107] The Nietzschean question is unavoidable here: why should scepticism go thus far and stop before these humanistic prejudices of justice, solidarity, and hope, if they are simply theological hangovers?

Yet we do not have to accept that the world is reducible to self-interest, that knowledge is aboriginally deception rooted in priestly trickery, and that cultivation and production are necessarily dominating. Such accounts of the origins of culture in terms of original violence, as always-already fallen, are as mythic and speculative as any others. Similarly if there is something truly other, another reality which is not just fiction, even if it cannot be observed, grasped or possessed, then we cannot discount mediation per se. For the traces of utopia beyond utility to which Adorno and Horkheimer point might not just be negative extrapolations but might actually be genuine mediations of this other reality. For we cannot rule out the possibility that the genuinely new *will* come, even that it might already have been made flesh and dwelt among us, for those with eyes to see. In the next chapter we will seek to explore what such a participatory theological aesthetics, beyond absolute negativity, might look like, and what it might yield in terms of our ideas about the relationship between labour and utility.

---

[107] *Critical Theory*, pp. 129–30. See also the apparent agreement with Nietzsche's claim, quoted in D of E, p. 44, that people should become 'priests with a bad conscience ... unmistakeably aware that everything they do is sheer falsehood.'

Martha, Martha, you are anxious and troubled about many things; one thing is needful. Mary has chosen the good portion which shall not be taken away from her.

6

The End of Work: Rest, Beauty and Liturgy

The Catholic Metaphysical Critique of the Culture of Work and its Incorporation into the English Romantic Tradition: Josef Pieper, Jacques Maritain, Eric Gill and David Jones

In the last chapter we explored some of the attempts of Marxists to escape the reductionist legacy of scientism, and uncovered further evidence that the aesthetic and the theological might lie at the roots of any critique of work under capitalism. In this chapter we return to the more explicitly theological and aesthetic tradition of social criticism in English Romanticism which we left in chapter 4. While, as we indicated at the end of that chapter, Ruskin and Morris had many possible heirs in the twentieth century, the theo-aesthetic currents with which we were particularly concerned in their work bore most fruit in the writings of the Roman Catholic artist and essayist Eric Gill. In his essays the theological basis of social critique is brought to the foreground and given greater precision through the use of Catholic metaphysical categories derived from Scholastic philosophy via the writings of Jacques Maritain. Here, finally, the foundational question of *teleology*, of what is the 'end' of work, what are we working for, comes to the foreground. While Maritain was interested in social questions, Gill was most dependent upon his writings in the philosophy of art, so that it was only through combining him with Morrisian ideas that Gill produced his distinctively theological analysis of the ideal nature of work as art. We will argue that the introduction of more metaphysical discussion serves to clarify and develop Morris's vision, while making more explicit its theological foundations. Nevertheless, before turning to Maritain's philosophy of art, there is another Catholic philosopher who also employs traditional metaphysics to criticize the contemporary culture of work: Josef Pieper. His reassertion of the classical priority of leisure over work raises questions about whether the Romantic and Marxist traditions we have been considering go far enough in their critique of the culture of work, or whether they merely repeat in a different form its idolatry of labour. At the same time, questions can be raised about the implicitly aristocratic and hierarchical metaphysics at work in Pieper, and whether this is inherent in any metaphysical critique of labour. Similar ambiguities are evident in Maritain's formalistic separation of art from life, despite his concern for the autonomy of art which echoes Adorno. We will seek to show that Gill overcomes these static hierarchies and dualisms through his indebtedness to Morris, although in a way that is an authentically Christian supercession of pagan metaphysics through the unity of opposites, while preserving a certain theological priority of contemplation in a way that was not possible for Morris. Similarly his more dynamic teleology avoids the formalistic separation to which Maritain seems prone. His account of the ideal supercession of the work/leisure opposition gains expression particularly in his account of liturgy, developing hints present in both Pieper and Maritain. Finally we will turn to the poet, artist and writer David Jones, to explore further how an account of humanity as fundamentally liturgical can serve to counter the modern totalizing and dehumanizing logic of labour and the utile.

JOSEF PIEPER (1904–97): THE METAPHYSICAL PRIORITY OF LEISURE AND CONTEMPLATION.

We work in order to be at leisure.[1]

At first sight the German Catholic philosopher Josef Pieper might seem an unusual figure to introduce here. While he is certainly a critic of the modern world of work and recognizes in it the logic of utility, the remedy he proposes seems quite different from the one we have been developing. First it is to the nature of thought that he looks for a realm of resistance to utility, rather than to aesthetics and the beautiful. Second, and more significantly, the authors we have been considering have looked for the *transformation* of labour, the liberation of work from utility so that distinctions between work and play, labour and leisure are transcended. Pieper, however, seems to prefer to *strengthen* the demarcation between work and leisure, to restrain work within defined limits in order to make room for a higher realm of freedom from work. If Morris would make every day into a joyful working Sabbath, Pieper fears this will simply make every day a working day, and so confines himself to the task of rescuing the Sabbath. In some ways Pieper's more modest proposals for the restraint rather than the transformation of alienated labour sound similar to the position of the later Marx, as we noted in chapter 3. The dangers of such a position are evident: first it leaves the majority of the worker's time under the reign of utility, merely establishing an unsatisfactory truce with the world of work which is then abandoned to its own secular devices, in return for a modest foothold of resistance; second as we shall see there are disturbingly

---

[1] Josef Pieper, *Leisure as the Basis of Culture*, trans. Gerald Malsbary – hereafter simply 'Pieper' – (South Bend, Indiana: St Augustine's Press, 1998), p. 4.

aristocratic elements to such a vision which can see work as the necessary precondition for leisure and then distributes this division to different groups of people, so that the leisure of a small elite necessary for culture and civilization is only possible through the slavery of the many. We will seek to show however that Pieper is not simply operating with a purely phenomenological distinction between activity and inactivity but with a more complex vision linked to the question of worship which renders his apparent separation of spheres no longer so absolute. At the same time the metaphysical priority he accords to rest restores a crucial element which was in danger of neglect among the nineteenth-century figures we have been considering.

The world of total work

Pieper's 1948 essay *Musse und Kult* (trans: Leisure: The Basis of Culture) is an attempt to recover the true meaning of leisure in 'today's leisureless culture of "total work"' where it has been all but forgotten. Pieper agrees with Weber's diagnosis of the modern bourgeois world that 'One does not work in order to live, but one lives for the sake of one's work'; a situation which is an exact inversion of the ancient and medieval view for which, as Aristotle put it: 'We are *not-at-leisure* in order to be-at-leisure.'[2] This is not just one feature of our world among others but entails an entirely different worldview, and a different conception of humanity as essentially 'the Worker', as Ernst Jünger had portrayed him. This then is a question of metaphysical importance. In such a world effort becomes the criterion of value, and there follows an 'over-valuation of the "difficult" as such'.[3] Life is viewed as a Herculean labour, as it was for the proto-modern Cynic Antisthenes. For Pieper this disciple of Socrates is the embodiment of the modern working man, someone who 'had no feeling for cultic celebration, which he preferred attacking with "enlightened" wit, he was "a-musical"...he felt no responsiveness to *Eros* (he said he "would like to kill Aphrodite"); as a flat Realist, he had no belief in immortality...'[4] 'Rational utility' is the foundational principle of this total world of work and hence no 'useless' activities can be tolerated. The paradoxes that we noticed earlier in chapters 2 and 5 apply here: the refusal of an objective teleology where things have real value in themselves through their (non-instrumental)

---

[2] Pieper 1998, p. 4, quoting Zinzendorf.

[3] Pieper 1998, p. 19.

[4] Ibid., p. 16. Here and elsewhere in Pieper's writings there are echoes of Heidegger's critique of technology and efforts to recover thinking and art. See Martin Heidegger, 'The Question concerning Technology' and 'The Origin of the Work of Art' in *Basic Writings*, ed. David Krell (London: Routledge, 1993). For an excellent theological engagement with Heidegger on these questions, see Jean-Yves Lacoste, *Experience and the Absolute*, trans. Mark Raferty-Skehan (New York: Fordham University Press, 2004) and *Le Monde et l'absence d'oeuvres* (Paris: Presses Universitaires de France, 2000).

relation to God leads at first to a situation where nothing has any value in itself except as an instrument to some subjective end arbitrarily determined by the agent (the triumph of formalist rationalism); then from this, because the ends are without real difference in value, the instrumental means come to be equally valued as ends in themselves, whether this be effort, profit or survival (the triumph of irrationalism). In another classical image, Pieper speaks of the modern worker as a Sisyphus 'chained to his labour without rest, and without inner satisfaction.'[5]

It should be noted here that Pieper does not seem to object to the existence of a realm of utility as such; indeed he presumes that servile work is a necessary part of existence, and must always have been so. Rather the problem for Pieper is the totalitarian claims of such a realm in the modern period. No longer a necessary but subordinate element of human living, the world of utility and work seems to be in danger of becoming the only horizon. In the world of total work there is no room for any activities that do not conform to the logic of utility, and so those other realms of non-utility are either abolished or forced to conform to this alien logic. Thus, for example, thinking, the business of philosophy, is reduced to technical knowledge that fulfils some immediate function, and leisure can only be understood as a break from work for the sake of work, with no inherent value in itself. Yet properly understood, these non-utilitarian regions of culture are for Pieper essential to our very humanity, and so he seeks to defend their integrity and even superiority. The attack of the world of work upon these cultural traditions represents for him nothing less than a threat to human culture and civilization as such, and so their defence is an urgent task. His persistent question is: 'Can human existence be fulfilled in being exclusively a work-a-day existence?'[6] To this he replies with the ancients that 'there rightly exist non-useful forms of human activity', or as Hegel put it: 'there is not only use, there is also blessing.'[7]

Knowledge and leisure

Pieper argues first that 'intellectual labour' is a modern oxymoron, premised upon an aggressive, possessive, activist epistemology after Kant. For the older Western tradition represented by Plato and Aristotle, and the Christian philosophers of the Middle Ages, the highest form of knowledge was utterly unlike labour, consisting rather in a passive receptivity more akin to vision, so that one could say that it is 'like a gift; it is effortless and not burdensome.'[8] Indeed it was of the very essence of thought that it required a certain freedom from work, a connection that is evident in the roots of words such as 'school' in the Greek word for leisure, σχολη. Plato

---

[5] Pieper 1998, p. 55.
[6] Ibid., p. 24.
[7] Ibid., p. 25.
[8] Ibid., p. 18.

in the Theaetetus opposed the philosopher both to the hand-worker and to the man overly caught up in the vanity of worldly business. The medieval philosophers, meanwhile, built on Aristotle to develop their theory of the 'liberal arts'.[9] The liberal arts were knowledge valued for its own sake rather than being employed for some other purpose and were opposed to the servile arts: 'The "liberality" or "freedom" of the liberal arts consists in their not being disposable for purposes, that they do not need to be legitimised by a social function, by being "work."'[10] This had served as the basis for the entire Western ideal of education, restated in the nineteenth century by Newman in his *Idea of a University* in terms of the knowledge that befitted a 'gentleman', a man of leisure.[11] If this sounds like a purely pagan, academic agenda, these categories were taken up within the medieval Christian tradition, for which the contemplative life – the *vita contemplativa* – was the highest form of knowledge and the ultimate goal desired by all humans: the beatitude of the vision of God. For St Thomas Aquinas this vision belonged to the more receptive, almost angelic *intellectus*, rather than to the more worldly, discursive, effort-laden operations of *ratio*. Thus Pieper claims that:

> Human knowing has an element of the non-active, purely receptive seeing, which is not there in virtue of our humanity as such, but in virtue of a transcendence over what is human, but which is really the highest fulfilment of what it is to be human, and is thus 'truly human' after all.[12]

Similarly, despite the influx of a 'Stoical' heroism into Protestant Christianity, Pieper insists that for the traditional Catholic vision, effort was not celebrated for its own sake. Rather, citing St Thomas again, 'The essence of virtue consists more in the Good than in the Difficult', and discipline only exists to serve happiness.[13] If the heart of the modern culture of total work is that 'man mistrusts everything that is without effort; that in good conscience he can own only what he himself has reached through painful effort; that he refuses to let himself be given anything', then we must recognize that this over-emphasis on effort is ultimately a Faustian refusal of the idea of life as Grace.[14] We can now

---

[9] Cf. Aristotle's *Metaphysics*, I, 3; and St Thomas Aquinas's commentary.
[10] Pieper 1998, p. 22.
[11] Ibid., p. 25.
[12] Ibid., p. 12; cf. St Thomas, *De Veritate*, q. XV, 1.
[13] Pieper 1998, pp. 17 and 19; cf. St Thomas Aquinas, *Summa Theologiae*, trans. The English Dominican Province (London: Eyre and Spottiswoode, 1963), IIa IIae, q. 123, a. 12, ad 2, and q. 141, a. 6, ad 1. Pieper also notes St Thomas's important argument that love of enemies is not commended for its heroism, indeed an effortless love of enemies would be even higher still (p. 18, cf. *Quaest. Disp. de Caritate* 8, ad 17).
[14] Pieper 1998, p. 19.

see what Pieper calls the 'abyss' that separates this attitude from the inheritance of Christian Europe.[15]

Leisure and worship

Having argued that the deepest meaning of thought is to be found not in the analytic and manipulative efforts of *ratio*, but in the more integrative and receptive *intellectus*, in a more passive contemplation the very dignity and freedom of which depends on it not being reduced to questions of utility, and which has leisure as its necessary precondition, Pieper turns to consider the nature of leisure. Similarly he insists that leisure cannot be accounted for in terms of utility, as is the case in the world of total work. Rest may well be good for our health, make for more efficient and productive workers, and so on, but leisure cannot be reduced to this function without ceasing to be truly leisure. Recalling Aristotle again, we work for the sake of leisure rather than vice versa. Leisure in the true sense is incapable of being instrumentalized, it belongs outside the realm of utility, indeed it is fundamentally opposed to its logic. Thus Pieper tells us: 'leisure is not there for the sake of work, no matter how much new strength the one who resumes working may gain from it.'[16] Likewise: 'Leisure is not justified in making the functionary as "trouble-free" in operation as possible, with minimum "downtime"'; rather if it is to be 'justified' at all, it must be simply on account of it being essential to our very humanity.[17]

Leisure then is 'not the same thing as the absence of activity', it is not merely an external state that can be socially engineered and empirically observed; rather it is a 'condition of the soul'.[18] It is exactly the opposite of the approach to life that characterizes the modern worker in the world of total work: 'Leisure is the disposition of receptive understanding, of contemplative beholding, and immersion – in the real.'[19] It is neither controlling and grasping, nor anxious; rather it is trusting and affirmative. Leisure is 'not the attitude of one who intervenes but of the one who opens himself; not of someone who seizes but of one who lets go, who lets *himself* go'; it is 'considering things in a celebrating spirit', it 'lives on affirmation . . . it is rather like the stillness in the conversation of lovers'.[20]

Thus leisure is not to be identified with the inactivity of idleness, as the modern world of work is so ready to do. Rather as the medieval moral theologians recognized, the opposite is the case: 'it was precisely lack of leisure, an inability to be at leisure, that went together with idleness; that

---

[15] Pieper 1998, p. 20.
[16] Ibid., p. 34.
[17] Ibid., p. 35.
[18] Ibid., pp. 33, 31.
[19] Ibid., p. 31.
[20] Ibid., pp. 32–3.

the restlessness of work-for-work's-sake arose from nothing other than idleness.'[21] This is one of the seven deadly sins: acedia, a despair, or *tristitia saeculi*, and *pace* Sombart, it is not opposed to an industrious work ethic, but rather to 'the cheerful affirmation by man of his own existence, of the world as a whole, and of God', it is a sin against the Sabbath.[22] Therefore 'idleness and lack of leisure belong with each other; leisure is opposed to both.'[23]

This linking of the true meaning of leisure with a condition of the soul and with celebration and even Sabbath leads into Pieper's claim that: 'The festival is the origin of leisure, its inmost and ever-central source. And this festive character is what makes leisure not only "effortless" but the very opposite of effort of toil.'[24] Festival includes relaxation, effortlessness, and the transcendence of mere function and utility; it is what distinguishes true leisure from mere inactivity. Festival is not only integral to our humanity, as was noted above with leisure, but it reveals how leisure actually lifts us beyond our mere humanity, being 'at once a human and super-human condition'. For this reason, Pieper insists that leisure cannot ultimately be comprehended in purely secular, humanist terms. In the face of the merciless logic of utility he asks whether 'an appeal to the *humanum* as such can suffice against the demands of the "total world of work"', agreeing with Aristotle's view of the life of leisure that: 'man cannot live this way insofar as he is man, but only insofar as something divine dwells within him.'[25] The source and ultimate justification of all true festival and leisure is thus cultic (as the German title of the essay implies), or, we might say, liturgical: it exists in order for worship to take place – a link that is still preserved in the origin of the English word 'holiday'. This was the meaning of non-working days in the Ancient world and in the Bible: time set aside from everyday labour for the possession of the gods, just as temples were places set aside from the usefulness of cultivation. Thus Pieper boldly insists:

> The most festive festival that can be celebrated is religious worship, or 'cult', and there is no festival that does not get its life from such worship or does not actually derive its origin from this. There is no worship 'without the gods', whether it be *Mardi gras* or a wedding.[26]

While there have been persistent attempts in the modern period to invent secular festivals, Pieper dismissively observes that 'they all demonstrate, through the forced and narrow character of their festivity, what religious

21 Ibid., p. 27.
22 Ibid., pp. 28–30; cf. *Summa Theologiae*, IIa IIae q. 35, a. 3, ad 2.
23 Pieper 1998, p. 30.
24 Ibid., p. 34.
25 Ibid., p. 36; Aristotle, *The Nichomachean Ethics* (Oxford: Oxford University Press, 1998), X, 7 (1177b27–28).
26 Pieper 1998, p. 51.

worship provides to a festival.'[27] Such invented festivals are pseudo-celebrations, actually serving the logic of utility, mere 'circuses' to keep the workers subservient. Leisure cannot be instrumentalized, because worship cannot be instrumentalized: 'The celebration of God's praises cannot be realised unless it takes place for its own sake.'[28] Plato is cited with approval here, in a passage that also forms the frontispiece to the essay:

> But the gods, taking pity on human beings – a race born to labour – gave them regularly recurring divine festivals, as a means of refreshment from their fatigue; they gave them the Muses, and Apollo and Dionysus as the leaders of the Muses, to the end that, after refreshing themselves in the company of the gods, they might return to an upright posture.[29]

Pieper comments that worship cannot just be manufactured because it has to be given *by the gods themselves*, as is the case for Christians supremely in the Eucharist: 'Worship itself is a given – or it does not exist at all.'[30]

Segregation of work and leisure?

It should be clear by now that while Pieper has the same target in mind as the other authors we have been considering – the modern world of work in which rational utility reduces people to slaves – the liberation from utility that he proposes is significantly different. Instead of opposing another type of *activity* – that of the artist-craftsman – to alienated labour, he draws attention instead to the resistance offered by that which is usually opposed to work, namely leisure. Following from this, he looks not for the transformation of labour into something less subject to the rule of utility such as artistic creation, but rather for the delimitation of labour by the parallel realm of leisure, of the 'extra-utile', which seems currently in danger of being lost. It seems we are faced here with two quite different approaches: something like the transcendence of the opposition between work and leisure, on the one hand; and the restraint of labour within clearly defined bounds that make room for leisure, on the other. There is a choice to be faced between transformation or segregation, and it rests upon the question of whether utility is fundamentally and inescapably part of the nature of human work. If we were in any doubt about these differences, Pieper makes them abundantly clear in his attacks on Carlyle who had been such an influence on Ruskin and Morris. For Pieper, Carlyle is the 'prophet of the religion of

---

[27] Pieper 1998.
[28] Ibid., p. 58.
[29] Ibid., p. 2.
[30] Ibid., p. 59.

Work', who celebrates the world of total work by making a cult of work for its own sake and trying to invest it with transcendent meaning.[31] The problem with such an approach from Pieper's perspective is that the celebration of work for its own sake fails in its intention to relieve the inhumanity of labour, by simply suppressing its necessarily servile nature.[32] This is inescapable because some actions must always be oriented towards utility and, therefore, necessarily servile. It is only the distinction between the liberal and the servile arts, creating spaces of non-work in people's lives, that can be the foundation of any authentic deproletarianization, not the pretended abolition of this distinction.[33] What are we to make of this debate? We might well concede that Pieper has put his finger on a very real danger in the Romantic tradition of social criticism and its idealization of labour, and that from a theological point of view he is quite correct to assert in some sense the metaphysical priority of contemplation over action, the Sabbath over the working day. Yet at the same time, as we have noted above, there are also problems with his alternative of segregation: most obviously that it seems little more than a stand off with the world of total work, leaving most of the worker's time unaffected and still under the rule of utility.

We will return to this question throughout this chapter, however for now it is worth noting that there are certainly moments where Pieper appears to suggest that the realms of utility and leisure are not quite so discrete and unrelated as we might have thought. The first thing to be observed is that there are clearly, for Pieper, forms of inactivity that partake more of the quality of work than leisure – what he terms idleness. Inversely there are forms of action that partake to some degree in the quality of leisure – for example, the liberal arts. This must be understood in accordance with the point already noted, that true leisure is a quality of the soul rather than something reducible to the external reality of inactivity. However, as we have seen, this does not mean that it is purely subjective: talk of the liberal arts suggests that certain activities objectively participate more in the nature of leisure than others. Already we seem to be talking more in terms of a hierarchy of participation than two utterly distinct realms. Despite the emphasis on the passivity and receptiveness of true leisure, the liberal arts remain *arts*, i.e. something to be *done*, and Pieper recalls on a number of occasions the Greek usage 'to *do* leisure' (*scholen agein*), suggesting that even the highest leisure partakes in the nature of action in some sense.[34] Equally important in this respect is Pieper's linking of leisure with the 'activity' of liturgical worship. Liturgy, while certainly not a purely human activity, nevertheless

---

[31]   Ibid., pp. 16 and 55.
[32]   Ibid., p. 44.
[33]   Ibid., p. 45. See also his critique of the destruction of the sacred in recent liturgical reforms, Josef Pieper, *In Search of the Sacred* (San Francisco: Ignatius, 1991), and of the destruction of true hope by this-worldly utopianism: Josef Pieper, *Hope and History* (San Francisco: Ignatius, 1994).
[34]   Pieper 1998, p. 48.

has significant parallels with notions of art in the other authors we have been considering, while also perhaps drawing out the true meaning of art, as Pieper suggests elsewhere.[35] At the other end of the hierarchy, Pieper concedes that even the most servile art is not purely servile in that it is a *human* action, so that it seems even the most base work can in some sense partake of the liberty, the celebratory spirit, the dignity and non-grasping peacefulness of true leisure.[36]

Pieper is also aware of the elitist and class-ridden overtones of his argument for the strict separation of the servile and liberal arts, addressing this question in an excursus on the proletariat and deproletarianization. He insists that all the references to Plato and Aristotle do not indicate any desire to restore a leisured intellectual class parasitic upon the servile majority. On the contrary he claims that 'one should do everything in one's power to overcome such an opposition [between the labouring and leisured classes] immediately', but that at the same time 'we should take care not to do something wrong, something completely nonsensical, in order to attain that goal.'[37] What Pieper legitimately fears is that the concern for social unity and the overcoming of class distinctions will take place through the total 'proletarianization' of society, rather than the deproletarianization of the proletariat. The Romantics' concern to dignify labour and liberate it from utility will simply lead to the abolition of all realms of resistance to utility, effectively making everyone into slaves. Yet this leads Pieper to insist that the distinction between the liberal and servile arts is the foundation of any authentic deproletarianization, and its abolition leads to the proletarianizing of everyone. However, at the same time he insists that deproletarianization should involve the widening of the space of the liberal arts, and it is not clear why this should be stopped at a certain point. For example, he speaks of the distinction between an honorarium and a wage as corresponding to that between the liberal and servile arts, and rightly criticizes Sartre's proposal that intellectuals should conceive of their work as wage-labour; yet he does not give any reason why there should exist any wage-workers at all, rather than a society where all received honoraria, as Ruskin had proposed.

It seems in conclusion that, while Pieper's reintroduction of traditional metaphysical categories can humble the idolatrous potential of much Romantic rhetoric about the transformation of labour, recalling that work finds its true meaning beyond itself in the theological horizon of leisure, nevertheless, when work is understood as a distinct sphere subordinate, yet intrinsically unrelated to leisure various problems ensue. As we shall now see, Maritain also reveals similar problems about the relation between utility and the extra-utile in his account of beauty.

---

[35] See Josef Pieper, *Only the Lover Sings: Art and Contemplation,* trans. Lothar Krauth (San Francisco: Ignatius, 1990).
[36] Pieper 1998, p. 46.
[37] Ibid., p. 41.

JACQUES MARITAIN (1882–1973): THE THEOLOGICAL METAPHYSICS OF *ARS*

Beauty is one of the divine attributes.[38]

Maritain stands in the same tradition of Thomist Catholic philosophy as Pieper; however, writing slightly earlier, he is of interest to us not for any views on labour but rather for his properly metaphysical account of beauty and art published as *Art and Scholasticism* (1924), an account taken up by Gill, enabling him to go beyond some of the confusions of the nineteenth-century aestheticians we have been considering. Yet Maritain's aesthetics are not without their own problems in relation to utility and teleology, as we shall see. In particular his attempt to extract an account of art in general, beyond the fine arts and their orientation towards the beautiful, leads him to assert an autonomous formal end to art *qua* art, which seems paradoxically almost identical to the utility it opposes, and dangerously in conflict with humanity, the good, and God. We will argue that these problems in accounting for the relationship between utility and the inutile in Maritain are similar to those we discerned in Pieper, and also have parallels in the modernist assertion of the autonomy of art. In Maritain's case they appear to be derived from an overly categorical Aristotelian perspective, and while Gill inherits some of these problems, in other ways, as we shall see, his more dynamic, theurgic metaphysical vision enables him partially to overcome them.

Beauty as one of the transcendentals

In chapter 3 we argued that beauty and goodness persisted in Marx's writings as traces of transcendence by which the current material order could be in some sense judged, yet their ultimate status and their relationship to truth and reality were always somewhat imperilled by Marx's hostility to theology and metaphysics and his denial of transcendence. Maritain provides a modern rearticulation of the ancient metaphysical view for which Beauty is one of the transcendentals and thus intrinsically related not only to the Good, but also to Truth and Being.[39] It is worth

---

[38] Jacques Maritain, *Art and Scholasticism with Other Essays (1924)*, – hereafter 'Maritain' – trans. J. F. Scanlan, p. 24. For a somewhat hagiographical account of Maritain's life, see Ralph McInerny, *The Very Rich Hours of Jacques Maritain: A Spiritual Life* (Notre Dame: University of Notre Dame Press, 2003).

[39] It is worth noting that Maritain's 'Thomist' aesthetics involve a constructive rather than purely exegetical reading of the tradition, and while it has become very widespread, not least through the writings of Przywara and Balthasar, it remains controversial; see Irène Fernandez, 'Beauté' in Jean-Yves Lacoste (ed.), *Dictionnaire Critique de Théologie* (Paris: Presses Universitaires de France, 2002).

noting how different this is from many contemporary subjectivist accounts of aesthetics.

Maritain begins with what sounds an uncontroversial definition of beauty as 'what gives pleasure on sight, *id quod visum placet*'.[40] Yet this apparently subjective definition of beauty from St Thomas only describes it *per effectum*, not essentially. Even at this stage however the mention of vision and delight points towards the True and the Good. Next Maritain claims, against materialist accounts of beauty as an irrational, sensual, emotional experience, that beauty is 'essentially the object of *intelligence*'.[41] Against Romantic accounts of art, beauty is experienced by the mind, it is rational and derives from order and harmony not chaos, as is particularly evident in, for example, the proportions of a Greek statue or the mathematics of a great piece of music. Yet this is not to say it is purely rational, unlike the more Angelic *scientia*; rather it also involves our senses, so that 'the beauty which is *connatural* to man is that which comes to delight the mind through the senses and their intuition.' Hence art 'has the savour of the terrestrial paradise because it restores for a brief moment the simultaneous peace and delight of the mind and the senses.'[42] St Thomas's three essential characteristics of beauty are: 'integrity, because the mind likes being; proportion, because the mind likes order and likes unity; lastly and above all brightness or clarity, because the mind likes light and intelligibility.'[43] It is now clear that while beauty is experienced by the mind, it is not a purely mental experience, but rather consists 'essentially in a certain excellence or perfection in the proportion of things to the mind', that is, it also concerns things, reality, ontology.[44] The first two 'essential' characteristics of beauty indicate it to be something ontological and rational rather than purely subjective or emotional, yet the third characteristic indicates that the human subject *is* properly involved: indeed beauty is the shining forth of the reason in things recognized by a rational mind, a natural harmony between the subject and object that only a theological worldview could imagine. Maritain explains: 'The mind rejoices in the beautiful because in the beautiful it finds itself again', reason recognizes the Divine Reason and Art in all things.[45] Beauty on this account presumes that the human mind is fundamentally 'at home' in the world, that the human reasoning is not going 'against the grain of the universe', because this world is creation rather than chaos.

Claritas, the third and most important essential characteristic of beauty is understood as the 'splendour of intelligibility', or the shining forth of divine rational forms in matter, as the Platonists had put it. This

---

[40] Maritain, p. 19; *Summa Theologiae*, Ia, q. 5, a. 4 ad 1.
[41] Maritain, p. 19.
[42] Ibid.
[43] Ibid., p. 20; *Summa Theologiae*, Ia, q. 39, a. 8.
[44] Maritain, p. 20.
[45] Ibid.

is Augustine's *splendor ordinis*, or what St Thomas calls *splendor formae*.[46] Maritain explains that form should be understood as the principle of intelligibility, a divine trace: 'the principle determining the particular perfection of everything which is, constituting and completing things in their essence and their qualities, the ontological secret, so to speak, of their innermost being, their spiritual essence, their operative mystery...'[47] Once again we see how the account of beauty at stake here entails an entire metaphysical doctrine of creation. For Maritain beauty is both rational *and* objective or ontological, unlike the purely epistemological *splendor* of the Cartesians. Yet if Beauty is intrinsically related to Truth, it is, as the medieval philosophers insisted, ultimately a kind of good, not of truth, a kind of delight in the truth, rather than a piece of knowledge. Beauty pleases, it is 'essentially delightful'.[48] Beauty stirs desire and love, drawing things out of themselves in an ecstasy of love, a movement that applies even to God himself (although his love causes beauty whereas ours is caused by it) as Denys the Areopagite had argued.[49] Beauty is related to Truth and Goodness for Maritain as for the medievals, because it ultimately belongs to the order of transcendentals: 'that is to say, of concepts which surpass all limits of kind of category and will not suffer themselves to be confined in any class, because they absorb everything and are to be found everywhere.'[50] Beauty is simply a property of Being itself, under one aspect, like the one, the true, and the good. In a certain sense we must say that 'everything is beautiful, as everything is good.'[51]

If in a certain sense everything is beautiful, it is also necessary to say at the same time that none is beautiful save one, just as none is good save one, God alone; or as Martian puts it: 'Beauty is one of the divine attributes'.[52] All the transcendentals are only properly predicable of God alone, and then of all other things secondarily, derivatively. Beauty in creation is thus 'essentially *analogous*', found in all things to the extent that they participate in God's beauty.[53] Here we come to the heart of Maritain's theo-aesthetic metaphysics:

> God is beautiful. He is the most beautiful of beings, because, as Denys the Areopagite and St Thomas explain, His beauty is without alteration or vicissitude, without increase or diminution: and because it is not like the beauty of things, which have all a particularised beauty, *particulatam pulchritudinem, sicut et particulam naturam,* He is beautiful by Himself and in

[46] Ibid.
[47] Ibid.
[48] Ibid., n.56; cf. *Summa Theologiae*, Ia, q. 5, a. 4, ad 1, IIa IIae, q. 27, a. 1, ad 3.
[49] Maritain, p. 22; De Div. Nom. IV.
[50] Maritain, p. 24.
[51] Ibid., p. 24.
[52] Ibid.
[53] Ibid.

Himself, absolutely beautiful...He is exceedingly beautiful (*superpulcher*), because there is pre-existent in a super-excellent way in the perfectly simple unity of His nature the fountain of all beauty...He is beauty itself, because He imparts beauty to all created beings.[54]

While all creation participates in God's beauty, humanity has a unique role in Maritain's theo-aesthetic vision as the only creature which can also actively share in God's work of creation, through the virtue of art. Human art is defined as: 'fundamentally constructive and creative...the faculty of producing, not of course, *ex nihilo*, but out of a pre-existing matter, a new creature, an original being capable in its turn of moving a human soul.'[55] The special dignity of the artist, therefore, is that he or she 'is as it were an associate of God in the making of works of beauty'.[56] Art does not only apply to God in terms of his actions *ad extra* towards creation, but also in a more mysterious way to the inner life of the Trinity itself. Here Maritain notes that St Thomas appropriated beauty particularly to the divine Son, who is 'so to speak, art of the Almighty God'.[57] For the ancients and medievals, this virtue of *ars* is not confined to a few individualistic geniuses as for the post-Renaissance cult of the artist; rather, as Morris had also observed, this virtue was found 'not in Phidias and Praxiteles only, but in the village carpenter and blacksmith as well.'[58] Hence it was no accident to the mind of the medieval philosophers that Christ willed to be an artisan prior to his public ministry: 'the virtue of art is to be predicated peculiarly of God, like Goodness and Justice, and that the Son, plying His poor man's trade, was still the image of the Father and of His action which never ceases.'[59]

If this sounds like an overly exalted, idealized account of art, Maritain qualifies this by recalling that human art still belongs to the order of manual drudgery, and that 'the production of beauty belongs to God alone as His true property.'[60] As with beauty, so with art: God alone is the only true artist – '*unus est artifex, Deus*' – all other art derives from this and participates in it. Once again, there are degrees of participation: Maritain reiterates the medieval distinction between *servile* arts, where the work to be done 'was an effect produced in matter' and thus *factibile*

54 Maritain, p. 25.
55 Ibid., p. 49.
56 Ibid.
57 Ibid., p. 25; See *Summa Theologiae* Ia, q. 39, a. 8, where St Thomas follows St Hilary in identifying the Son with *species* or beauty in his discussion of the *vestigia trinitatis* in all creation, noting how the three attributes of beauty (integrity, proportion, and brightness or clarity) apply to the Son, and how it is in virtue of the last of these three that the Son is also spoken of by St Augustine (*De Trin.* 6:10) as the 'art' of God; cf. also St Augustine, *De Doc. Chr.* I:5.
58 Maritain, p. 16.
59 Ibid., p. 17; cf. St Thomas, *Sum. con. Gen*, 1:93.
60 Maritain, p. 28.

proper, and the *liberal* arts, such as logic or poetry, where the work is a 'purely spiritual composition remaining in the soul'.[61] Yet even in the latter case the distinction between divine and human art remains: 'The human artist or poet whose mind is not, like the Divine Mind, the cause of things, cannot draw this form complete out of his creative spirit'.[62] Human art cannot be *ex nihilo*, and, therefore, must always be derivative and secondary: 'by developing the faculties with which the Creator has endowed him – "for every perfect gift cometh from on high and down from the Father of light" – and making use of created matter, [the human artist] creates as it were in the second degree.'[63] It is the forgetting of this distinction that has led, for Maritain, to the worst hubristic delusions of post-Renaissance art, the 'idealist vertigo' that believes it can escape the material and subjective conditions of its own production.[64] When Maritain writes that 'Artistic creation does not copy God's creation, but continues it', he clearly does not mean that somehow human art extends, supplements or adds to God's creation from its own independent position. Indeed while Maritain argues against crudely photographic, reproductive views of art – the essence of art is making not material imitation he insists – nevertheless there is a certain imitation as the transmission of the 'brilliance of a form' that is proper to human art. In this sense human art *does* imitate nature, precisely because, unlike God, it can no more produce form *ex nihilo* than it can matter. Maritain is scornful towards the debased realism of the academicians, insisting that nature should be a free stimulus, imitated in its very action rather than slavishly reproduced; yet he also insists, against the idealism of some contemporary art, that human art is entirely dependent upon the priority of God's art, and in exactly this point is different from divine art: '*operatio artis fundatur super operationem naturae, et haec super creationem*'.[65]

The autonomy of art: Conflicting ends?

We have presented Maritain's theo-aesthetics as a persuasive metaphysical account of beauty and art, making explicit much of what we were groping for in earlier, less philosophical authors. However this is not the entire picture, as was mentioned earlier: there are various difficulties within Maritain's account of art, to which we shall now turn. These problems focus around his overly formal definition of art *qua* art, by which he understands something quite distinct from our more usual use of art in the sense of the fine arts. Maritain begins by noting, as had

---

[61] Ibid., p. 17; *Summa Theologiae* Ia IIae, q. 57, a. 3, ad 3.
[62] Maritain, p. 48.
[63] Ibid., p. 49.
[64] Ibid., p. 48.
[65] Ibid., p. 49; *Summa Theologiae* Ia, q. 45, a. 8.

Morris before him, the much broader use of the medieval term *ars*, which could include shipwrights, carpenters, grammarians and logicians alongside painters, sculptors and musicians, compared to the more narrow modern usage of art. However, while Ruskin and Morris had concluded from this that the production of beauty had been an end aimed at not just by a few, but was integral to all labour, Maritain takes a different position. Maritain distinguishes the fine arts, which are orientated to beauty, from art *as such*, which is not.[66] The goal of art *qua* art is simply the work to be done, nothing more. This requires some careful explanation. Art *qua* art, is defined by Maritain as '*recta ratio factibilium* . . . the *undeviating determination of work to be done.*'[67] Art is a 'habit of the practical intellect'; that is to say, it belongs to the practical sphere, the realm of *uti* rather than *frui*, unlike contemplation, yet it is a virtue of the intellect, so that Maritain can insist surprisingly that art *qua* art is entirely unrelated to physical skill, and that an artist with a trembling hand produces imperfect work, but may still possess the virtue of art faultlessly.[68] The formal element in art consists in the imposition of regulation upon matter; hence rules, '*viae certae et determinatae*', were always regarded as the essence of art by the ancients.[69] It should be clear that such a definition makes it much more obvious why shipwrights and grammarians are also artists, in the older sense, and what little it has to do with more modern notions of creativity and imagination.

If the sole goal or telos of art *qua* art is the work to be produced, then this raises difficult questions about what relation if any this has to higher ends or goals. On Maritain's account, the goal of art appears entirely autonomous and independent from such higher ends. Art as such is entirely indifferent to the value of the thing made; it does not matter whether the thing made is ultimately good or not, but simply that it is a good whatever-it-was-supposed-to-be. The moral questions this position raises should be evident: on Maritain's account, the virtue of art could be just as evident in the production of weapons of mass destruction as in life-saving drugs (in clear opposition to Ruskin's views). It is evident that art is described as a virtue here not in any moral sense, but simply in terms of being an excellence. Maritain does not shy away from these tensions, stating explicitly that the pure artist, considered abstractly, is 'completely immoral'.[70] This is because art 'is ordered to such-and-such a definite end, separate and self-sufficient, not to the common end of human life; and it relates to the peculiar good or perfection not of the man making, but of the work made'; or elsewhere: 'Art has no concern with our life, but only with such-and-such particular and extra-human ends which in regard to Art are an ultimate goal.'[71] This is elaborated in

[66] Cf. Maritain, pp. 26, 38, and *passim*.
[67] Ibid., p. 7.
[68] Ibid., pp. 9, 11.
[69] Ibid., p. 31.
[70] Ibid., p. 13.
[71] Ibid., pp. 6, 12.

terms of the contrast, going back to Aristotle's *Nichomachean Ethics*, between making and action, which together make up the practical life: making (*factibile*, ποιητον) is the sphere of art, concerned solely with the work made; while action (*agibile*, πραχτον) is the sphere of freedom, the will, morality, oriented to the good of humanity and directed by the virtue of prudence, instead of art.[72] Art is more exclusively intellectual than prudence, being a rectitude of reason rather than the will. It is no more concerned with the moral will and the good for humanity than a grammatical solecism, which provides a good example of a 'sin' against art. At the heart of this opposition between art and morality is the teleological question of the distinction of ends and the radical autonomy of the end of art. Thus Maritain tells us: 'Prudence operates for the good of the worker, *ad bonum operantis*, Art operates for the good of the work done, *ad bonum operis*, and everything which diverts it from that end adulterates and diminishes it.'[73] Elsewhere he restates this in terms of the scholastic distinction between the worker's end (*finis operantis*) and the end of the work (*finis operis*) to speak of how a worker might work purely for the sake of a wage and yet still produce work that is in no way affected by this but is properly oriented to its own end.[74] While such a distinction is clearly intellectually possible, it is precisely these disjunctions – of the worker from his work, and of both from any ultimate good – that so many of the authors we have been considering have identified as alienating qualities, distortions of the true nature of work, with disastrous social and ethical consequences. Maritain admits something of this sinister nature to his account of art when he speaks of its 'despotic and all-absorbing power', or describes it as 'the devouring idol' in the soul of humanity.[75] He recognizes that this entails a raging conflict in the artist's being between his own nature as a human with obligations to the good, and his commitment to art which is indifferent to such concerns.[76] Because art *qua* art and the good are in no way intrinsically related, they can only be reconciled extrinsically, by violent coercion, the exercise of arbitrary control from without.[77] At this point it is worth noting that an absolutely autonomous art, so-called 'pure' art, which one might expect to be the exact opposite of utility, appears startlingly almost dialectically identical to utility: an entirely formal and immanent realm, sundered from all concerns with the good, purporting to be an end-in-itself, iconoclastic and with totalizing ambitions. Maritain is certainly not unaware of the socio-ethical question of the cult of utility, as the following description of the problems of the modern world indicates:

[72]   Cf. Maritain, pp. 5–6.
[73]   Ibid., p. 12.
[74]   Ibid., p. 60.
[75]   Ibid., pp. 6, 12.
[76]   Ibid., pp. 12, 65.
[77]   Ibid., p. 59.

the *unnatural* principles of the *fecundity of money* and the *finality of the useful*, multiplying its needs and servitudes without any possibility of there ever being a limit, ruining the leisure of the soul, withdrawing the material *factibile* from the control which proportioned it to the ends of the human being, imposing on man its puffing machinery and its speeding up of matter, the modern world is shaping human activity in a properly inhuman way, in a properly devilish direction for the ultimate end of all this frenzy is to prevent man from remembering God.[78]

Is Maritain's account of art *qua* art persuasive with respect to these problems? His position appears to be a blend of late scholastic views, ultimately deriving from Aristotle and interpreted rather formalistically, and more modern views regarding the autonomy of art. There are certainly moments where Maritain makes other claims that appear to stand against these views. For example, he insists that the 'independence' of art is a nineteenth-century delusion and that art is not 'pagan' by birth, which would seem to contradict his earlier portrayal of art as an entirely secular realm in conflict with God.[79] He also notes that no virtue can ultimately be opposed to the good: 'virtue can incline only to good: it is impossible to make use of a virtue to do evil: it is essentially *habitus operativus boni*.'[80] Likewise *all* human actions are properly ordered to the end of contemplation, which suggests that even art always exceeds itself and is ultimately oriented towards a higher good than the work to be done.[81] Equally crucially, there can be no good, including the good of art, opposed to God or the ultimate Good of human life; hence art must be subordinate to God.[82] If art is part of God's good creation, rather than a consequence of sin, if it is rightly ordered to producing anything rather than nothing, then it cannot be ultimately opposed to God. Elsewhere Maritain appears to qualify the absolute distinction of art from morality, when he says that prudence, the virtue of living well, is metaphorically an art, the art of the good life, or *ars recte vivendi*, as St Augustine put it.[83] Here we might well ask Maritain why the good life is only metaphorically an art and not in fact the supreme and exemplary art, as the original passages he is using in St Thomas can be read as saying.[84] Equally we might ask why Maritain insists on separating the fine arts from art *qua* art, as if their orientation towards beauty was

---

[78]   Cf. Maritain, p. 29.
[79]   Ibid., pp. 60, 53.
[80]   Ibid., p. 10; *Summa Theologiae*, Ia IIae, q. 55, a. 3.
[81]   Maritain, p. 63; St Thomas, *Sum. con. Gen.* II, 37, 6.
[82]   Maritain, p. 58.
[83]   Ibid., p. 11; n. 16: St Aug. *De Civ. Dei* iv:21; cf. Aristotle *Nich. Eth.* 6, and *Summa Theologiae*, IIa IIae, q. 47, a. 2, ad 1, Ia IIae, q. 21, a. 2, ad 2, and q. 57, a. 4, ad 3.
[84]   N.B. particularly *Summa Theologiae*, Ia IIae, q. 68, a. 4, ad 1, where St Thomas argues that the gifts of the Holy Spirit in human lives are as it were his art. While

simply an accident of one sub-group of arts, rather than in some sense exemplary of the nature of all art. Surely if beauty is one of the transcendentals, an aspect of all being, then Maritain should be even more ready than Ruskin and Morris to affirm that all true art, inasmuch as it aims at making anything, *must* be oriented towards the telos of beauty, just as it must be oriented towards truth, goodness, unity and being. Yet, rather surprisingly given his belief in the convertibility of the transcendentals, Maritain does not seem to think that even the fine arts are free of hostility towards morality by virtue of their orientation to beauty. On the contrary, he says that the opposition between art and prudence becomes *more* acute with the fine arts.[85] Similarly he speaks of Beauty in this context as a 'wild beast' which could only be contained by Faith using enchantment.[86] Such language is hard to reconcile with his earlier claim that beauty is a divine attribute, and seems more indebted to the very modern secular views of art whose damage he is lamenting.[87] Perhaps, to give Maritain the benefit of the doubt, he is speaking here of art not absolutely, but only from the perspective of fallen humanity. Such a conclusion is encouraged by his comments about the inspired art described in the scriptures and continued by the saints, the role of love in the humbling and right ordering of art, and the nature of the Liturgy as 'the transcendent, super-eminent type of Christian art-forms'.[88] Most crucially, he does argue that the divorce between Art and Prudence is ultimately the result of the turning away of both from the contemplation of Divine Wisdom: 'So Wisdom, being endowed with the outlook of God and ranging over Action and Making alike, alone can completely reconcile Art and Prudence.'[89] Perhaps then, in God at least, these problematic oppositions are transcended for Maritain. God's creative power is not in conflict with his goodness. If however, as the references to the saints and the liturgy suggest, we are able to share to some degree in this divine transcendence of the opposition of art and prudence, Maritain gives little indication what form this might take. He is so concerned with

---

St Thomas does follow Aristotle in speaking of material making as definitive of human art, he does not seem to see the ends of art and prudence as only extrinsically and accidentally related, but rather as part of the hierarchy of ends which all end in God.

[85] Maritain, p. 64.

[86] Ibid., p. 18.

[87] We might note here the similarities between this 'secular' view of art and Maritain's political views which Gutiérrez helpfully characterizes as the 'distinction of planes model'. See Gustavo Gutiérrez, *A Theology of Liberation* (London: SCM., 2001), chapters 4 and 5. For more on Maritain's complex political views, see his response to the *Action Francaise* affair: Jacques Maritain, *The Things that are not Caesar's*, trans. J. F. Scanlan (London: Sheed and Ward, 1930), and Waldemar Gurian, 'On Maritain's Political Philosophy' in *The Thomist* V, 1967.

[88] Maritain, p. 38. Among inspired artists, Beseleel ben Uri ben Hur and Ooliab ben Achisamech of Exodus, the Blessed Virgin Mary, St Hildegarde, Fra Angelico, and Bach are all mentioned: Maritain, pp. 64, 63, 55, 12, 47, and 38.

[89] Ibid., p. 67.

what influence morality might have upon art that he does not pause to consider what his theory of art might have to say to our moral life, to our socio-economic relations and the meaning of labour.

ERIC GILL (1882–1940): THE SYNTHESIS OF SOCIAL CRITICISM AND METAPHYSICS

> Play is more proper to man than work, and it is only when work is play that it is really good and right.[90]

It was the English artist, sculptor, engraver and essayist Eric Gill who integrated the two divergent traditions of continental Catholic metaphysics and Romantic English social criticism. Gill was indirectly a disciple of Morris and Maritain and we will need to consider how he differs subtly from each. Gill was an eccentric who gathered something of a personality cult around him during his lifetime, yet he was not a great original thinker. His essays are highly polemical and often repetitive and almost all his ideas can be traced to one of the two sources mentioned. D. H. Lawrence, whom Gill admired, described him in a review as a 'crude and crass amateur', a verdict Gill admitted to be largely true.[91] Nevertheless, his importance as the person to bring together aesthetic social criticism with Catholic metaphysics should not be underrated. As we have seen, the English Romantic tradition of social criticism had always been characterized by a significant medievalism, yet, perhaps because of English anti-Catholic and anti-Scholastic prejudices, this had never extended to an interest in medieval Catholic thought.[92] Yet we have sought to argue that it was precisely metaphysical questions concerning the nature of humanity and its labour, transcendent values and ends, which have been lurking problematically unnoticed throughout this tradition. Maritain's Thomism provides, we might say, the vocabulary that the English tradition has lacked in its self-articulation.[93] Likewise, as we noted above with Pieper, this

---

[90]   'Quae ex Veritate et Bono' (1921) in Eric Gill, *Art Nonsense and Other Essays* (London: Cassell and Co., 1934), p. 69; cf. Proverbs 8:30–31.

[91]   Fiona MacCarthy, *Eric Gill* (London: Faber and Faber, 1989), p. 257. MacCarthy's biography remains the most detailed, yet she has done a lot to destroy any serious interest in Gill through her efforts to counter the earlier hagiographical interpretations of Gill's life by his friends and disciples. While Gill's own meticulous record of his sexual practices, which MacCarthy made public, evidently has a bearing on his personal integrity as a hero-figure among Roman Catholics and his long-known views on gender and sexuality, I fail to see what relevance it has to his role as a social critic, or to his philosophy of art and of labour. A less salacious account is provided by Malcolm Yorke, *Eric Gill: Man of Flesh and Spirit* (London: Tauris Parke, 2000), while Gill's own version remains worthwhile reading: *Autobiography* (London: Jonathan Cape, 1940).

[92]   I am grateful to Janet Soskice for drawing this antipathy to my attention.

[93]   Gill puts it thus in his *Autobiography*, p. 137: 'Well, following Morris, following Ruskin, following the universal practice of the world, except in eccentric periods such

metaphysical tradition has the potential to correct a dangerous 'over-activism' in the English romanticizing of labour. However, at the same time, on the other hand, we have seen certain socio-ethical concerns in the metaphysical tradition, where certain spheres (the servile arts for Pieper or the realm of art for Maritain) are accorded a spurious autonomy which renders them virtually immune to the demands of ultimate ends and thus potentially outside of redemptive transformation and moral ordering. On these concerns, despite moments to the contrary, Gill seems much closer to Morris in having a more integrated and dynamic view of human life that prevents such formalistic distinctions. At times the tensions between Morris and Maritain persist unresolved in Gill's writings, as he himself recognizes when he speaks of the apparent contradictions between two views of art in his essays. Yet, he explains, these are partly due to the different purposes and audiences to which he was aiming: 'In the earlier essays I was more concerned to extricate the artist from the hot-house of the art-school, whereas in the later I was more concerned to extricate him from the ice-house of an atheistic industrialism.'[94] Throughout, Gill expresses his synthesis of the two traditions with persuasive argumentative force in his essays and practically in the idiosyncratic form of his own life as an artisan.

Social criticism and the artist

Gill's account of the ills of modern industrial capitalist society is almost entirely identical with that of Morris, whose ideas he had imbibed while still in his youth. In 1899 he had begun to learn lettering at the London Central School of Arts and Crafts, where one of Morris's greatest pupils, W. R. Lethaby was principal. From 1905 he was involved in the Fabian Society while living in Hammersmith, where the same views were also prevalent.[95] While Gill's position on the metaphysical roots and hence also the nature of the solution of these social problems was to change over the years, particularly following his conversion to Catholicism in 1913, his basic phenomenological analysis remained the same. What form did this take?

Writing in the mid-1920s, Gill attempts to 'define' capitalism, almost in the manner of a scholastic text book, as: 'that system in which goods are made and services rendered at the initiative of and for the profit of the lenders of "money"'.[96] He notes that capitalism proper is to be distinguished from mere money-lending in that the capitalist usually makes the majority of his living purely from the lending of capital, the

---

as that induced by our irreligious commercialism...we were in revolt against the whole conception of art as being irrational. Without knowing it we were Thomistic and Aristotelian.'
[94] *Art Nonsense*, p. vi.
[95] MacCarthy, pp. 63–79 and *Autobiography*, pp. 94–130.
[96] 'Responsibility, and the Analogy between Slavery and Capitalism' (1925) – hereafter: 'Responsibility' – in *Art Nonsense*, p. 134.

capitalist retains control of how his capital is used, and that the activity of capital in generating profit dominates the economy, rather than being subordinate to any other economic transactions. Hence it applies particularly to the systems of modern Britain, northern Italy, France and Belgium, the USA and Germany, and its historical emergence is linked, among other things, with the invention of double-entry book-keeping.[97] Gill accepts the standard account that such a system leads to the existence of a class of capitalists, concerned directly with profit rather than the making or use of goods, and a Proletariat, depending upon their labour, yet concerned only directly with their wages and not with the technical or intellectual quality of their activities.[98] He then proceeds to define industrialism in a similar manner as: 'that system in which goods are made or services rendered in the mass', employing means such as 'the subdivision of labour, the factory, machine production and "scientific management"'.[99] We might note here that what is normally termed post-industrialism, i.e. the situation after the decline of heavy mechanical industry, seems still to come within Gill's definition of industry. He concedes that the merits of such a system are its orientation towards profitableness and economy, and that this benefits the consumer through cheapness and convenience, and the worker through regularity and simplicity of employment.[100] Gill concludes that there is 'not necessarily' any sin 'in any individual instance' of capitalism or industrialism.[101] This verdict, already perhaps influenced by the attempt to imitate the 'objective' style of Catholic moral teaching, may seem surprising from one who only a few years previously had produced a highly controversial war memorial with Christ driving money-changers in the dress of modern English bankers from the Temple, and an inscription that read: '*Agite nunc, divites, plorate ululantes in miseriis vestris, quae advenient vobis. Divitiae vestrae putrefactae sunt* – Go now, you rich men, weep and howl in your miseries which shall come upon you. Your riches are putrid (James, 5:1).'[102] Yet behind the more moderate analysis of the later essay a similar sentiment is still very much present, as the title, 'Responsibility, and the Analogy between Slavery and Capitalism', indicates. For capitalism and industrialism are, for Gill, little better than slavery. Slavery is defined as the loss of freedom and responsibility for one's actions through subjection to the will of others, while freedom is not opposed to discipline (as in decadent accounts of freedom as arbitrariness), but only to irresponsibility. Diminished responsibility is an inevitable consequence of capitalism and industrialism, most particularly in the worker, but also in the capitalist. This question of diminished

---

[97]   'Responsibility', pp. 134, 138 f.
[98]   Ibid., p. 135.
[99]   Ibid., p. 136.
[100]   Ibid., p. 137.
[101]   Ibid., pp. 136–7.
[102]   MacCarthy, pp. 166–7, Yorke, pp. 221–3.

responsibility is a matter of life and death, as Gill affirms, quoting St Thomas: 'The highest manifestation of life consists in this: that a being governs its own actions... Now a slave does not govern his own actions, but rather they are governed for him. Hence a man, in so far as he is a slave, is a veritable image of death.'[103]

It is here that the familiar Morrisian aesthetic categories come into play: If the factory workman is a slave without responsibility for his labour, there is another form of activity which stands at the opposite end of the spectrum from him: 'The type of the free workman is the artist... All free workmen are artists. All workmen who are not artists are slaves.'[104] The artist is the paradigm of the free worker because he has freedom in expressing himself and is responsible for what he creates, even if commissioned by another; he also takes delight in his work, and this delight is manifest as beauty in the thing made.[105] Artists properly understood are not just an elite group of talented individuals pandering to luxury tastes, but rather: 'Every man is called to be an artist'.[106] This is because beauty is not just an optional embellishment to life, and an artist is nothing more than someone who makes things well: 'simply a person who, being a responsible workman, is concerned for the rightness and goodness of his work, and in whose work beauty is the measure of his concern.'[107] In this respect the 'professional' artist, often contemptuously referred to by Gill as the 'Royal Academician sort', concerned only with the production of luxury 'fine arts' without real value or use, is as much a departure from the ideal as is the factory worker and the products of modern industry. If contemporary machine-made industrial products are so devoid of real artistic input as to be inhuman and ugly; then equally most modern art is governed by a debased purely subjectivist notion of beauty, so that it is nothing more than the artist's self-expression. As Gill puts it: 'The factory article reeks of the machine, the painting and sculpture reek of the man.'[108] The removal of the artistic dimension in all labour, and the related restriction of art to the fine arts, the divorce of art from ordinary life is a typically central Morrisian theme beloved of Gill:

> The ordinary productions of men have been so denuded of humanity as to be no longer works of art at all; they are no longer works of deliberate skill... Art is now the exclusive domain of picture-makers, sculptors, poets, and musicians –

[103] 'Responsibility', p. 133.
[104] 'Essential Perfection' (1918) in *Art Nonsense*, p. 5.
[105] Ibid., p. 4; Ecclesiastes is cited with approval: 'And I have found that nothing is better than for a man to rejoice in his work, and that this is his portion.' Gill gives a vivid account of his own discovery of this truth when he made his first sculpture in 1905: *Autobiography*, pp. 158–2.
[106] 'Art and Love' (1927) in *Art Nonsense*, p. 198.
[107] 'Quae ex Veritate et Bono', p. 71.
[108] 'The Criterion in Art' (1928) in *Art Nonsense*, p. 278.

there is now no art but fine-art . . . We expect nothing from the
commercial thing but its serviceableness; we place an exaggerated value upon the self-expression of the 'work of art'.
The objective nature of a work of art, its own being, is
forgotten.[109]

Phrases such as 'no longer . . . now . . . forgotten' in this passage hint at the
typical Romantic genealogy given to this crisis, which again is virtually
identical with that of Ruskin and Morris. Gill tells us that it is 'an
abnormal condition of things wherein we differentiate between ordinary
workmen and artists', a distinction that would have been unknown to
most of the great pre-modern civilizations of the world.[110] Gill claims
that it was virtually unknown in England until the eighteenth century,
and only became dominant in the nineteenth. However, by considering
art history, he argues that the real origins of this separation lie in the
Renaissance: 'The impersonal quality of all the great pre-Renaissance art
is obvious. The Renaissance discovered man and made the most of
him.'[111] The sculptures of Chartres are contrasted with the 'sentimen-
talism and anecdotage' which climaxed in the nineteenth-century acad-
emies and salons to indicate the disastrous consequences of the
separation of beauty from utility in modernity.[112] Before the Renaissance however,

picture-painting and sculpture (even music and poetry) were
part of the ordinary production of buildings and furniture.
You did not buy a picture for the sake of such and such an
artist's prowess, in spite of the notoriety of individual artists
here and there. You bought it because you had need of it, and
you naturally employed the best man known to you.[113]

At the heart of this Copernican revolution was a change in the view
of humanity: 'Man became critic whereas formerly he had been creator.'[114] By this Gill means the following: 'A critical mind is one that
looks on things from the outside. As a result of the Renaissance man
found himself outside Nature.'[115] The divorce of humanity from being
an integral part of nature to somehow outside it is one we have already
encountered in Morris and more explicitly in Adorno and Horkheimer's
Dialectic of Enlightenment. Gill also echoes the latter in his argument
that such a separation leads eventually to a utility that is only concerned
with bestial survival, so that the man who seeks to separate himself from

[109] 'The Criterion in Art', p. 278.
[110] Ibid. p. 281.
[111] Ibid., p. 284.
[112] Ibid., p. 287.
[113] Ibid., p. 286.
[114] 'Quae ex Veritate et Bono', p. 75.
[115] 'The Criterion in Art', p. 288.

nature in order to dominate the latter is ironically transformed into his own caricature of that which he wishes to dominate.[116] The consequences of this revolution are far-reaching: 'intrinsic values give place to extrinsic – absolute to relative.'[117] The Renaissance celebration of man's power and riches leads into the Reformation refusal of traditional authorities, which in turn unleashes the man of business who had formerly been subordinate, but is now uncontrolled, bringing the process to its logical conclusion in the industrial revolution. Here, Gill tells us: 'The workman became merely a tool and ceased to be a responsible initiator owning and working at his own work. Master and Man became exploiter and exploited in a world of commerce and without love.'[118]

Business and commerce are not evil activities in themselves; the tragic difference in the modern period is that these activities are no longer subordinate to higher ends and greater social goods but have been released from traditional restraints and made the ultimate horizon of human living: 'That men of business should be our rulers is bad enough; that their way of thinking should permeate and possess the minds of whole nations of men is a tragedy compared with which war, pestilence and famine fade into insignificance.'[119] When Gill claims that such a 'civilization' is little more than slavery and whoredom, Morris could hardly have expressed himself better!

Contra Arts and Crafts: The root of the question is religious

However, while Gill's debts to Morris were considerable, he grew increasingly disillusioned with the Arts and Crafts movement that claimed to continue Morris's legacy, and increasingly pessimistic about the social reformism of the Fabians. As early as 1910, writing in the *Socialist Review* much to the annoyance of Lethaby and others, Gill clearly saw the ironies which had haunted the later Morris concerning the failure of Arts and Crafts to have any real social impact, let alone reunite art with ordinary things. Unable to escape the economic logic of the surrounding society, the handicraft people were forced to sell their products at prices which insured they remained luxury items for the rich, which were then mass-reproduced by factories anyway. Thus Gill writes with bleak honesty: 'that was the main result of the Arts and Crafts Exhibition Society – to supply beautiful hand-made things to the rich, and imitation ditto to the not-so-rich. But as for wrecking commercial industrialism and resuscitating a human world – not a hint of it.'[120] Gill continued to recognize the 'mass of good intention' in the movement, but regarded it as 'intellectually muddled', a mixture of 'forlorn hope'

[116] 'Art and Love', p. 193.
[117] 'Quae ex Veritate et Bono', p. 75.
[118] Ibid., p. 76.
[119] 'Responsibility', p. 141.
[120] *Autobiography*, p. 270.

and 'idle fancy', and hence little better than 'fiddling while Rome burns'.[121]

Part of this hostility to the Arts and Crafts movement consisted in what we might call a more modernist aesthetic. For all his medievalism, Gill was not as devoted to Gothic as Ruskin and Morris had been. Indeed, he insisted that 'Artistically, the Gothic revival is played out, and we may be grateful to architects for that.'[122] Similar sympathies are evident in his judgement that the post-Impressionists after Cezanne were more successful in returning to the basic values of pre-Renaissance art than ever the Pre-Raphaelites were.[123] More surprising is Gill's admiration for the Forth Bridge as more of a work of art than Tower Bridge; or his insistence that churches, just as much as factories, should be built of iron and concrete and should not hide it.[124] Yet these positions are in a sense merely the functionalist outworking of the refusal of the notion of beauty as redundant ornament that, as we have seen, goes back to Pugin. Gill shares Pugin's loathing of the dishonesty of the false internal dome of St Paul's *and* the fake gothic facades of the nineteenth century. Whereas Pugin had believed that beauty and utility should be unified, Gill believed that beauty followed from utility, or as he was fond of saying: 'If you take care of Truth and Goodness, Beauty will take care of itself.'[125] This is because beauty is understood by Gill, in accordance with Maritain's Thomist rationalism, as 'order, unity, clarity', or simply things well made.[126] From this it follows that the machine-built 'newest locomotives' are more beautiful in being honest and free of all 'art nonsense' than the stained-glass doors of suburbia.[127] Gill, like Morris, was not a Luddite opposed to all technology in itself: 'It is no more immoral to make things by machinery than by hand. It is immoral to make things badly and pretend that they are good and no amount of 'hand' is an excuse for stupidity or inefficiency.'[128]

However we should be careful not to misunderstand Gill here, who after all remained hostile to much of the working conditions and products of industrialized mechanized society, and was himself a craftsman working with his hands to produce beautiful things for most of his life. Gill did ultimately agree with Morris, as we have seen, that the condition of the artisan was more natural to humanity than that of the factory slave. What then was his disagreement with the Arts and Crafts Movement? First, while sharing their ideal, Gill had a much more pessimistic

[121] 'The Revival of Handicraft' (1924) in *Art Nonsense*, pp. 118, 115.
[122] Autobiography, p. 203, Peter Faulkner, *William Morris and Eric Gill* (King's Lynn: William Morris Society, 1975), p. 20.
[123] 'Quae ex Veritate et Bono', p. 73.
[124] 'Art Nonsense' (1929) in *Art Nonsense*, pp. 313, 320.
[125] 'Quae ex Veritate et Bono', p. 65; 'Indian Sculpture' (1922) in *Art Nonsense*, p. 102.
[126] 'Quae ex Veritate et Bono', p. 65.
[127] 'Art Nonsense', p. 318.
[128] Ibid., p. 314.

judgement upon the present situation and the artist's capacity to do anything to change it. There can be, he says, no 'putting back the clock':

> We've jolly well got to take things as they are – we artists. The time is past when it seemed worth while to band ourselves into 'Arts and Crafts Movements' and to join 'Fabian Societies,' or 'Art Workers' Guilds'. The business of 'social reform' is outside the sphere of artists.[129]

There is a tragic conditionality to Gill's advocacy of pure utility. Our times, which aspire to nothing higher than the pursuit of self-interest and money, may well be sad times that do not produce truly great works of art; nevertheless, we can at least be honest, and it would be 'sadder still to continue the worn out pretence'.[130] Such a situation leads Gill, the sculptor, to argue that sculpture probably belongs to the museum in our age. The restoration of beauty to ordinary labour requires nothing less than 'the complete destruction of a civilisation in which money is god and men of commerce are our rulers.'[131] Gill rejects the belief of the early Morris that civilization can be changed by the revival of arts and crafts, because: 'the competition with the factory involved is too great and the position of the "artist-craftsman" too artificial.'[132] More crucially, following Maritain's separation of art and morality, social reform is *in essence* no business of the artist, the criterion in art is *not* morality. Even more explicitly, Gill insists that the artist *qua* artist has no interest in beatitude and is indifferent to the societal demands he must satisfy.[133] Such a position raises the same questions regarding the relation of the Beautiful to the Good that we considered above in Maritain's thought, but more of this shortly.

Gill also rejected the later Morris's view that a change of civilization would come about through a violent revolution.[134] Gill believed that a change in civilization *would* come, but not through the efforts of reformers, violent or artistic. *Meanwhile* then, the artist must live as well as possible in the age of the machine and commerce: *vanum est vobis ante lucem surgere.*[135] Thus the position of an artisan remains a possibility, handicraft can be revived, but not as a programme for social reform. Instead it remains an option that could be practised more as a form of counter-cultural resistance. Gill expressed this political stance in terms of a prophetic call in a key passage in 1924:

---

[129]   'The Future of Sculpture' (1928) in *Art Nonsense*, p. 308.
[130]   'The Future of Sculpture', p. 307.
[131]   'The Criterion in Art', p. 291.
[132]   Ibid.
[133]   Ibid., p. 298; *Art Nonsense*, p. 317.
[134]   'The Criterion in Art', p. 291.
[135]   '*In vain do you rise up before the light*'; *Art Nonsense*, p. 320.

Let us, then, cut ourselves out. Let us go out of Babylon – 'go out from her, my people.' Babylon, much as it needs us to give a saleable appearance to its goods, to swell its foreign trade to be sure! – much as it dotes upon us, provided only we flatter it sufficiently – Babylon can very well be left to go to Hell its own way. It is a waste of time adorning a house built on sand. The Revival of Handicraft, then, is practical politics only 'in the mountains'. Alone, or in ones and twos, flight must be taken. Then, again, in the wilderness, earning our bread by the sweat of our brow, the wilderness shall blossom as the rose. But, 'Quicumque vult . . .'[136]

This was in fact exactly what Gill did, first in the village of Ditchling in Sussex, then at Capel-y-ffin in the Welsh Black Mountains, and finally at Piggotts near High Wycombe. In all these places he sought to establish, with varying degrees of success, a mode of life and pattern of work with his family and various other sympathizers in accordance with his beliefs and in semi-monastic withdrawal from the values of the surrounding society. This was most pronounced in the period on Ditchling common where, shortly after his conversion to Catholicism, Gill attracted a community of like-minded artisans and their families which at its largest numbered around 40. In 1918 Gill and his wife joined the Dominican order of tertiaries, and many other members of the community followed them. It was in this environment that Gill was introduced by Fr Vincent McNabb to Catholic social teaching, particularly Leo XIII's *Rerum Novarum*, and to Thomist metaphysics and aesthetics through Maritain, whose *Art and Scholasticism* was translated by McNabb and published by Gill's St Dominic Press at Ditchling. It was also here that in 1921 Gill founded the Craft Guild of St Joseph and St Dominic, a workers' guild in the guild socialist tradition going back to Ruskin's Guild of St George, but with much more explicitly theological foundations, and its own elaborate liturgical life, focused in their chapel in the midst of the workshops and houses on Ditchling Common.[137]

It would however be mistaken to portray Gill's withdrawal from society to create alternative communities as an apolitical option without any vision for the wider re-ordering of society. Gill's mature political philosophy was a form of Distributism, the anti-centralist social philosophy of radical Catholics such as G. K. Chesterton, whom Gill had known since his pre-conversion days in Hammersmith, and Hilaire Belloc, whose *Servile State* and *An Essay on the Restoration of Property* were the most persuasive accounts of their position.[138] The Distributists placed great importance on personal responsibility and were opposed to

---

[136]   'The Revival of Handicraft', p. 122.
[137]   MacCarthy, pp. 116–75; *Autobiography*, pp. 205–15.
[138]   MacCarthy notes continuities with the Chartist agenda of the 1840s and the New Life Carpenterianism of the 1880s; p. 142.

all forms of accumulation of power and capital. For this reason they were equally hostile towards capitalism and state socialism. Gill provides a good account of this agenda in his own terms in his 1919 *Grammar of Industry*, where he argued in favour of four fundamental principles in economics and politics: 'Freedom, Responsibility, Ownership and Union'.[139] Freedom and responsibility are contrasted with the injustice and slavery of the condition of the modern factory worker as we have already seen. From the necessity of responsibility Gill deduces that the worker must be an owner, owning his own tools and workshop, his own home, the work he produces, and his own trade.[140] It is their non-ownership of these things that has made the workers slaves to those who do, the capitalists. Only thus owning his own means of making his living can the worker be independent of middle-men, and become free and potentially responsible. Gill recognizes that not everyone can or should be perfectly autonomous and equal, there will always be masters and disciples, but insists:

> Nevertheless it is necessary that ownership should preponderate in the community not merely for the material good of the community – that is comparatively unimportant – but for the safety of men's souls. The present state in which there are few owners and many slaves is founded on injustice, and therefore not only corrupt but corrupting.[141]

Given that even responsible and free workers will need to collaborate with one another, Gill concludes that cooperation and unionization follow from ownership: 'if men are to control a trade and be independent of middle-men, they must be banded together in unions or guilds. The union is a corporate society.'[142]

Unions or guilds, like nations, should exist for the sake of their members, not the other way round as in fascist states. Yet the union or guild does resemble an individual in that it too must be ordered responsibly, orienting itself not towards self-interest but towards justice and the good. Here Gill echoes Ruskin's account of how professional guilds committed to social goods and substantive traditions of virtue pointing towards transcendent values differ from unions purely based upon the defence of group interest. This was the philosophy of labour upon which the Guild of St Joseph and St Dominic was based, and which Gill attempted to embody throughout his life.[143]

[139] 'A Grammar of Industry' (1919) in *Art Nonsense*, p. 14.
[140] 'A Grammar of Industry', p. 12; cf. the notion of the 'proprietary state' in Hilaire Belloc, *An Essay on the Restoration of Property* (London: Wheats, 1984), p. 20.
[141] 'A Grammar of Industry', p. 13.
[142] Ibid.
[143] Gill also celebrates the family and other forms of corporate and collegiate living, something he learned to love first when he lived at Lincoln's Inn: *Autobiography* pp. 127–9.

This mention of transcendent values and the question of responsibility bring us to the heart of Gill's difference from the Arts and Crafts movement. For, as we have seen, this difference between Morris and Gill is not ultimately reducible to the psychological difference between 'activity and optimism' and 'isolationism and mere protest', as Nicolete Gray argued.[144] At various points in their lives, they were in fact much closer to each other on these questions than the standard view of either would allow. The real difference, as Gill himself certainly saw, was more fundamental, a difference in philosophy, in basic beliefs about the nature of the world and humanity. The Catholicism evident in the life of Gill's communities and in his essays was in no sense an accidental ornament, but rather was the foundation and source of all his aesthetic and political views. When Gill referred to the Arts and Crafts Movement as 'infidel', he meant this quite precisely.[145] In the revealingly titled *The Necessity of Belief*, looking back on the nineteenth century, and those such as Cobbett, Disraeli, Carlyle, Ruskin and Morris, whom he believed to have begun the revolt against materialism, Gill gives his final judgement on Morris:

> The criticism of the nineteenth century had to begin at a point nearer to the beginning of things than any criticism advanced by William Morris. That great man, that most manly of great men, as sensitive and passionate as he was fearless and hot-tempered, had not the mind to see the roots of the disorder. For all his humanity, he did not see at what point it was that humanity was corrupted. An agnostic in revolt against a complacent Anglicanism, a Socialist in revolt against a meanly mercantile parliamentarianism, an artist in revolt against mechanical industrialism, but an unbeliever! He saw no being behind doing; he saw no city of God behind an earthly paradise; he saw joy in labour but no sacrifice.[146]

Whereas it was necessary to discern the implicit theo-aesthetic in Morris and to a lesser extent Ruskin, particularly through their advocacy of Gothic, Gill has less interest in Medieval Gothic, but, as he himself said: 'we are much less scornful than they of the philosophical achievements of the time.'[147] Social questions for Gill were ultimately moral and metaphysical questions, and in this respect he was somewhat closer to Ruskin than Morris, as he also recognized: 'Ruskin saw clearly that the roots of human action, and therefore of human art, are moral roots.'[148] There can be no real political action or social reform without agreement

---

[144]   Faulkner, p. 23.
[145]   'Christianity and Art' (1927) in *Art Nonsense*, p. 230.
[146]   Cited in Faulkner, p. 21.
[147]   *Autobiography*, p. 203, cited in Faulkner, p. 20.
[148]   Speech at the Ruskin Memorial Dinner of 1934, cited in Faulkner, p. 22.

on fundamental questions such as 'What sort of a thing is man?'[149] A consensus on the religious questions of what and why must precede the political questions of how, metaphysics before pragmatics. Without this Gill believed there could only be 'confusion leading inevitably to dissipation and disintegration', and 'the merest palliative to the cancer.'[150] Thus Gill's *Grammar of Industry* begins by looking to the Catholic 'Penny Catechism' for answers to these questions and concludes that: 'Man is a reasonable creature capable of knowing, loving and serving God.'[151] The affirmation of freedom and responsibility, from which the rest of this 'grammar' as so much else of Gill's thought flows, is not something necessary and self-evident. It is an affirmation of faith, based upon the teaching of the Catholic Church that humanity is both free and responsible, because we were created to know, love and serve God. The *Grammar of Industry* describes what 'kind of industrial system should be built upon Catholic dogma'.[152] Responsibility is a Catholic belief, just as Gill draws his very definitions of freedom and slavery directly from St Thomas Aquinas.[153] Capitalism is to be condemned not because the majority of people are dissatisfied with it; indeed Gill recognizes that the power of capitalism is so insidious that the appetite of most workers for freedom and responsibility has atrophied, and the system replaces these desires with false 'demands' which it can satisfy.[154] Rather capitalism stands under judgement because it is fundamentally opposed to the *truth* about humanity, as revealed by Catholic Christianity. As soon as one bases critique on the more profound level of distinguishing between 'true' and 'false' desires and demands, a claim is being made that cannot be demonstrated on purely empirical grounds, and thus embodies some implicit 'super-natural' metaphysical view of humanity and the world. This same metaphysical claim is the basis for Gill's confidence that the current civilization must ultimately self-destruct without the intervention of artists or revolutionaries: 'The present civilization is founded upon an unnatural condition and will come to a natural end.'[155] Gill's favourite analogy for this opposition between capitalism and the truth-claims of Catholic Christianity is the early Church's attitude to slavery. While the Church never explicitly condemned slavery as such, nevertheless 'the effect of the influence of the Church was the diminution and eventually the abandonment of slavery, for the two could not permanently co-exist.'[156] Thus, given that capitalism and industrialism are systems which reduce and degrade responsibility, and responsibility is one of the distinguishing notes of Catholicism, so likewise Catholicism

---

[149] 'A Grammar of Industry', p. 6; 'The Revival of Handicraft', p. 116.
[150] 'A Grammar of Industry', p. 6; 'The Revival of Handicraft', p. 117.
[151] 'A Grammar of Industry', p. 8.
[152] Ibid., p. 9.
[153] 'Responsibility', pp. 132–133.
[154] 'The Future of Sculpture', p. 303; 'Quae ex Veritate et Bono', p. 79.
[155] 'The Criterion in Art', p. 291.
[156] 'Responsibility', p. 133.

and capitalism are essentially opposed and cannot ultimately co-exist.[157] Gill confidently prophesies that:

> as it was Christianity and the Church which was ultimately the destroyer of the physical slavery upon which the civilisations of antiquity were built, so it will be Christianity and the Church which will destroy the even worse and more devilish slavery of the mind and of the soul upon which are built the commercial empires of to-day.[158]

A Christian metaphysic or worldview will entail a crucially different teleology in conflict with that of capitalist society. For if it is human nature to know, serve and love God, or, as Gill puts it elsewhere, the final end for humanity is 'the marriage of [the] soul to God', then everything he does must be judged in relation to that end.[159] Gill thus insists: 'Every activity of man must be directed to those ends; otherwise man is false to himself, for he is acting against his nature, and false to God, for he is acting against his maker.'[160] The Christian God is a jealous God who insists that we cannot serve two masters. For a Christian metaphysic, God must be the only final and ultimate end of all human actions: 'things that do not envisage God as their end are like arrows not even aimed at the target.'[161] By contrast, Gill tells us, most activities in which the modern man is engaged have their end 'not in the love of God but in the love of money' which is the root of all evil simply because: 'money in itself is nothing and the love of nothing is the exact opposite of the love of God.'[162] In all things humans should seek first the Kingdom of God, which requires the pursuit of justice and the exercise of love in all our works and relations.[163]

To recall themes raised in earlier chapters, such a reference to ultimate values and the transcendent end of human actions immediately takes us beyond purely naturalistic and materialist accounts of humanity which reduce all actions to expressions of self-interest. Humanity for Gill, in accordance with Catholic Christian doctrine, is 'matter and spirit'.[164] This means that, unlike animals, our nature, our desire, and our proper end all go beyond the purely material: 'Man does not live by bread alone', which Gill glosses to mean 'man does not live only that life which bread subserves, but another life also, and one ministered to by

---

[157] 'Responsibility', pp. 132, 136, 137.
[158] 'Indian Sculpture', pp. 107–8.
[159] 'Quae ex Veritate et Bono', p. 68; cf. 'Art and Love', p. 192.
[160] 'Art and Love', p. 192.
[161] 'Stone-Carving' (1921) in *Art Nonsense*, p. 82.
[162] 'Quae ex Veritate et Bono', p. 68.
[163] 'Art and Love', p. 194; 'Quae ex Veritate et Bono', p. 78.
[164] 'Christianity and Art', p. 232; Gill cites Nietzsche here with qualified approval – 'What is great in man is that he is a bridge and not a goal, a bridge leading from animal to beyond man.'

spiritual food.'[165] In addition to the 'necessities' of earthly life, such as food, shelter, clothing, founded upon the earthly instincts for survival and procreation, humans also desire, produce and engage in a great many gratuitous activities and things which are superfluous to these basic animal instincts. These things which exceed the logic of utility, go beyond our 'needs', are either useless in the sense that they should not exist, or are 'useless' in that they exist purely for their intrinsic goodness. This latter category of 'unnecessary' things, things which are good in themselves, point towards the theological: 'The only reason for the existence of a thing which does not subserve earthly life is that God needs it.'[166] Gill's famous and rather flippant example of such a thing is custard: 'Man can do very well without it here below. But God is the great consumer of custard, and he made man chiefly to the end that sweets should grow in Paradise.'[167] To summarize, humanity for Gill is intrinsically oriented in its nature, desires and work to ends that exceed the materialist logic of utility and point towards transcendence. The materialist reduction of humanity to animals governed by no concerns higher than utility is a distortion of our true nature, which while it might be less empirically evident, is nevertheless ultimately more real: 'So, though it be true to say that man's primal instincts are for preservation and procreation, it is "truer" to say that man's first need is God.'[168] The excessive nature of human activity, the 'surplus-value' of human labour which Marx noted, is for Gill a pointer to the super-abundance of the divine.

Gill's critique of labour in modern society depends upon the horizon of ultimate values which makes it possible, beyond mere semblance, to attempt to distinguish between good and bad, true and false forms of production and consumption. If God is the final end to which all our work must be oriented, then there is also an absolute standard by which it can all be objectively judged. 'There is nothing to be said against slavery except that it is not the will of God' Gill says at one point, just as 'There is nothing to be said for freedom except that it is the will of God', whose service *is* perfect freedom.[169] Gill is quite clear on this necessarily theological nature of the affirmation of absolute value: 'The essence of religion is the affirmation of absolute values... the affirmation of an absolute value is a religious affirmation.'[170] Or elsewhere: 'the agnostical socialist cannot see further than death.'[171] The theological horizon is the necessary precondition not only of the

---

[165] 'Of Things Necessary and Unnecessary' (1921) in *Art Nonsense*, p. 60.
[166] 'Of Things Necessary and Unnecessary', p. 61.
[167] Ibid.
[168] 'Stone-Carving', p. 82; cf. 'Essential Perfection', p. 3: 'The essential perfection of man is not in his physical functions – the proper material exercise of his organs – but in his worship of God.'
[169] 'Slavery and Freedom' (1918) in *Art Nonsense*, p. 2.
[170] 'Christianity and Art', p. 232.
[171] *Autobiography*, p. 112.

negative social critique of alienated labour, but equally of its necessarily implied opposite pole, the positive vision of true labour as art. As Gill puts it very bluntly: 'If we want art we must again get religion.'[172] Of all the things that transcend the order of utility, beauty is the most prominent. We have seen how the artist was for Gill, as for Morris, a foretaste and paradigm of free, unalienated labour. This is linked much more explicitly by Gill with Maritain's theological and metaphysical account of aesthetics, so that any true account of beauty and art must be inescapably theological. For Gill, 'Beauty is...a thing of religious significance, ineffable...'; more than this, following Maritain, it is one of the transcendentals and a divine attribute.[173] Consequently beauty, for Gill, is objective and ontological, it is part of the rational structure of reality, not the subjective epistemological affection sought by post-Renaissance art: 'Beauty is not to be confused with loveliness. Beauty is absolute, loveliness is relative.'[174] Whereas false art is concerned with loveliness, true art is concerned only with beauty, which is necessarily theological:

> That which is beautiful relatively to man's love of it is relatively beautiful (more strictly called lovely). That which is beautiful relatively to God's love of it is beautiful absolutely. Therefore the sole test of absolute values is God, and this is of necessity, for God is in fact and by definition the only absolute being.[175]

Beauty ought to belong to *all* things made, not just a narrow class of things such as the fine arts, because it consists simply in things being well-made: 'Proximately a work of art is simply "a thing well made"...in every work of man Beauty is its essential perfection.'[176] Beauty properly inheres in all true and good work, whether divine or human: 'Beauty is not an accidental perfection either of God's creation or of man's handiwork. Beauty is an Essential Perfection of Creation and of handiwork.'[177] The 'true' nature, in the sense of the divinely intended ideal, of humanity as worker and maker is then revealed as the artist:

> Man is artist, man is normally the artist – the maker of things. Man naturally desires good and therefore good things. Man as artist naturally desires to *make* good things – things good in themselves – like God, he would survey his handiwork and see that it is good.[178]

---

172 'Christianity and Art', p. 247.
173 'Indian Sculpture', p. 104.
174 'Essential Perfection', p. 3; cf. 'Quae ex Veritate et Bono', pp. 72–4.
175 'Christianity and Art', p. 242.
176 'Indian Sculpture', p. 104.
177 'Essential Perfection', pp. 3–4.
178 'The Future of Sculpture', p. 300.

In this sense Gill endorses Maritain's analogy of divine and human creation: 'The artist purely as such is the creator; he collaborates with God in creating.'[179] Not just collaborator though, but also respondent, in the sense of lover and worshipper, for art is 'the peculiar and appropriative activity of man as the lover of God.'[180] As charity, love of God and love of neighbour, is the essential perfection of any human act, so true art is ordered by love: 'a work of art is the work of a lover. It is lover's worship'; or elsewhere: 'a work of art is simply a thing made by a lover, and God alone is beloved.'[181] Once again it is worth noting the necessarily theological nature of this account of art: it is not merely an expression of love, but love *of God*, precisely because it exceeds the logic of utility. Something that is made gratuitously, good for its own sake, good 'for nothing', must, like the custard, be good for God: 'Only from the point of view of God is it worth while to make a thing as well as it can be made. Hence to make a thing well for its own sake is tantamount to making it so for God's sake.'[182] Or again: 'Beauty is, even in its most humble aspect, not the expression of man's love for man, but of man's love for God. It is an oblation and, however unconsciously, as an act of worship that man gives Beauty to the work of his hands.'[183]

At its most profound level, art for Gill, like leisure for Pieper, is rooted in worship, it is fundamentally liturgical. It is only because art is at root liturgical that it is able to transcend the order of utility, and this reveals its necessarily theological nature. Beauty is ultimately simply the 'the Love of God and his praise and worship sensible in the work of man's hands'.[184]

Beyond Maritain? Transcending oppositions

In the discussion of Maritain's aesthetics above, we noted the problematic question of the supposed 'autonomy' of art, i.e. its separation from ethics and God as the Supreme Good and Final End. From a specifically *theological* perspective, we questioned the coherence of this teleological absolute distinction of ends to create a realm isolated from and indifferent to God. We have also seen how Gill, particularly in his later criticisms of the moralism of the Arts and Craft movement, repeats these arguments of Maritain, contrasting art with prudence, the artist with the moralist, and insisting that the artist has no interest *qua* artist in ethics, society, or even final beatitude.[185] When Maritain's aesthetics are employed *politically* by Gill, as a vision of emancipated labour, then

---

179 Ibid., p. 299.
180 'Art and Love', p. 196.
181 Ibid., pp. 196, 194.
182 Ibid., p. 197.
183 'Indian Sculpture', p. 108.
184 'Essential Perfection', pp. 3–4.
185 For example, 'The Criterion in Art', p. 298, 'The Future of Sculpture', p. 301, *Art Nonsense*, p. 317.

these theological problems are translated into the same sort of *political* problems which we observed in Pieper's definition of leisure over-and-against work: namely, that the attempt to defend and consolidate a realm of non-utility against utility instead merely reinforces the realm of utility and inoculates it against the potential transformative influence from outside itself. Whereas in Pieper this expressed itself in a certain indifference to the transformation of work; in Gill it seems at times as if the majority of the population cannot hope to find the joy in labour which belongs to the artist, while the chosen few who are granted this privilege can have nothing directly to say as artists to the condition of that society. It is worth noting in passing that while using Maritain's categories, Gill the artist seems not to conceive of art as a potentially Godless idolatry in the way Maritain does, so that for Gill the separation of art from morality is more of an exaltation of the spiritual otherworld-liness of art against the prosaic worldly concern of morality, whereas Maritain generally regards prudence as closer to God than art.[186] In both cases however the difference and relationship between utility and non-utility is thought in a relatively static way, limiting the transformative capacity of the non-utile, and apparently leaving the world largely doomed to the hegemony of utility.

And yet, just as we noted that there were elements in Pieper and Maritain which resisted this direction to their thought, so there are many significant moments in Gill's writings which likewise suggest a more complex picture that overcomes these simple oppositions. In both Pieper and Maritain it was in the highest of human activities, such as the works of the saints, or the liturgical celebration of the *opus dei*, that the simple oppositions between work and rest, art and prudence seemed to break down, and even more particularly for Maritain, in the work of God himself. This perhaps suggests some sort of heavenwards ascent from the opposition of utility and non-utility towards the unity of opposites. Something like this can be detected in similar passages of Gill. More generally, Gill's continuing Morrisian instincts for the trans-formation of labour, combined with his less aristocratic sympathies, and frankly more muddled anti-categorical mind, rescue him from the overly formalist views of Pieper and Maritain, and enable him to develop a more properly integrated aesthetic-theological teleology of work, one true to the convertibility of transcendentals and the participatory ana-logy of divine and human labour.

The first evidence of a more integrated view that resists these overly simplistic oppositions comes in hints that for Gill the beautiful and the useful are difficult if not impossible to separate in reality, i.e. beauty and utility are somehow integral to all human creations, in varying degrees. Thus Gill sometimes refers to the non-utile value of something (its intrinsic beauty and goodness) as the mental or spiritual 'utility' as

---

[186] This could well be in part because Gill, in contrast to Maritain, but closer here to Morris, seems never to conceive of art which is *not* oriented to beauty.

opposed to the physical utility.[187] This is in itself a helpful and revealing turn of phrase which suggests a certain continuity between the useful and the beautiful, while indicating the higher value of the latter in terms of intrinsic and more absolute truth, goodness, and beauty, rather than the merely derivative or even false value of material utility or self-interest. However, the latter is, of course, more immediately empirically evident and less demanding than spiritual utility, which is precisely the attractiveness of materialism. Nevertheless, in specific concrete things Gill observes that the physical and spiritual, utility and beauty, are virtually impossible to separate: after observing that chairs appear to be objects of utility and paintings things of beauty, he goes on to recognize that,

> some chairs have more than merely physical utility (e.g., a bishop's or even a grandfather's) and some paintings have more than merely mental utility (e.g., a painted reredos or a postage stamp – such things subserve and influence the physical life of men).[188]

Similarly, clothes, which might appear to be one of the most basic useful things, are for Gill much more about 'dignity and adornment' than 'physical convenience'.[189] And if Gill argues that even the most useful things are and should be at least as much things of beauty, similarly he is sceptical about the prospect of 'pure' art, free of any usefulness to humanity, which he regards as a decadent ideal that has probably never been achieved, if only because of the fallen nature of humans, who will not expend energy or money for things that are not in some way in their interest.[190] Thus in an important passage Gill points towards a more dynamic and transformative relation between utility and the non-utile:

> It is clear that any art can become 'fine' and any fine art may become 'servile.' It would be better if, in the ordinary way, we dropped the distinction altogether and criticised each thing on its merits. We should thus perhaps get the picture painters and sculptors, musicians, architects and men of letters off their pedestals and, on the other hand, raise the engineers and crossing sweepers and dentists to a higher level of self-respect.[191]

---

[187] 'The Criterion in Art', p. 282.
[188] Ibid.
[189] Ibid., p. 283.
[190] Ibid., p. 290.
[191] *Art Nonsense*, p. 321.

It is obvious that in a very real sense for Gill, 'all things are mixed – art and prudence inextricably', or we might add, utility and non-utility.[192] Underlying the observation that pure utility is nowhere to be found is the larger metaphysical claim, which we have already seen to be derived from Maritain, that 'beauty is resplendent Being' and that, therefore, it is present in all things.[193] Gill believes in the convertibility of the trans-cendentals, so that: 'in reality everything has a threefold significance for everything combines in itself Truth, Goodness and Beauty'.[194] While Maritain would have agreed with such claims, he seems not to have recognized that it follows from this that *all* art, not just the fine arts, is oriented towards beauty in as much as they are oriented towards making anything, and thus all human work is properly oriented towards God. Gill on the other hand insisted that beauty 'properly pertains to all the works of men', questioning the sense in which any art can be truly 'autonomous' from God.[195]

If the creation of beauty is intrinsic to all human work, then the properly subordinate role of utility in labour should not be scorned either. The curse of necessity haunts all work after Adam's fall, accord-ing to Gill; people *must* labour in order to survive. Yet even such works of necessity can (and perhaps, as we shall consider shortly, *must* inas-much as they are human works) exceed necessity and become 'the occasion of countless works of glory'.[196] Gill is quite content for utility to be a criterion in human labour, insisting only that 'serviceableness shall be strictly criticised and utility taken in its widest sense.'[197] In an anticipation of more recent developments in consumer politics, Gill realizes that this requires discerning consumers who can resist the false utility that serves nothing other than the greed of the manufacturers.[198] True utility, labouring for food, shelter, survival, has its role to play as what Gill calls an 'immediate or *proximate* end', subordinate to the ultimate end, which can never be utility but only ever God.[199] These proximate ends, which have the character of utility, are not, rightly discerned, accidentally related to God, but intrinsically, as to the Final End of all things, and thus they equally have the potential to participate to some degree in the non-utility of God. Gill sees such an ordering of proximate and ultimate ends in Christ's command to 'Seek ye first the kingdom of God and his justice and all these things shall be added unto you.'[200] He glosses this passage in the following manner:

[192] 'The Future of Sculpture', p. 301.
[193] 'The Criterion in Art', p. 294.
[194] 'Quae ex Veritate et Bono', p. 66; cf. 'Id Quod Visum placet' (1926) in *Art Nonsense*, p. 146.
[195] 'The Criterion in Art', p. 294.
[196] Ibid.
[197] Ibid.
[198] Ibid., p. 295.
[199] 'Art and Love', p. 192.
[200] Ibid., pp. 193–4.

Food and shelter are not the ends for which man works. On the contrary, man's work is the end to which food and shelter are the means. We say that man's work is the end. That is to say, it is the immediate or proximate end. The ultimate end, the final end is God. All food and shelter are things to help man in his work; all work is to help man to his God.[201]

Here we see something of Gill's integrated teleology: God alone, as the Final End, truly exceeds utility, however, in that all ends are intrinsically related to God as the Final End, there can be no 'autonomous' realms, but rather all activities are oriented towards God and the transcendence of utility, by which they can also be judged.

What does such a transcendence of utility in labour mean in practice? We have already seen how Gill believed that in a free society all workers would be like artists in working freely, responsibly, and taking delight in their work which would be expressed as beauty. Yet he also looks for the overcoming of the opposition between work and play as a mark of the redemption of work, and, apparently contrary to Pieper, for a paradoxical reversal of the opposition of work and leisure. Thus in a famous passage, Gill expresses the difference between work and leisure under slavery and in a state of freedom as follows:

That state is a state of Slavery in which a man does what he likes to do in his spare time and in his working time that which is required of him. This state can only exist when what a man likes to do is to please himself.
That state is a state of Freedom in which a man does what he likes to do in his working time and in his spare time that what is required of him. This state can only exist when what a man likes to do is to please God.[202]

It should be evident that this is not just a reversal of activities, but a transformation of each: In the state of freedom there could be no false necessities, no serving greed or injustice. People neither want to do things, nor are required to do things that are not *truly* useful or good. This transformation that liberates work from the false idol of utility is perhaps best expressed by Gill in terms of the claim that play is the deepest meaning of work, echoing certain elements of Adorno, and hence that this is what the liberation of work must resemble:

play is more proper to man than work and it is only when work is play that it is really good and right. And the reason is this: Play when consciously undertaken (when it is not merely physical exuberance) is more exactly an expression of free

[201] Ibid., p. 192.
[202] 'Slavery and Freedom', p. 1.

will than is the thing called 'work'. For the idea of work is inextricably bound up with necessity... Play is more proper to man than work because man's distinguishing character is that of a creature having free will.[203]

DAVID JONES (1895–1974): *HOMO SACRAMENTALIS*, NOT *ECONOMICUS*

Mere utility is in strict literal fact, impossible to man.[204]

The final figure in this chapter's quartet continues the Catholic meta-physical-aesthetic critique of work under modern capitalism, albeit primarily through poetry rather than essays. Like Gill, David Jones was an artist and engraver of considerable note before turning to poetry in 1937 with *In Parenthesis*, a meditation on his experience in the trenches during the First World War. It was here that he had experienced the first stirrings of an interest in Catholicism which led him to convert in 1921. In the same year he joined Gill in Ditchling where he was to spend the next four years, during which time he joined in the discussions of contemporary civilization and Maritain's aesthetics. Jones produced his own greatest account of art and Western Civilization in his epic poem *The Anathemata* (1952). In this work, and in a number of essays from the same period, particularly *Art and Sacrament* and *The Utile*, and various other fragments of poetry, Jones developed an account of humanity as fundamentally the artist, the sign-maker, for whom all labour, all activity is inescapably sacramental, liturgical. He painted a picture of a modern world which seeks to deny this fact and bring everything under the rule of mere utility, which is in fact just the will to domination, and is as old as time. If Jones was less explicit than Gill in setting forth a positive political and economic vision, he crucially realized, perhaps here going beyond the other figures we have been considering, that, precisely because humanity is *inescapably* sacramental, the capitalist project can never truly succeed, pure utility *never* exists in reality.[205]

---

[203] 'Quae ex Veritate et Bono', p. 69; Gill cites here Proverbs 8:30–31: 'My delight was every day playing in his sight through the round of the earth', and Maritain's quotation from Aquinas: 'The operations of play are not ordained to anything else but are sought after for their own sake'. See also David Jones's use of this text below.

[204] 'The Utile' (1958) in David Jones, *Epoch and Artist,* ed. Harman Grisewood (London: Faber and Faber, 1959), p. 181. Overviews of Jones's work include: Thomas Dilworth, *The Shape of Meaning in the Poetry of David Jones* (Toronto: University of Toronto Press, 1988), Kathleen Henderson Staudt, *At the Turn of a Civilisation: David Jones and Modern Poetics* (University of Michigan Press, 1994), Keith Alldritt, *David Jones: Writer and Artist* (London: Constable, 2003), and Rowan Williams, *Grace and Necessity: Reflections on Art and Love* (London: Continuum, 2005), pp. 56–90.

[205] Jones's political views have come under much scrutiny due to his reading of *Mein Kampf* and advocacy of appeasement. While he was always opposed to Hitler's pagan racism and glorification of violence, he, like many of his generation, had

THE END OF WORK: REST, BEAUTY AND LITURGY

The culture of the utile

The Anathemata opens with the image of a priest in a church, 'at the sagging end and chapter's close' of history, where:

> 'The utile infiltration nowhere held
>   creeps vestibule
> is already at the closed lattices, is coming through each door.'[206]

Like a plague, the utile is pictured by Jones as a spirit of deathliness and destruction ('Ossific', 'sterile'[207]), opposed to all that is living, beautiful, gratuitous. In the essay *The Utile*, Jones clarifies that he is using this term not in the wider sense of useful or good, but according to the more specific meaning associated with utilitarianism, that is, of *mere* utility, functionality, opposed to questions of goodness and beauty. In this sense 'utile' applies more to 'carburettors and gull's pinions' than to Stonehenge or the Lord's Prayer.[208] More polemically however, it is the spirit of rationality and ruthlessness, of quantification and commodification, of sameness and indifference, of control and hoarding, opposed also to all that is ancient, particular, differentiated, all that is free, child-like, celebratory, worshipful, cultic, holy.[209] This contrast can be best seen in Jones's passionate litany to the *Tutelar of the Place*, linked with the Mother of God, for deliverance from all the curses of utility:

Queen of the differentiated sites, administratrix of the demarcations, let our cry come unto you.
    In all times of imperium save us when the *mercatores* comes save

---

initially hoped that these new totalitarian forces might be harnessed so as to bring about the overthrow of the capitalist system. When the true nature of these forces became clear, he admitted how dangerously mistaken he had been. For a highly critical perspective, see Elizabeth Ward, *David Jones: Mythmaker* (Manchester: Manchester University Press, 1983); and for a balanced defence see Thomas Dilworth, 'David Jones and Fascism' in John Matthias (ed.), *David Jones: Man and Poet* (Orono, Maine: The National Poetry Foundation).

[206] David Jones, *The Anathemata* (London: Faber and Faber, 1952), p. 50.
[207] Ibid., p. 49.
[208] 'The Utile', p. 180.
[209] This opposition between utility and gratuity is explored by Dilworth (pp. 64–6), who claims Jones learnt it initially from the art criticism of Roger Fry and then from Maritain; Dilworth also links it with the opposition between civilization and culture in Oswald Spengler's *Decline of the West* which influenced Jones around the time he wrote *The Anathemata*. For the importance to Jones of Spengler, but also Jones's rejection of his determinism, see: Kathleen Henderson Staudt, 'The Decline of the West and the Optimism of the Saints: David Jones's reading of Oswald Spengler' in Matthias; and Kathleen Henderson Staudt, *At the Turn of a Civilisation: David Jones and Modern Poetics* (University of Michigan Press, 1994), pp. 121–38, where the influence of Christopher Dawson and James Joyce upon Jones's view of history is also discussed.

us
    from the guile of the *negotiatores* save us from the *missi*,
        from the agents who think no shame
by inquest to audit what is shameful to tell
          deliver us.
When they check their capitularies in their curias
        confuse their reckonings.
When they narrowly assess the *trefydd*
        by hide and rod
        by *pentan* and pent
by impost and fee on beast-head
        and roof-tree
and number the souls of men
        notch their tallies false
disorder what they have collated.
        When they sit in *Consilium*
to liquidate the holy diversities
        mother of particular perfections
        queen of otherness
        mistress of asymmetry
patroness of things counter, parti, pied, several
protectress of things known and handled
help of things familiar and small
        wardress of the secret crevices
        of things wrapped and hidden
mediatrix of all the deposits
        margravine of the troia
empress of the labyrinth
        receive our prayer.[210]

In this more negative sense, mere utility, denying the existence of anything more, Jones believes the utile to be the goal sought by the
most characteristic works of what he calls 'our present technocracy'.[211]
The most distinctive thing about this modern utilitarian culture is the
attempt to divorce the utile from the sacramental to which it has always
been wed, albeit not without friction (but more of this shortly).[212] This
is not simple anti-modernism, for, like Gill, Jones can see the beauty in
the best of modern technology. Yet he recognizes that the insistence upon

[210] 'The Tutelar of the Place' (1960) in David Jones, *The Sleeping Lord and Other Fragments* (London: Faber and Faber, 1974), pp. 62–3.

[211] 'The Utile', p. 181.

[212] 'Art and Sacrament' (1955) in *Epoch and Artist*, p. 176. Rowan Williams describes this essay as 'one of the most important pieces of writing in the twentieth century on art and the sacred', Williams, p. 88. Williams recognises that Jones has 'used Maritain's categories to go beyond Maritain' here (p. 83), but is curiously dismissive of Gill's influence in this step (pp. 45–55).

utility and nothing else is a fatal narrowing of our humanity, and when he considers as fairly as he can our civilization he regrets that this is what he finds:

> I have watched the wheels go round in case I might see the living creatures like the appearance of lamps, in case I might see the Living God projected from the Machine. I have said to the perfected steel, be my sister and for the glassy towers I thought I felt some beginnings of His creature, but *A, a, a, Domine Deus,* my hands found the glazed work unrefined and the terrible crystal a stage-paste . . . *Eia, Domine Deus.*[213]

In his wedding poem, *The Epithalamion,* where the progress of history is seen through various symbolic women, we are given a Weberian vision of the origins of such a spirit in early Puritanism and the rise of the merchants and financiers:

> Stern Duty, that flat-breasted girl, sits yellow
> at the prow, but
> Fugger sets the helm, to
> prosperous shallows.
> (The sirens rape their locks to fit Genevan
> bonnets and Triton now begins to count his
> charges. Plenty spills her horn – to those who
> pay. They plug the moist nipples of our mother
> up with notes of credit. They manipulate the
> eternal fountains. They burn the fruit of Ceres'
> womb, that her reaper-lovers had got upon
> her – to suit their double-columned books.
> John Barleycorn must die a second death,
> when bankers rule, as Spengler shows, till
> Caesar comes.)[214]

Yet lest we should think that Jones simply identifies the utile with modernity, his most frequent image for this spirit is the Roman soldiers whose empire subdues all local cults, and who, of course, put to death the Son of God, becoming subsequently in the Book of Revelation the symbol of Satan's Empire. In *The Tribune's Visitation* the Roman Tribune delivers a speech to his troops that constitutes an iconoclastic call to the disenchantment of the world, urging them to cast off all such effete 'superstition':

---

[213] 'A, a, a, Domine Deus' (1966) in *The Sleeping Lord,* p. 9.
[214] 'Epithalamion' in David Jones, *Wedding Poems,* ed. Thomas Dilworth (London: The Enitharmon Press, 2002), p. 37.

> Old rhyme, no doubt, makes beautiful
> >   the older fantasies
> but leave the stuff
> >   to the men in skirts
> who beat the bounds
> >   of small localities
> all that's done with
> >   for the likes of us
> in *Urbs*, throughout *orbis*.[215]

Myth and sacraments must be left behind as childish things by the rationalist, dominating project of Roman *imperium*:

> >   Suchlike bumpkin sacraments
> are for the young-time
> >   for the dream-watches
> now we serve contemporary fact.
> >   It's the world-bounds
> we're detailed to beat
> >   to discipline the world-floor
> to a common level
> >   till everything presuming difference
> and all the sweet remembered demarcations
> >   wither
> to the touch of us
> >   and know the fact of empire.'[216]

Lest the soldiers should protest that surely their own Roman myths, their sacred places and treasured things should be spared this onslaught, the Tribune insists: 'Spurn from caul of fantasy, even if it be the fantasy of sweet Italy.' Disenchantment is not to stop at their own doorstep. For the Tribune fears that such recollection

> calls up some embodiment
> >   of early loyalty
> raises some signum
> >   which, by a subconscious trick
> softens the edge of our world intention.[217]

To believe in such things would be to become 'party members duped with your own propaganda'.[218] Here we can perhaps see something of how the logic of instrumental reason becomes reflexive: initially treating

---

[215]   'The Tribune's Visitation' (1958), in *The Sleeping Lord* p. 50.
[216]   'The Tribune's Visitation', pp. 50–1.
[217]   Ibid., p. 52.
[218]   Ibid., p. 54.

others as inanimate, it inevitably rebounds upon those who exercise it, as Adorno and Horkheimer argued. These soldiers are simply 'ministers of death' who 'but supervise the world-death being dead ourselves long since'.[219] Yet even this poem ends with the Tribune invoking the troops' mystical fellowship with one another and with Caesar, and their binding loyalty to their oath (*sacramentum*), which begins to raise questions about whether these soldiers have attained their goal of pure utility, or whether the sacramental remains even here, inescapable, distorted and misdirected perhaps, but not abolished. Similarly, even the Roman *Imperium* dimly foreshadows the universality of Christ's rule for Jones, and so can be taken up and used by it. Nothing, it seems, is beyond sacramental redemption.

Humanity the artist or sign-maker

Jones shares the cultural pessimism of many of the figures we have encountered, frequently employing apocalyptic images, or speaking of the 'days of the final desolations', the 'thirteenth hour', and the 'December of our culture'.[220] In such a situation those who seek to resist the advance of the utile will have an isolated, forlorn, defensive role to play, appearing as a childish anachronism, like the priest at the beginning of *The Anathemata* who is 'so late in time, curiously surviving':

> The cult-man stands alone in Pellam's land: more precariously than he knows he guards the *signa*.[221]

Likewise a similar defensive tone of preservation by the segregation and burial of the non-utile, with echoes perhaps of Pieper's defensive approach towards leisure, is evident in *The Tutelar of the Place*, where the benevolent mother is invoked in the following manner:

> In all times of *Gleichschaltung*, in the days of the central economies, set up the hedges of illusion round some remnant of us, twine the wattles of mist, white-web a Gwydion hedge'[222]

or again, shortly afterwards:

> ward somewhere the secret seed, under the mountain, under and between, between the grids of the Ram's survey when he squares the world-circle.

---

[219] Ibid., p. 56.
[220] 'Prothalamion' p. 32 and 'Epithalamion' p. 40 in *Wedding Poems*, 'The Tribune's Visitation', p. 64.
[221] *The Anathemata*, p. 50.
[222] 'The Tutelar of the Place', p. 63.

> Sweet Mair devise a mazy-guard
> in and out and round about
> double-dance defences
> countermure and echelon meanders round
> the holy mound
> > fence within the fence
> pile the dun ash for the bright seed
> > (within the curtained wood the canister
> within the canister the budding rod)
> > troia in depth the shifting wattles of illusion for the
> ancilia for the palladia for the kept memorials, because of the
> commissioners of the Ram and the Ram's decree concerning
> the utility of the hidden things.'[223]

It seems here that the only hope for the non-utile is to go underground, to be protected and hidden. Yet all is not quite as bleak as it seems. For *The Anathemata* tells a story of the whole of human history as always and everywhere, unavoidably, the making of signs, so that Jones can claim: 'We were then *homo faber, homo sapiens* before Lascaux and we shall be *homo faber, homo sapiens* after the last atomic bomb has fallen.'[224] The very word 'Anathemata' is used by Jones to suggest:

> the blessed things that have taken on what is cursed and the profane things that somehow are redeemed: the delights and also the 'ornaments', both in the primary sense of gear and paraphernalia and in the sense of what simply adorns; the donated and votive things, the things dedicated after whatever fashion, the things in some sense made separate, being 'laid up from other things'; things, or some aspect of them, that partake of the extra-utile and of the gratuitous; things that are the signs of something other, together with those signs that not only have the nature of a sign, but are themselves, under some mode, what they signify. Things set up, lifted up, or in whatever manner made over to the gods.[225]

From such a definition we begin to see that there is nothing in the world of humanity that is not in some sense 'anathemata', nothing which does not somehow signify. *The Anathemata* opens with exactly such a making of signs, echoing the actions of the celebrant in the mass, but also suggesting a timeless aboriginal and ineradicable nature to this action of sign-making:

---

[223] 'The Tutelar of the Place', p. 64 ('Mair' here is the Welsh form of Mary).
[224] 'The Utile', p. 184. It is interesting to note that Jones believes Neanderthal man to have been truly human because of the evidence of art and funerary rites, regardless of their being a different line of descent from *Homo Sapiens Sapiens*.
[225] Preface to the Anathemata, pp. 28–9.

We already and first of all discern him making this thing other. His groping syntax, if we attend, already shapes:

ADSCRIPTAM, RATAM, RATIONABILEM ... and by pre-application and for *them*, under modes and patterns altogether theirs, the holy and venerable hands lift up an efficacious sign.[226]

In the essay *Art and Sacrament*, Jones makes his position clear when he insists that all people are artists, and that all human productions and creations are art. This Morrisian theme, which we have often come across, apparently struck Jones during his years with Gill, and is summarized by him in the words of James Joyce: 'practical life or "art" ... comprehends all our activities from boat-building to poetry'.[227] Jones does not entirely endorse the clumsy slogan 'art for art's sake', and certainly not its elitist and restricted conception of art, but claims that the truth underlying this is the quality he terms 'Gratuity Ness' which is of the essence of all *Ars*.[228] Art, he claims, is 'the sole intransitive activity of man'.[229] This claim is then illustrated by considering in turn a strategy, a birthday cake, a painting and a ritual action. While even the greatest work of art may not be entirely free of transitive aspects (the artist still needs to earn his bread, the patron may want the art for some political or financial purpose), nevertheless it is the element of intransitivity, gratuitousness in its making that makes it count as art. In this sense the post-Impressionists were correct to argue that it is the 'abstract' quality in a work of art that makes it *ars*, *poiesis*; although the opposition between abstraction and realism is a false one, for every work of art also necessarily 're-presents' something.[230]

Ars, the gratuitous making of things, is not merely one human capacity among others, it is *distinctively* human, for humanity is a 'creature which is not only capable of gratuitous acts but of which it can be said that such acts are this creature's hall-mark and sign-manual.'[231] This is what distinguishes us from the animals, who, although they certainly make things, and things of beauty like bee-hives and spiders webs, never exceed the order of the functional, never produce evidence of the gratuitous, or of 'sign'.[232] Likewise in traditional thought, *ars* distinguishes us from pure intelligences, the angels, who, being immaterial, cannot

---

[226]   *The Anathemata*, p. 45; 'adscriptam ... etc' and 'holy and venerable hands' are quotations from the Roman Mass.

[227]   'Art and Sacrament', p. 172.

[228]   Ibid., p. 149.

[229]   Ibid.

[230]   Ibid., pp. 172–3.

[231]   Ibid., p. 148.

[232]   Ibid., p. 149. This is not to say that nature, as God's work, does not express gratuity, nor that natural things cannot be or become signs, just that other creatures do not *make* signs, create gratuitous abstract forms that also re-present things, as humans do.

'make' things.[233] If art is distinctive to humanity, then, Jones argues, this is because of the type of creatures we are, and this in turn already takes us into a quasi-theological anthropology: 'this mammal has an end other than that of the other mammals, or, as they say, this creature, because he is endowed with rationality (i.e. has a "rational soul") must have a supernatural end.'[234] Art then is not just one branch of human activity, but is 'truncal', and includes not just the fine arts but also 'the diesel engine, boot-making, English prose, radar, horticulture, carpentry and the celebration of the Sacred Mysteries.'[235]

If we are creatures of art, what is it that we distinctively make? Because our end is supernatural, humans are creatures who make things that are 'not only things of mundane requirement but are of necessity the signs of something other'.[236] Humanity is 'a sign-maker' and 'his art is sign-making', so that 'in every matter, trivial or of some consequence, to our harm or to our joy or indifferently, we all of us, all the time, make *signa* of the particular.'[237] Jones argues that when we get away from the restrictively narrow modern usage of the word 'sacrament', we realize that all art is properly sacramental as such, a 're-presenting', 'showing again under other forms', an 'effective recalling', because 'man is unavoidably a sacramentalist and . . . his works are sacramental in character.'[238] From the earliest cave painting 50 millennia or more ago, we are already in the realm of 'sign (sacrament), of anamnesis, of anathemata'.[239] More bluntly put: '*men make sacraments*.'[240] And this gratuity, this quality of surplus, this setting-aside, or marking out, or making-other, or lifting up, is always in some sense an offering *to the*

---

[233] 'Art and Sacrament', p. 150. We might wonder here whether this restriction of *ars* to the material, which we came across earlier in Maritain, is entirely true. For what are we to make of the songs of the angels, which are surely in some sense *poiesis*?

[234] Ibid., p. 147.

[235] Ibid., pp. 176, 153.

[236] Ibid., p. 150.

[237] Ibid., p. 154, Preface to Epoch and Artist, p. 15. For accounts of Jones's sacramental anthropology, see Thomas Whitaker, 'Homo Faber, Homo Sapiens' in Matthias, where this perspective is described as 'strikingly modern' (p. 415) and linked with Vico, Nietzsche and Bergson, but also with the sacramental, analogical ontologies of Irenaeus, Dionysius, Aquinas, Coleridge, Keble and Hopkins; and Staudt, pp. 39–49, where it is linked with Gregory Dix's notion of *anamnesis* and 'real presence' and situated between post-structuralist formalism and Marxist representationalism. For a similar sacramental response to modern semiotic debates which likewise stresses the real presence of the signified in the signifier, see Catherine Pickstock, *After Writing: On the Liturgical Consummation of Philosophy* (Oxford: Blackwell, 1998). Ward rejects Jones's basic distinction between utility and gratuity as a 'Manichaean dualism' reducible to the opposition between the primitive past and the technological present. For responses to this caricature, see: Whitaker pp. 472–5, Staudt, pp. 20–5, and Dilworth p. 66.

[238] 'Art and Sacrament', p. 155. René Hague, Jones's friend and commentator, tried to push Gill back into a more narrowly orthodox interpretation of sacramentality, to prevent the blurring of lines (Whitaker, p. 468).

[239] 'Art and Sacrament', p. 156.

[240] Ibid., p. 163.

gods, for: 'it is on account of the anthropic sign-making that we first suspect that anthropos has some part in a without-endness.'[241] Art, for Jones, is then a fundamentally 'religious' activity, and more than this, from the theological point of view it is a participation in Him '*per quem omnia facta sunt*', the Eternal Artifex, Pontifex, and Logos.[242] The 'gratuity-ness' of art is a particular sign of this, for Jones reminds us that the theologians say that the creation of the world was 'not a necessary, but a gratuitous, act', or even we might say 'for fun', in the same sense that we hear of Wisdom playing in the book of Proverbs – '*ludens in orbe terrarum*' – with the children of Adam for her 'play-fellows'.[243]

Crucially, this sacramentality is not confined by Jones to some things and not to others. The world cannot be tidily divided into the utile and the extra-utile or sacramental. There is 'no escape from sacrament'.[244] It is in fact the attempt to divorce the utile from the sacramental which has led to the particularly modern predicament, the rise of the *merely* utile.[245] The two are inextricably bound together and must not be crudely opposed, just like *Ars* and *Prudentia*. Here Jones is clearly going beyond Maritain, and even Gill, in the refusal of formalism. Just as there is no escape from sacrament, so likewise Jones argues that we cannot live outside of one 'prudentia' or another, in the sense of *mores*, forms of life, hence there is simply

> no purpose in posing the kind of questions which so often are posed touching Prudentia and Ars as though these were two comparable qualities in opposition to each other or two jurisdictions or figures in a hierarchy having claims against each other... I do not believe that such conceptions make sense.[246]

It is only as a 'sapiential', rational creature that we can be 'prudential', and equally that we can have any freedom, gratuity, *ars*. In other words: 'Man could not belong to Prudentia except as an artist and he could not be an artist but for that tie-up with Prudentia.'[247] At bottom, such simple oppositions – art and prudence, utility and the sacramental – cannot apply in reality, because they would require the existence of a secular realm isolated from God. As Jones insists: 'properly speaking, and at the root of the matter, Ars knows only a 'sacred' activity.'[248] Jones's logic here follows precisely the point we have been trying to draw out in Maritain and Gill, but which neither makes explicit for themselves:

[241] Ibid., p. 156.
[242] Ibid., p. 160.
[243] Ibid., pp. 153–4; Proverbs 8:30–31.
[244] 'Art and Sacrament', p. 167.
[245] Ibid., p. 176.
[246] Ibid., p. 147.
[247] Ibid., p. 150.
[248] Ibid., p. 157.

If being and goodness are convertible – '*Bonum et ens convertuntur*' – then there can be no 'value-free' realm of facts; in so far as art makes *anything* real, it makes something that is good in relation to God, therefore sacramental and not purely 'utile'. Likewise: 'a sign then must be significant of something, hence of some "reality", so of something "good", so of something that is "sacred".'[249] Nothing signifies nothing! This is Jones's final conclusion in his essay *The Utile*: that pure utility is non-existent, mere nothingness. This follows from the inescapability of sacramentality: '*if* man is the kind of creature here defined as "man-the-artist" then none of his works can, in strict, literal fact, be wholly and exclusively ordered toward mere utility.'[250] Utility, functionality in the non-derogatory sense, is found throughout creation, but only humanity, which is ordered to the extra-utile, can seek *pure* utility in the negative sense. And yet we will never attain it, for the simple reason that: 'mere utility is in strict literal fact, impossible to man.'[251] However bad things may get, however far the advance of utility may seem to reach, it can never ultimately triumph, for humanity cannot completely eradicate its nature as a sacramental animal. This sacramental nature is both God-given, and the mode in which God gives himself to us: 'He placed Himself in the order of signs.'[252] Thus *The Anathemata* ends as it began, with the celebration in signs of the greatest art of all, begun in the Upper Room and on Calvary, the '*Ars ut artem falleret*', as St Thomas called it; the greatest work of God, which, through His gift, becomes also the highest work of humanity, the work of the people (*Leit-ourgia*) while remaining still, more fundamentally, the work of God (*opus dei*), which He works in and through us:

> He does what is done in many places
> what he does other
>   he does after the mode
> of what has always been done.
> What did he do other
>   recumbent at the garnished supper?
> What did he do yet other
>   Riding the Axile Tree?'[253]

---

[249] 'Art and Sacrament'.
[250] 'The Utile', p. 180.
[251] Ibid., p. 181.
[252] *Epoch and Artist, frontispiece*. This phrase came from the theologian Maurice de la Taille, Whitaker, p. 479.
[253] 'Art and Sacrament', p. 168, *The Anathemata*, p. 243. Dilworth sees an echo here of the Grail questions, with the implication that they point towards a renewal of the wasteland of modern civilization. Whitaker (p. 482) notes here the ambivalence over whether the pronoun refers to Christ, the priest from the beginning, or humanity the sign-maker, and argues that this reflects a profoundly incarnational and participatory account of divine and human agency.

Do not labour for the food that perishes, but for the food which endures to eternal life

7

Concluding Remarks

Labour, Utility and Theology

This book began with various twentieth-century attempts to reflect theologically on work. In the subsequent chapters we have sought to gain a deeper understanding of the 'problem of labour' in the intellectual history of the past two centuries. We have focused particularly on two traditions of social criticism, the one deriving from Marx, and the other broadly belonging to English Romanticism. Through exploring the inter-relationships of these two traditions and their internal tensions and instabilities, we have sought to throw some light upon the question of what specifically *theological* reflection upon work might have to offer, what difference theology makes to such debates. It is now appropriate to attempt to offer some conclusions.

SOCIAL CRITICISM AND THEOLOGY: THE PUPPET AND THE DWARF

Since the nineteenth century the 'question of labour' has been at the heart of attempts to generate social critiques; that is, to understand the socio-economic forms and tensions of our world and, through under-standing them, in some sense to criticize or judge them, even to begin to imagine how things might be otherwise. Partly because of the political events of the twentieth century, but still even today after the 'collapse of communism' in Europe and in different ways in Asia and elsewhere, the figure of Karl Marx towers over this 'problem of labour'. It is largely due to him that we have subsequently generally regarded questions of labour as purely socio-economic and accordingly have addressed them by quasi-physico-scientific methods, purportedly dealing with positive 'natural' facts, in order to generate supposedly necessary pragmatic strategies for their manipulation and negotiation. This method has *deliberately* attempted to bracket out all considerations of value and meaning, of morals or ethics, and it should come as no surprise that it has often had an explicitly anti-theological agenda. This has been most evident in the anti-religious prejudices of certain critical and radical circles, for whom religion is *necessarily* aligned with the past, with tradition and primitivism, obfuscation and untruth, repression and reactionary politics.[1] On this account, the criticism and renewal of society, the transformation and liberation of labour from conditions of alienation and oppression are concerns for which theology can only be an obstacle to be cast aside. The future may well be bright, but it certainly has to be godless.

However this violent excision of theology from the picture of social criticism has not been an unproblematic one. Indeed we have sought to argue that this exclusion has been the bad conscience haunting the intellectual Left, the repressed secret at the origins of their tradition and henceforth the skeleton in the closet, constantly resurfacing throughout their history to trouble them. For ultimately the materialist, naturalist, rationalist worldview that the Left has adopted cannot adequately account for the practice of social criticism to which they are in reality more fundamentally committed. This is not only a question of intellectual consistency, for the problem is more acute: there is at least significant evidence that this materialist worldview which has been adopted by the mainstream Left is not simply an inadequate foundation for critique, but that it is also in some way deeply allied to the very alienation of labour in the modern world which they have sought to oppose. If this is so, then the alliance of social criticism with materialism may well prove to have been not just an unfortunate confusion, but a poisonous affair with the enemy. Likewise if there is an anti-theological, materialist heart to the problem of the alienation of labour under capitalism, then theology, far from being part of the problem, might actually be the key to the solution. If this is the case, then the exclusion of theology by the Left is a withering isolation from the very well-springs of their own critique.

This case – that theology, far from being a hindrance to social criticism, is its deepest source – can be made historically and theoretically, as we have endeavoured to show in the foregoing chapters. Historically, we have seen how Marxism arose out of that quasi-theological cocktail of ideas that was German Idealism and Romanticism, a milieu in which theology was often bound up with or mediated by aesthetics. While Marx believed himself to have made a clean break from his origins, these theological roots have resurfaced at various points throughout subsequent Marxism, even if only as an anxiety about how beauty, goodness and truth can be understood on a materialist basis. Thus we can point to Lukács's rediscovery of the importance of Hegel to Marx, the philosophical interests of the Frankfurt school, the aesthetic concerns of the New Left of the 'sixties, or the more recent curiosity

---

[1] Obviously such an intellectual yoking of religion and reaction was in no small part due to the very visible alliance of certain ecclesiastical powers with the oppressive political forces of the *Anciens Régimes* throughout Europe for much of the nineteenth century and beyond. However, that this yoking should be regarded as in some sense necessary and logical rather than simply partial and historically contingent, despite many counter-examples, indicates that meta-historical philosophical prejudices are at work here as well, and it is to these that we are objecting.

about post-secularism on the Left, as various examples of the irrepressibility of theological questions for the Marxist tradition and of the structural instabilities caused by Marx's grafting of political economy onto his romantic roots. Adorno and Horkheimer illustrate this particularly well, as we have seen, in their concern with the autonomy of aesthetics, their hostility towards positivism, and their genealogy of instrumental reason.

Theoretically the link between theology and social criticism can be seen in that criticism, judgement, is always committed to, or interested in, something *other* than what it is criticizing, some source or measure of judgement which is external to the reality being judged, in some sense not only over and against it, but also 'above' it. This could of course be some other material reality, as when for example the condition of French labourers is judged by the condition of English labourers. But what if there neither is, nor has been, any higher instance of the thing judged? It seems that somehow it is still possible to pass judgement on the best, the most 'ideal' labour, precisely in that it is never completely ideal. Likewise Marx wants to offer not just a critique of the alienated labour of chimney-sweeps or miners, but of *all* labour; not just using one form of labour to judge another, but somehow judging the entire history of human labour *as such*. Whence then comes his criterion of judgement? From which vantage point, and by what yardstick is he able judge? Of course Marx, and all the other social critics we have considered, do point to empirical realities that in some sense foreshadow unalienated labour, offer a hint of how things might be different, yet these realities never perfectly express the ideal to which they point, and in which they share partially. Criticism, then, *necessarily presumes* a certain ideal which is *not* empirically given.

More fundamentally, we can even say that this logic does not only apply to those particularly committed to social or political criticism. On the contrary, none of us can escape the business of judgement, discernment (which is just criticism on a more modest scale) which always points beyond itself to some ideal not empirically given in the material world. Precisely because there cannot be any 'pure', value-free description, *any* perspective on society is already implicitly committed to some form of ideality or another, which in turn makes possible certain judgements. This is both an anthropological claim (humans are the sort of creatures who cannot escape making value judgements, we are cultural animals whose world is necessarily value-saturated) and also a theological claim (Truth cannot ultimately be completely separated from Goodness, and nothing can be finally indifferent to God).

In the specific case of work, a particular 'aesthetic' vision or ideal of true, unalienated labour is implicit in Marx's critique, as we have seen. While this is certainly intimated by certain practices which are more free, more autotelic, etc, the ideal is never fully realized in these practices and so cannot be reduced to them. We have argued that behind this ideal is actually an idea of what labour is like for God, which Marx has inherited from older traditions. This vision of divine labour is the theological foundation of his ideal, unalienated labour, and it is thus the theological foundation of his entire critical project, and, by extension, those of his successors. While Marx himself does not recognize this theological source of his thinking and even tries to disavow it, we have argued that the alternative sources to which he points cannot deliver this ideal. For the ideal of unalienated labour is not immanently given either in 'nature' or in history. Nor, as was argued in relation to Adorno, can it be simply negatively extrapolated from 'bad' labour. Rather the true nature of labour is somehow excessive to human labour, properly ideal, *transcendent* even.

It seems then that Walter Benjamin was profoundly right when he spoke of the relationship between Marxism and theology using the image of an 'automaton' chess machine that was in reality a puppet operated by a hidden dwarf.[2] Marxist critique is in truth not automated and self-founding, but is actually animated by a hidden theological heart which is kept out of sight. Yet if he meant this largely negatively, referring to the debased 'historical materialism' of Soviet orthodoxy which encouraged a naïve historical confidence and Whiggish optimism, inherited from Hegel's 'theology', then we can certainly accept this criticism of the negative role played by debased theology – there is no *necessary* progress to human history – while insisting that precisely *because* of this, i.e. because the problem of alienation is not just going to resolve itself through the unfolding of history, the very possibility of any critique *has* to be moral, 'theological'. In this case Benjamin's image can be re-appropriated positively: theology might not be such a 'wizened' dwarf, and if she comes out of hiding, she might well be able to engage in real critique, properly to take on her opponent rather than simply engaging in a con-trick.

It is also worth asking why the theological core of the critique of labour came to be hidden in the first place. Marx's rebellion against theology can in part be understood in terms of the Young Hegelian refusal of idealist Kantianism, on the one hand, and of the ideological justification of the status quo in conservative Hegelianism, on the other. But Marx's further step towards scientistic materialism was also influenced by his reading in political economy. Ironically it seems the very authors who gave his ideas concrete political material and who were one of his most frequent targets were also the sources of the physico-scientific model with its materialist metaphysic which Marx bought into. These similarities between Marx's suppression of the theological and the materialism of the political economists is of particular significance if this exclusion of the theological is actually crucial to political economy and to capitalism more generally. It seems as if Marx's refusal of theological foundations to critique leads him to fall into naturalistic and materialistic accounts of 'use-value' by which means 'utility' (which we

---

[2]   *Theses on the Philosophy of History*, in Walter Benjamin, *Illuminations*, p. 45.

have argued is the real heart of capitalism) sneaks into Marxism by the back door, acting like a fifth column in the enemy camp.

THE 'SPIRIT OF UTILITY': THE HEART OF THE NATURE OF LABOUR UNDER CAPITALISM

What is meant by the 'Spirit of Utility'? We have used this term to connect a number of loosely similar critical characterisations of the modern socio-cultural-economic condition, and the situation of human work under such a condition. It enables us to see the family resemblances between Marx's phenomenological account of the alienation of labour under capitalism, the exclusion of beauty and pleasure from labour noted by Ruskin and Morris, Weber's history of the 'spirit of capitalism', the Frankfurt School's 'dialectic of Enlightenment' and 'instrumental reason', Pieper's description of the 'world of total work', Gill's account of the slavery of factory labour, and Jones's anti-sacramental 'Utile'. In the foregoing chapters we have noted how these accounts differ from each other, yet possess a certain commonality nevertheless. By qualifying each of them in various ways we have sought to show how they might complement one another to provide a more complex, integrated account. At the least, a certain pattern of critiques of utility emerges from the intellectual history of the past two centuries; but beyond this, while obviously the demonstration of this is beyond the scope of this book, it is hoped that this history of reflection generates a coherent and plausible account which throws light upon our own contemporary situation.

The logic of utility

It is now necessary to offer a summary of what can be understood by the Spirit of Utility, based upon the foregoing explorations. The notion is best approached historically as a useful and evolving idea which emerged initially out of the late eighteenth- and early nineteenth-century anxieties about the dehumanizing effects of Enlightenment rationalism and the rise of the factories and industrialization. Various figures in philosophy and the arts, loosely termed Romantics, noted similarities between these two phenomena: a rational, calculating, quantifying spirit, which seemed determinedly destructive of traditional modes of thought and life, with materialistic, anti-theological prejudices, levelling qualitative differences to one commensurable, measurable scale, bracketing out moral and theological concerns in order to occupy a purportedly 'neutral', empirically describable realm. This affinity between literary-philosophical-cultural currents and socio-economic trends can be seen nowhere so well as in the links between the political economy of Smith, Malthus, Ricardo and Mill, and the utilitarianism of Bentham and Mill. Before Bentham the term 'utility' had simply meant usefulness and as such was virtually interchangeable with 'goodness', although with an implication of instrumental rather than intrinsic goodness. While Bentham and Mill clearly intended this breadth of meaning to remain, often using 'happiness' as a synonym for utility, the wider context of their work indicated a narrowing of the term to *mere* utility, understood in materialistic, quantifiable terms, and it was in this sense that their Romantic opponents took up the term as a label for their enemies. For these figures, as we have seen, 'utility' refers to mere functionality, reducing humans to animals or machines, opposed to anything vital or transcendent, and it is in this critical sense that the term is being used here.

Implicit in these nineteenth-century debates was a certain history of utility which linked its rise to dominance with 'modernity', whether this was through the medievalism of Carlyle, Pugin and Ruskin, or the Marxist dialectical account of history and the identification of a capitalist epoch. Yet it is Weber and the Frankfurt School who are most helpful in offering a more detailed historical narrative of the rise of utility, and particularly in grasping the *theological* significance of this story. Before offering such a 'genealogy' of utility however, it is necessary to make the obvious caveat that such grand narratives can be useful in understanding links and affinities between many complex events, and the logical directions of these trajectories; nevertheless the realities are incredibly complex, self-contradictory and overlapping, so that there can be no crude epochalism. The spirit of utility cannot be found anywhere in its purity as such. But more of this shortly.

Despite the yoking of utility and modernity, any historical narrative of the spirit of utility must begin by recognizing that it is as old as civilization. While Weber, as we saw, appears to argue that only what he calls 'adventure capitalism' is as old as humanity, and rational capitalism is distinctively modern, we questioned the helpfulness of his distinction between these two forms, and noted examples he gave of the latter in pre-modern and non-Western cultures. Adorno and Horkheimer link this spirit of instrumental reason with Western civilization itself, so that even the Homeric epics are already proto-bourgeois, and, even more fundamentally, language and thought are already inescapably reifying and alienating, deceptive and dominating. While we questioned the pessimistic necessity of this dialectical view, we would nevertheless concede that the sinister potential must always have been there. In more theological terms, sin, while not necessary, is as old as history; from the first divine gift of authority to 'keep and till' the garden and name and 'have dominion' over the other creatures, the potential existed for this to degenerate into the *libido dominandi*.[3] As David Jones observed, while the virtuous transcendence of utility seems distinctively human, so likewise is the disordered capacity to seek *mere* utility. Humanity, as the creature with transcendent ends not immediately given, has the capacity to choose goals, and then *use* things to or for these ends. Humanity is the

[3] Genesis, 1: 28, 2:15.

tool-maker, *homo instrumentalis*, who can use things and distinguish between means and ends. This distinction is inscribed into many languages with the distinction between transitive and intransitive actions, and the use of dative and instrumental cases. The same distinction of means and ends has been central to much of Western philosophy, from Plato's distinction of the intrinsically good realm of being from the only derivatively good realm of becoming, through Aristotle's teleological analysis, and Augustine's *uti-frui* distinction.[4] As this indicates, there is a benign logic of utility or instrumentality, integral to human action in varying degrees, which is in itself entirely unproblematic, equivalent to the 'tilling and keeping' of Eden, or the 'cunning' that is commended by Christ to his disciples.[5] Its harmlessness consists in its occupying its proper, subordinate place, as at most a formal virtue of method, serving higher transcendent goods. Here utility is operating within the right relation between means and ends, corresponding to an ontological, rather than subjective, teleology in which all things belong to a chain of *intrinsic* goodness, ending ultimately in God, who alone is absolutely Good. Usefulness, efficiency, profit and rational organization are not evils in themselves; neither however are they gods, as they seem to be for so much modern work.[6]

The genealogy of the modern world of total utility

While the usurping of the worship of God by utility is again as old as history, nevertheless it is still plausible to claim that never before has it enjoyed such a triumphant extension to become almost effectively the total worldview of an entire culture as in the modern West. In other places and other times, as Tawney observed, this idolatry, however widespread, was always recognized and judged as such, which is perhaps the most telling indication of what is distinctive in modernity. The broad outline of this cultural shift, of the advance of subjective utility at the expense of traditional values and complex *ontological* teleologies, to a position of apparent dominance, is narrated by most of the figures we have considered. While this is primarily a cultural shift, we have seen that it appeared to the participants to correspond with social and economic changes in society, and Tawney's claim that at the least it collaborated with and encouraged the rise of such changes remains plausible. We can picture this shift in terms of stages of disenchantment, beginning

---

[4] On the subsequent importance to Christian thought of Augustine's *uti-frui* distinction in *De Doctrina Christiana* and its problems, see Oliver O'Donovan, *Resurrection and Moral Order* (Leicester: Inter-Varsity Press, 1986), pp. 234–5, and 'Usus and Fruitio in Augustine', *Journal of Theological Studies*, 33, 1982.

[5] Cf. Matthew 10:16: 'be wise as serpents', and the parables of the Talents (Matthew 25:14–30), the Ten Virgins (Matthew 25:1–13), and the Dishonest Steward (Luke 16:1–9).

[6] I am grateful to Chad Pecknold who, perhaps more than anyone else, made me realize this, with his defence of a modest pragmatism, not opposed to ontology.

with the removal of value from the material world, as in the more extreme forms of Protestant voluntarism, where the only value of anything is imposed upon it accidentally by divine fiat (for the Puritan no sacraments or signs have any intrinsic meaning, and even the saved cannot be recognized by any intrinsic qualities or appearances, as Weber notes). This corresponds to a sundering of means and ends, which are no longer 'naturally' intrinsically fitted to one another, but are arbitrarily related by acts of subjective willing.[7] The entire material universe has become an indifferent collection of 'means', *utenda*, to be utilized for the (invisible) end of salvation. The philosophical counterpart to this theological vision is the Cartesian universe, and its consequences can be seen in the instrumentalizing and casual pillaging of the natural world: seeing 'every tree as potential wood', as Arendt puts it.[8] From here, it is only a short step to elevating human subjectivity to an equal level to divine subjectivity, so that material things can be given value *either* by God *or* by human acts of will (cf. Locke's theory of labour-value). And once the human subject is regarded as an end-in-itself, it does not take much for the weak and unmediated ontological horizon to drop out altogether. Thus God himself is regarded as merely a means to the more immediately evident end of the subject, a necessary idea posited by the subject (Kant), or just simply dead (Nietzsche), leaving the Faustian human will as the only source of all value, and the only end-in-itself.[9] The ancient subordination of action to contemplation, of labour to receptivity, has been overturned here and human labour has become Herculean. Utility as efficiency of means and indifference to ends has become hostile to any ends external to itself, and thus become pure self-interest.[10] Yet in this final move from Kant to Nietzsche, an important series of shifts takes place, as Adorno and Horkheimer noted in their comments on Sade: from rationalist formalism to irrationalist, bestial self-interest; or, in Weber's terms, rational 'ascetic' capitalism transforms itself into hedonistic 'sport', or adventure capitalism. Here the deconstructive logic of absolute utility turns upon the dominating rational subject itself, demystifying it and objectifying this last realm of value and meaning hiding in the 'soul' as itself utterly worthless. The dominator falls victim to his own logic. People are

---

[7] O'Donovan provides a good account of the various voluntarist attacks on ontological teleology, and offers a defence of the latter in terms of Biblical and Patristic doctrines of creation and the priority of ontology over epistemology, *Resurrection and Moral Order*, pp. 31–52.

[8] Hannah Arendt, *The Human Condition* (Chicago: University of Chicago Press, 1998), p. 158.

[9] Arendt, pp. 155–8, notes the paradox that the 'anti-utilitarian' Kant cannot escape the 'Protagorean' utilitarian logic he is reacting against, and how different he is here from Aristotle and especially Plato, in, e.g., the *Theaetetus*.

[10] The anthropologist Marcel Mauss suggests we can almost date the invention of 'interest' in the modern sense to Mandeville's *The Fable of the Bees*, Mauss, *The Gift*, trans. W. D. Halls (London: Routledge, 2002), p. 97.

reduced to commodities whose 'usefulness' can be measured in terms of profit and efficiency, and who will be disposed of accordingly. The world of work has become total, seeking to obliterate all other accounts of the world. Absolute utility reveals itself as nothing but violent self-interest and nihilism.

Christianity's bastard child?

One of the interesting corollaries of this story of the advance of utility is that it presents the exaltation and extension of utility to a total world-view as something distinctive to the modern West, i.e. to the Christian and post-Christian world. While we should be cautious of any causal claims, it does seem that the world of total utility, which we have argued is in many ways an anti-Christian development, is also in a certain sense a bastard child of Christianity, although not a necessary development. Weber is of course the most famous advocate of this affinity, but we should also recall the account which Adorno and Horkheimer offer of the shift from animism and polytheism to monotheism as the removal of divine intrinsic value from the material, empirical world, and its concentration in the supra-empirical transcendent. Both Weber and *The Dialectic of Enlightenment* point to corrective tendencies to this drift within orthodox Christianity, most notably the doctrine of the incarnation, and the consequent re-establishment of the mediation of the transcendent by the material through the sacramental. We might even describe Christianity in this sense as properly a sort of post-critical animism.[11] Such debates however indicate how the problem of utility might be conceived as internal to Christian thought, in which case theology is particularly well placed to address it.

ONLY THEOLOGY OVERCOMES UTILITY

If utility is at the heart of the nature of the problem of modern labour, then only something that adequately addresses this nature will provide a serious critique. We have seen in the above sections that utility seems to be bound up with a hostility to theology, and that there are suppressed theological roots at the heart of the Marxist critique of labour, but the question remains: how exactly can theology provide a critique of utility? To answer this we have explored the theo-aesthetic currents in the English Romantic tradition of social criticism. This parallel tradition of thinking about labour, in Ruskin and Morris, does not suppress its theological foundations but openly speaks of art as a foretaste of emancipated labour and a trace of divine labour.

---

[11] This was suggested to me by John Milbank. It is also implicit in the truly Catholic vision of David Jones, in which the pagan gods and nature itself, once taken captive, can be celebrated for their foreshadowing of the mysteries of Christ.

The theo-logic of beauty as the non-utile.

Why is this critique 'aesthetic'? Because beauty seems, phenomenologic-ally, the most natural opponent to mere utility, and so has become the obvious banner for rallying opposition to the world of total utility. Beauty comes to represent the non-utile. As has been argued by many, the aesthetic becomes for much of the nineteenth century a refuge for the theological concerns that have been banished from other areas of dis-course. The phenomenon of the beautiful exceeds the logic of utility, transcends material self-interest, points to something more. It recalls us to the gratuitous, super-natural nature of humans, that our desires exceed our immediate material survival, suggesting that our Final End is more than this, that it is something we are free to turn from, unlike the animals. Hence it is a *moral* matter, as Ruskin grasped; it cannot be empirically discovered, and so it must be culturally mediated. Beauty, the non-utile, on this account, points to the theological; it is sacramental in the sense of being the shining forth of invisible form through visible matter, as Maritain, Gill and Jones argued. It cannot be adequately accounted for on subjectivist, naturalist or materialist terms, and so, precisely because it is bound up with goodness and truth, it points to the transcendent ontological nature of all three. From being the subjectivist refuge for theology in early Romanticism, beauty has come full circle to be the one that has to recall truth and goodness to their ontological, but supra-empirical, and, therefore, culturally mediated nature.[12] Beauty points to transcendence, to another reality, and this is precisely the source of its critical capacity, as Adorno and Horkheimer indicate. Art, as the gratuitous, intellectual, responsible, delightful creation of things that are beautiful, because they are useful *and* good, rather than merely useful, points to an entirely different way of working that stands in judgement upon all this-worldly ways of working, as particularly Morris and Gill grasped.

---

[12]   I am conscious of the criticisms that have been raised about the use of aesthetics in theology in recent times, but I am convinced that it remains a helpful point of entry into wider discussions, not least here because, as I have sought to show, this was the mode in which theological questions persisted in philosophical terms in order to become the foundation of the critique of labour. Part of the argument I have attempted to make in the course of this book is that these notions of the 'aesthetic' must be understood ontologically, rather than purely subjectively, and that ultimately they find their fulfilment in the category of the liturgical, where it becomes partici-patory rather than purely human, social rather than private, and, in the Eucharist, finds its concrete reference in the Passion and Resurrection of the Incarnate Word. See Irène Fernandez, 'Beauté' in Jean-Yves Lacoste (ed.), *Dictionnaire Critique de Théologie* (Paris: Presses Universitaires de France, 2002), Catherine Pickstock, 'Lit-urgy, Art, and Politics' in *Modern Theology* 16:2, 2000, and Stanley Hauerwas, *Performing the Faith: Bonhoeffer and the Practice of Non-Violence* (London: SPCK, 2004), pp. 151–65 ('Suffering Beauty: The Liturgical Formation of Christ's Body').

The nothingness of pure utility

Theology can do more than simply set up a counter vision to the world of utility in the theo-aesthetic; it can also deconstruct the very notion of pure utility itself. For in itself, utility is simply *nothing*. It is no accident that utility, when separated from larger concerns and set up alone as supreme, turns against itself, as we saw above. For pure utility is an incoherent notion. 'Utility' properly means usefulness, which always begs the question usefulness *for what*? Utility cannot escape the commitment to higher goods, and when it attempts to do so, by opposing itself to higher notions of goodness and claiming to be an end-in-itself, it becomes nonsense. Utility cannot be made 'value-free', because questions of utility are always necessarily parasitic upon prior, presumed values.[13] Likewise its hostility to traditions in the name of a supposed timeless human nature always merely conceals the particular traditions upon which it must depend. As we saw in the discussion of Marx, there is no extra-cultural human nature which can be empirically invoked; all considerations of nature for humanity are necessarily culturally mediated.

Nothing in reality operates according to *pure* utility. Even the most apparently efficient, neutral and rational method must presume some irrational or super-rational, unnecessary, *moral-metaphysical* prejudice, presupposition or trust at its base. The most perfectly functional machine will still have been built for *this* reason rather than that one, in this way and not that one, and functional justifications of these decisions cannot go all the way down, without reaching a point where they flounder. The most perfectly efficient profit-maximizing corporation has still chosen to produce these things in these places at these times by these methods, choices which are never finally reducible to utility and necessity.[14] This is clearly evident in the refusal of criminal methods of maximizing profit, but we should insist that the legal realm of business possibilities is not, therefore, a morally indifferent range of equal alternatives. Businesses cannot escape from ethics into a neutral realm of utility. The most common appeal to such a realm goes under the name of

---

[13] Arendt makes this point very well, p. 154: 'This perplexity, inherent in all consistent utilitarianism, the philosophy of *homo faber* par excellence, can be diagnosed theoretically as an innate incapacity to understand the distinction between utility and meaningfulness... Obviously there is no answer to the question which Lessing once put to the utilitarian philosophers of his time: "And what is the use of use?" The perplexity of utilitarianism is that it gets caught in the unending chain of means and ends without ever arriving at some principle which could justify the category of means and end, that is, of utility itself... in other words, utility established as meaning generates meaninglessness.'

[14] Mauss notes that there is a symbolic 'surplus' in human production, exchange, and consumption which precludes such an account; making, eating and buying always mean something more to us than simply this: p. 92.

the 'free market', naturalizing the desires of people as a morally indifferent given 'demand' which *must* simply be met by supply. We should certainly not underestimate the inertia of these demands as they now stand, nor over-estimate our capacity to alter them, which was Gill's complaint against the moralism of Ruskin and Morris. Yet nevertheless we must insist, as is perhaps more evident in our hyper-real consumerist society than ever before, that these desires are culturally constructed, are in no sense necessary, and are certainly not morally indifferent. Sometimes even if we know that our refusal to collaborate will change nothing, will merely leave others to supply these desires, and will be to our own cost, we must still nevertheless make this stand.

Pure utility, as David Jones puts it, is a strict impossibility for humans; it is a fiction, a myth, which deceptively tries to hide the real ends to which it necessarily remains committed. This is partly of course a counsel of consolation: we need not despair, for pure utility is so contrary to our 'nature' that we will never completely descend to it. Yet it is also no cause for complacency, but rather a spur to action; for it is certainly possible for things to be oriented towards utility, and thus for the influence of utility to increase. This may be a myth, but it is a dangerous and idolatrous one.

DIVINE *ARS*: A VISION OF UNALIENATED LABOUR

We have argued that human labour cannot be understood in terms of pure utility, but rather that it has within itself an excessive logic that points beyond itself, a certain 'ideality', a rational, aesthetic, moral nature, not empirically evident, but standing in judgement against the current realities. It is only by virtue of this nature that social criticism is possible; there could be no critique at all if labour were nothing but pure utility. Labour as utility in this sense, despite all liberal claims of reformism, is never truly radical but always merely a recipe for dehumanization. This is because labour whose only end is efficiency and functionality, free of responsibility, intellect and delight, is *sub-human* work.

Criticism depends, then, on a *vision* of true labour, a transcendent vision, intimated by all labour which points towards it, although manifest more in some forms than others. Yet this vision is no more empirically evident or simply given than pure utility. We cannot 'see' ideal labour, perfect work, with which to criticize false work, alienated labour. All that we see is labour which is a mixture of utility and the inutile, with aspects pointing towards one or the other end-goal in differing degrees. In this sense it is a judgement of faith and hope, impossible to prove, yet tested in the living out of this vision, that one reality is ultimately *real* – the non-utility of divine labour – and the other is ultimately *nothingness* – utility. It remains possible for humanity to choose death rather than life. Only the eye of faith can see the invisible things of God in the visible.

The difference from Marx

We have argued that it was this vision of ideal labour – what work must be like for God – which was glimpsed in the Romantic tradition of social criticism, more or less explicitly, often under the form of art. We have also sought to show the advantages that such a theological-moral-aesthetic vision has over the Marxist materialist vision allegedly based upon history or nature. First, the theological vision has no naïve confidence that this vision will necessarily materialize of its own accord, and so no justification of the sins of the present or past as necessary preconditions for the 'progress' of the future. The sinister consequences of these presuppositions were only too evident in the history of twentieth-century 'Marxist' politics. Beneath this, there is no violent ontology of necessary conflict, present in Marx himself, and revealing his hidden Hobbesian materialist prejudices, imported via political economy. Simply put, the theological vision trusts that the happiness of one does not necessarily depend on the misery of others. Furthermore, it preserves the emphasis in the earlier Marx, somewhat neglected in his later writings, that the transformation of human labour would involve greater personal responsibility and autonomy, and that this in turn would entail a *qualitative* phenomenological transformation of labour to become more free, more intellectual, more delightful, rather than merely its restriction by ever-greater hours of leisure. The failure to preserve these insights can be seen in the relentlessly centralist tyrannous tendencies of so much utilitarian socialism. Finally, and perhaps most significantly, there is in this theological vision no idolatrous Herculean celebration of labour as itself the end of all human living, reducing rest to mere recreation or 'idleness', existing at the service of work, as Pieper so powerfully described it. Rather, work itself must serve the higher end of worship and contemplation of the divine, the eternal Sabbath of the Beatific Vision.

The attributes of divine labour beyond utility

This vision, we have argued, finds its best articulation not just in the celebration of the spirit of Gothic in Ruskin, or Morris's utopian visions of the future, but rather when it is no longer shy of using the language of metaphysics, as in the writings of Maritain, Pieper, Gill and Jones. What then is this vision? What can we say of God's work? We can begin with the claim that the artist is one of the best analogues we have for the divine labour of creation: from Jeremiah's image of the potter, to Aquinas's claim that 'the knowledge of God is to all creatures what the knowledge of the artificer is to things made by his art.'[15] Art resembles

---

[15] St Thomas Aquinas, *Summa Theologiae*, trans. The English Dominican Province (London: Eyre and Spottiswoode, 1963), Ia, q. 14, a. 8, rep. Aquinas is very cautious about this analogy however, insisting, for example, that, strictly speaking, humans do

God's work in that, as Aquinas puts it again, God 'does not act for his own utility', his work has nothing of the qualities of human toil.[16] God creates purely for the sake of the thing being created, gratuitously, out of sheer delight. He does not create out of any need or lack in himself, nor instrumentally for any other purpose. God works for no other reward than his love for the thing made. God creates without loss or exertion, without failure and with perfect delight in the thing made. He simply says 'Let it be' and it is, and he sees immediately that 'it was good.' God creates without alienation because his 'thoughts' are themselves efficacious; his work cannot fall short of his 'plan'. All the traditional polarities with which we think of human labour are transcended here: God's work cannot be opposed to thinking, as if it were more action than contemplation, for it is both simultaneously, without division. Likewise God's work cannot be contrasted with rest, for God remains unchanging in his action, and his life which is pure act is also perfect rest. Again, God's work cannot be contrasted with play, for its very gratuity and immediate delight is precisely best understood as a form of play (as the famous description of Divine Wisdom in Proverbs 8:30–31 indicates). More fundamentally, God's work is somehow not accidental to God; rather, he *is* what he does, and so it is proper to speak of art as not just extrinsic to God, part of his relations with matter, but somehow also integral to his inner Trinitarian life, where the eternal Word is the 'image' or 'art' of the Father.[17] Our language is clearly breaking down in the face of these paradoxical realities. And yet what is at stake here is the ontological claim that at the deepest level there is no violent division of labour upon which all human social oppositions are founded.[18] The distinctions which must exist for us *can*, therefore, be imagined as

---

not create. For a good discussion of these issues in his thought, see Robert Miner, *Truth in the Making* (London: Routledge, 2004), pp. 2–11.

[16] *Summa Theologiae*, Ia, q. 44, a. 4, ad 1.

[17] Armand Larive, *After Sunday: A Theology of Work* (London: Continuum, 2004) offers a recent attempt to provide a systematic Trinitarian theology of work. Despite an impressive range of extra-theological reading and an admirable concern to oppose the privatization and clericalization of Christian faith, Larive seems primarily concerned with this familiar intra-ecclesial debate and so falls into the opposite danger of providing a 'translation' of various contemporary issues in secular work into the language of doctrine, emptying Christian faith of its content and critical capacity at the same time. To take just two examples, it is far from obvious to me what is gained by making 'co-creativity' the 'chief duty of every Christian' (p. 154), or that it is necessary or desirable to evacuate Christian ethics and eschatology of the language of 'perfection' (pp. 73–87). For a much more sophisticated and critical exploration of the analogy between human work and the life of the Trinity, see Dorothy Leigh Sayers, *The Mind of the Maker* (London: Continuum, 2002), especially pp. 177–84, which sets forth the thesis of this book *in nuce*.

[18] This is where I disagree with what I understand to be the argument of Arendt in *The Human Condition*. Simply put, I am sympathetic with her critical account of the degeneration of notions of human activity in modernity through rational utilitarian instrumentalization to bestial self-interest, however I am not persuaded by her argument that these developments are natural consequences of Christian

potentially harmonious rather than necessarily conflicting. Labour is not a reality which makes injustice necessary and inescapable.

Our analogical participation in divine labour

It is important to insist, particularly against the more idealist currents in the Romantic tradition that we have been considering, that this perfect labour is not attainable for us in this life. 'One alone is Good', and therefore we cannot completely escape the logic of utility. As Gill reminds us, to think that we could do so would be to succumb to the Pelagian angelic view of humanity which has been such a temptation to artists. We are temporal creatures, so the eternal unity of rest and action can only be figured by us through the diurnal alternation of rest and action, and never entirely by their perfect unity in time. The distinctions between work and play, rest, or thought cannot be completely transcended this side of Heaven, and any attempts to impose such an abolition of distinction from without will probably be sinister, as Pieper feared. Yet with all these caveats we can still say that human labour is able to participate in divine labour, precisely because there is an analogy between divine and human making; we are still called to 'be perfect as our Father in Heaven is perfect'.[19] This can happen to greater or lesser degrees; our work can become more 'divine' through the partial

---

'otherworldliness' and interiorization. More fundamentally, I am not convinced by her typology of labour, work and action. It is not clear to me that manual subsistence labour is necessarily sub-human, nor that fabrication need be violent, nor that either are somehow 'private' and sub-political, as distinct from the active life of the *polis*. The attempt to separate these three must entail a hierarchical division of labour founded upon the delegation of 'sub-human' labour to a slave-class, as in the ancient Greek societies which seem to be Arendt's ideal. Christianity's insistence upon the necessary intermingling of these three can best be seen in the Eucharist, where our most animal-like activities of consumption are also the highest art, and the very creation of community. Even subsistence is cultural for humanity, and as such, like art, is also always social and political, and crucially need not be agonistic. This also relates to the question, discussed above in relation to Maritain, of whether the Aristotelian distinction of *praxis* from *poiesis* is ultimately sustainable.

[19] See Dorothy L. Sayers, *The Mind of the Maker*, pp. 21–2. I am convinced that the dangers which Lacoste and others see in the Romantic and Idealist visions of human creation, and which we have also seen in the Marxist tradition (i.e., ateleological, arbitrary self-expression for its own sake), are not purely reducible to the Barthian charge of ignoring the ontological distinction. As Sayers notes, the highest forms of human labour are almost *ex nihilo*, and this is not a problem. Rather, if this *analogia actionis* is to make sense, then we might note, after Bulgakov, that even in God's case, *ex nihilo* should not be understood in an arbitrary, voluntarist sense (which is perhaps the Idealists' error), but as grounded in the Sophic eternal ideas in the divine mind. See Jean-Yves Lacoste, 'Travail: Théologie Historique' in Lacoste (ed.), *Dictionnaire Critique de Théologie* (Paris: Presses Universitaires de France, 2002), Philip Blond, 'Prolegomena to an Ethics of the Eye' in *Studies in Christian Ethics* 16:1, 2003, pp. 52–6, and Sergius Bulgakov, *The Bride of the Lamb*, trans. Boris Jakim (Edinburgh: T. & T. Clark, 2002), pp. 3–123. I hope to explore these questions further in the future.

transcendence of utility. This is precisely what we mean by the transformation or redemption of work, and as our work participates more fully in divine labour so to some extent the oppositions we have noted begin to be overcome, even if never finally. So in the highest forms of human activity, perhaps especially in the lives of the saints and in the liturgy, we see 'work' that is also thoughtful, playful, restful and delightful. The service of God is a 'slavery' which is also 'perfect freedom'. In a certain sense, such a transvaluation of values, the transcendence of utility, is cast by the gospel over all the activities of life, so that we can begin to say, as in the Benedictine motto: '*laborare est orare*'; all our life's work becomes a liturgical offering to God, and as such moves beyond utility.[20] Thus under the New Covenant, the Sabbath is no longer a rest after creation, but is the day when the sick are healed, looking forward to the new creation, for as Christ says: 'my Father is working still, and I am still working.'[21] Even the eternal rest of Heaven should not be thought of statically in terms of inactivity, but as the ceaseless restful 'work' of liturgical praise and celebration continued by the saints in bliss. Even more radically, the categories of necessity and superfluity become transformed here on earth: what appears most superfluous to the 'natural' eye – charity – is, seen by the light of the Gospel, the 'one thing necessary', as Christ says to Martha, nothing more than 'what was our duty', as the unworthy servants recognize; while that which seems 'necessary' to the eye of nature – survival – becomes superfluous to the saints who realize that 'he who loses his life for my sake will find it.' This is the logic of the Cross, or as Ruskin and Gill put it, the logic of self-sacrifice which stands opposed to the self-interest of utility. For the life of faith, lived liturgically, everything is superfluity, grace, and yet, when we have done everything, offered all our work, we must still say that 'we are unprofitable servants', precisely because all true work, inasmuch as it participates in God's work, is not ours but is given to us. Likewise, while we can have no control over the issue of our labour in this life, cannot secure it against being thwarted; nevertheless, we trust, in the hope of the Resurrection, that no good work will ultimately be lost.

---

[20]   Lacoste, Jean-Yves, *Experience and the Absolute*, trans. Mark Raferty-Skehan (New York: Fordham University Press, 2004), p. 79.

[21]   See Paul Beauchamp, 'Travail: Théologie Biblique' in Jean-Yves Lacoste (ed.), *Dictionnaire Critique de Théologie* (Paris: Presses Universitaires de France, 2002): 'L'agir cotidien rejoint le service liturgique, non finalise par le produit: "le jour du sabbat, les prêtres dans le Temple violent le sabbat sans être en faute". Cet ordre nouveau n'est ni un état, ni a proprement parler une fin à atteindre, mais un commencement posé.' Philo and the Rabbis also worked out ways of understanding how God could be paradoxically still at work while taking his Sabbath rest from creation; see Gerhard Kittle (ed.), *The Theological Dictionary of the New Testament*, trans Geoffrey W. Bromiley (Grand Rapids: Eerdmans, 1964-), vol. II, p. 640.

THE REDEMPTION OF WORK: THE ORDERING OF PRODUCTION, EXCHANGE AND CONSUMPTION TOWARDS HOLINESS

What are the 'practical consequences' of the foregoing conclusions? This book has sought to oppose the myth of labour as utility which claims that the entire economic realm of production, exchange and consumption is a neutral realm of necessity independent of moral concerns. We cannot be indifferent towards the ends of our labour; our work, and indeed our entire economy, stand under judgement. Everyone, at every level, is responsible for these things, and cannot evade accountability for them: workers, employers, managers, traders, consumers, share-holders, legislators; however much the structures of our particular society may lead us to feel bereft of this responsibility in the face of implacable systems and 'necessary' courses of action.

Thus we must say that there can be no standing on the side-lines: 'He that gathereth not scattereth', as Ruskin insisted. All our economic relations are also symbolic-cultural, and, as such, they can either point towards God, human flourishing, 'wealth' in the Ruskinian sense, or they will point towards 'illth', violence and death. 'Profit', in itself and unconnected to wider values, cannot be the final end of our work or our trade, any more than it could be the final end of our consumption. All our work and trade are in some sense oriented towards consumption in the widest meaning of the term, and are distorted by being separated from this reality. We consume not only food and drink, but also the things we use, symbolic and cultural values, and even one another. For this reason, the right-ordering of our labour and trade depends upon the right-ordering of our consumption, or desire. In this sense traditional Christian moral discussion of avarice, covetousness, gluttony, temperance and the elevation and purification of desire remains fundamental to the 'problem of labour'. Christianity entails what we might call an education in right-eating. Part of this education in eating is to say that not all consumption is good, and therefore consumption cannot be an end in itself.

Consumption for humans is not simply a natural given; we do not simply eat for its own sake, we always eat with gods or demons, to our own salvation or to our damnation. 'Man does not live by bread alone', and ultimately we are called to labour for the food which does not perish, the bread of Life which comes down from Heaven, Christ who is the gift of obedience to the Father's will. The service of God, justice and charity in our relations with one another and with the universe, is the truest food for which we must learn to hunger, and which will feed us 'unto everlasting life'.

This is not achieved however simply by explicitly naming God as the supposed end of all our works (although this is necessary in some contexts to counter the culturally widespread myth of utility); indeed, the most holy work will be directed towards the Highest End entirely unconsciously and without show, like the best artists, as Gill notes. Similarly, proximate and subordinate ends have their proper place under God and need not be pietistically abolished by the insistence that everything be done directly 'for God', without mediation.

The question naturally arises at this point, as it has done with many of the figures we have been considering: how this alternative vision of labour could ever be 'implemented', given our current, quite different economic system. We have sought to argue throughout that the alternatives are not quite as absolute as they seem, because it is impossible to live according to utility, despite what is claimed. Much of what we are seeking to encourage is already implicitly or vestigially operative, despite pressures to the contrary. Nevertheless, it is claimed that any further advances are impossible, either because the necessary consensus on the foundational premises could not be obtained on account of the contested nature of religion; or because agreement on the vision would not secure the necessary transformation of practices, human selfishness being too powerful a force to tame. In the first case we might respond that the breakdown of any superficial 'neutral' rational consensus opens a space for us seriously to enter these debates, and that, as some of our authors indicated, this is a vision which, while Christian in origin, might well be able to gather much support from other perspectives. To the second point we would simply note that such an argument could be used against any virtue at all, and that it matters whether a culture has the vocabulary to name injustice, even if this naming has no *direct* effect upon the levels of injustice (this is what I take Tawney's modification of Weber's thesis to mean). These counter-points notwithstanding, we must concede that total changes of system are almost impossible to achieve. More crucially no change of economic system could itself solve the problem (this is one of the classic mistakes of utilitarian socialism). Wickedness and utility will always be with us. No system could securely establish righteousness itself, formally from above, precisely because, as so many of our authors have reminded us, the transformation of labour is ultimately a matter of personal responsibility. Nevertheless we remain under obligation to act rightly regardless of our chances of success, and, particularly according to the Christian logic of cross and resurrection, even if it comes at personal cost to ourselves. Holy working, trading, and eating are in this sense a prophetic witness in the wilderness, ascetic and sacrificial. Furthermore this is not just a solitary stance of despair; rather the establishment and maintenance of communal discourses and practices by which these questions are kept open at every level is a vital task of hope for the whole world. Throughout the book we have drawn attention to certain counter-cultural practices that witness to the possibility of the transcendence of utility: the responsible craft of an artisan, the liberal arts vision of education as more than technical, the cooperative contemplative working life of a religious community, the corporate commitment to certain values even at the expense of personal interest in the service-professions, the gratuitous delight of child's play, the sacrificial and non-competitive relations of maternal love, the Sabbath rest understood as more than mere recreation at the service of work, the transcendent logic of the liturgical and sacramental.[22] In the last chapter we argued, against tendencies in Pieper and Maritain, that these practices of non-utility should not simply be defended as fortresses, but rather their distinctive qualities should be extended as far as possible to all our work, and indeed to all of life. This corresponds to Barth's comment that the Sabbath ought not to be an exception from ordinary time, but the key to the meaning of every day. While we have not touched much upon it here, it is my belief that this is what the Church's tradition of social teaching has sought to encourage in society: a list of external characteristics which, while not definitive of non-utility in work, are pointers towards this.[23] Just wages and conditions of working, fair prices and honest trade have been central to this tradition. Cooperation and subsidiarity have also been key principles, encouraging distribution of property, unionization and shared ownership wherever possible, although not at the expense of individual ownership and responsibility, but only on this foundation, as the distributivists pointed out. Against the alienation from the fruits of one's actions created by distance, many of the authors considered here have advocated the increase of forms of immediacy, proximity and locality, as ways of encouraging greater responsibility. In particular the use of humans to perform monotonous, servile actions without responsibility, which could be undertaken by machines, needs to be challenged, as does the costly transportation of goods, which could be produced locally, over vast distances for the sake of supposed 'cheapness'. Similarly the disconnection of capital from its real personal costs encouraged by an increasingly unregulated system of lending and debt represents another form of economic irresponsibility. Perhaps the ever-more-virtual spiralling of debt, at every level of society and as much in the developed world as the developing world, should cause us to reconsider something of the Church's traditional unease with usury, at the same time as Islamic communities in the West are exploring positive alternatives to such practices. The Church has also always insisted, in different ways at different times, that certain activities and occupations are simply incompatible with Christian faith, and there remain situations today where all people of good will should have the confidence to refuse to participate in

[22] Mauss looks to archaic societies to find a similar critique of political economy and a social ethic of solidarity and radical generosity: pp. 83–107.

[23] In this respect, the report of the Council of Churches for Britain and Ireland, *Unemployment and the Future of Work* (London: Inter-Church House, 1997) is a particularly good example, combining a detailed analysis of the present situation and concrete proposals with faithfulness to the radicality of the theological tradition (see especially pp. 77–81 on gift exchange economies, the proposals on pp. 158–74, pp. 219–28 on the historical development of Christian reflection on work, and pp. 285–7 on Simone Weil).

activities such as the production of weapons of mass destruction, either through their labour, or through their capital. Capital itself, profit and surpluses, should not, according to our authors, be sought for its own sake nor hoarded pointlessly, but rather always returned back into the economic cycle, while at the same time opening up this cycle to the service of human flourishing. Production, exchange and consumption cannot simply pretend innocently to follow the slavish whims of popular desire, but must all be subjected to an endless discernment based not upon the question 'what can I get out of this', but 'is this truly good and useful?', 'is it serving its true end?', 'is this in accordance with the divine will?'. Similarly, just as we have seen that it has been the attempt to conceive of humanity as somehow separate from creation, over and against nature imparting whatever value he pleases to everything, which has been so damaging not only to the environment but also to our notions of ourselves and our labour, so likewise the redemption of work must entail a right relation to the created world we inhabit and to which we too belong, rather than the merciless, selfish and irresponsible pillaging which we see at present.

In the lives of individual workers it is often claimed that there has been a shift in recent years in the West from oppressive static models of labour (one job for life with the same firm, doing the same thing) towards more liberating mobile models of labour (casual work, frequent changes of job, retraining, etc.).[24] Yet neither 'staticness' nor mobility are solutions in themselves; for the latter can be as dehumanizing (de-skilled, insecure) as the former (no freedom or flexibility). Variety and stability, freedom and security need to be held together in working lives. We might point here to the current in the Romantic tradition we have been considering which, against the increasing specialization and ever-greater division of labour according to class, has insisted that true human flourishing consists in varied and integrated lives, overcoming this division of labour and the one-sided humans it produces by encouraging all to engage in many types of activity as far as possible, neither merely intellectual nor physical for example. Such a move should be combined, they believed, with the responsible creativity and sociability that all workers need in their labour, and which together might just begin to grant to our labour that quality of serious playfulness, of delight, which they believed characterizes the work of God. Then our work might be more truly capable of being offered up to God as an offering pleasing in His sight, only to be received back from Him in its true fruits, both now, and in eternal life.

---

[24] Cf. Volf, in chapter 1, and Richard Sennett, *The Corrosion of Character: The Personal Consequences of Work in the New Capitalism* (London: Norton, 1998) for a critique of these perspectives.

Bibliography

Adey, G. and D. Frisby, (eds) *The Positivist Dispute in German Sociology* (Heinemann: London, 1976).

Adorno, Theodor Wiesengrund and Max Horkheimer, *Dialectic of Enlightenment*, trans. John Cumming (London: Verso, 1997).

Adorno, Theodor Wiesengrund, 'Theses upon Art and Religion Today', *The Kenyon Review*, VII:4, 1945.

Adorno, Theodor Wiesengrund, *Negative Dialectics*, trans. E. B. Ashton (New York: The Seabury Press, 1973).

Adorno, Theodor Wiesengrund, *Kierkegaard: Construction of the Aesthetic*, trans. Robert Hullot-Kentor (Minneapolis: University of Minneapolis Press, 1989).

Adorno, Theodor Wiesengrund, *Aesthetic Theory* (London: Athlone Press, 1997).

Adorno, Theodor Wiesengrund, *Minima Moralia: Reflections from Damaged Life*, trans. E. F. N. Jephcott (London: Verso, 1978).

Adorno, Theodor Wiesengrund, *Hegel: Three Studies*, trans. Shierry Weber Nicholsen (Cambridge, MA: MIT Press, 1993).

Alldritt, Keith, *David Jones: Writer and Artist* (London: Constable, 2003).

Arendt, Hannah, *The Human Condition* (Chicago: University of Chicago Press, 1998).

Arnal, Oscar, *Priests in Working-class Blue: The History of the Worker Priests (1943–1954)* (New York: Paulist Press, 1986).

Aristotle, *The Nichomachean Ethics* (Oxford: Oxford University Press, 1998).

Aron, Raymond, *Main Currents in Sociological Thought* (London: Penguin, 1990).

St Augustine, 'On Christian Doctrine' in Philip Schaff (ed.), *Nicene and Post-Nicene Fathers*, vol. 2 (Peabody, MA: Hendrickson, 1999).

St Augustine, 'On the Holy Trinity' in Philip Schaff (ed.), *Nicene and Post-Nicene Fathers*, vol. 3 (Peabody, MA: Hendrickson, 1999).

St Augustine, 'On the Work of Monks' in Philip Schaff (ed.), *Nicene and Post-Nicene Fathers*, vol. 3 (Peabody, MA: Hendrickson, 1999).

Balibar, Etienne, *The Philosophy of Marx* (London: Verso, 1995).

Ballard, Paul, *Towards a Contemporary Theology of Work* (Cardiff: University College, Cardiff, 1982).

Von Balthasar, Hans Urs, *The Glory of the Lord* (Edinburgh: T. & T. Clark, 1982–91), vols. I–VII.

Barth, Karl, *Church Dogmatics III:4*, ed. G. W. Bromiley and T. F. Torrance (Edinburgh: T. & T. Clark, 1961).

Batchelor, John, *John Ruskin: A Life* (New York: Carrol and Graf, 2000).

Baxandall, Lee and Stefan Morawski (eds), *Marx Engels: On Literature and Art* (New York: International General, 1974).

Beauchamp, Paul, 'Travail: Théologie Biblique', in Lacoste (ed.), *Dictionnaire Critique de Théologie*.

Belloc, Hilaire, *An Essay on the Restoration of Property* (London: Wheats, 1984).

Bendix, Reinhard, *Max Weber: An Intellectual Portrait* (London: Methuen, 1966).

St Benedict, *The Rule of St Benedict*, trans. Cardinal Gasquet (London: Chatto and Windus, 1936).

Benhabib, Seyla, Wolfgang Bonss and John McCole (eds), *On Max Horkheimer: New Perspectives* (Cambridge, MA: MIT Press, 1993).

Benjamin, Walter, *Illuminations* (London: Pimlico, 1999).

Bernstein, J. M., *Adorno: Disenchantment and Ethics* (Cambridge: Cambridge University Press, 2001).

Bloch, Ernst, *The Spirit of Utopia* (Stanford: Stanford University Press, 2000).

Blond, Philip, 'Prolegomena to an Ethics of the Eye', *Studies in Christian Ethics*, 16:1, 2003.

Botterweck, G. Johannes, and Helmer Ringren (eds), *The Theological Dictionary of the Old Testament*, trans. John T. Willis (Grand Rapids: Eerdmans, 1975–), vols. VII, VIII, X, XI and XII.

Bowie, Andrew, *From Romanticism to Critical Theory: The Philosophy of German Literary Theory* (London: Routledge, 1997).

Bulgakov, Sergei, *Sophia: The Wisdom of God* (Hudson, NY: The Lindisfarne Press, 1993).

Bulgakov, Sergei, *Philosophy of Economy: The World as Household*, trans. Catherine Evtuhov (New Haven: Yale University Press, 2000).

Bulgakov, Sergius, *The Bride of the Lamb*, trans. Boris Jakim (Edinburgh: T. & T. Clark, 2002).

Carlyle, Thomas, *Past and Present* (London: Routledge, 1888).

Carver, Terrell (ed.), *The Cambridge Companion to Marx* (Cambridge: Cambridge University Press, 1991).

Carver, Terrell (ed.), *Marx's Later Political Writings* (Cambridge: Cambridge University Press, 1996).

Chenu, Marie-Dominique, *The Theology of Work: An Exploration* (Dublin: Gill and Son, 1963).

Chenu, Marie-Dominique, 'La sacerdoce des prêtres ouvriers', *La Vie Intellectuelle* February 1954, pp. 175–81.

The Council of Churches for Britain and Ireland, *Unemployment and the Future of Work* (London: Inter-Church House, 1997).

Dilworth, Thomas, *The Shape of Meaning in the Poetry of David Jones* (Toronto: University of Toronto Press, 1988).

Dilworth, Thomas, 'David Jones and Fascism', in Matthias.

Eagleton, Terry, *The Ideology of the Aesthetic* (Oxford: Blackwell, 1990).

Engels, Frederick, 'Socialism: Utopian and Scientific', in *Karl Marx and Frederick Engels: Selected Works*.

Faulkner, Peter, *William Morris and Eric Gill* (King's Lynn: William Morris Society, 1975).

Fernandez, Irène, 'Beauté', in Lacoste (ed.), *Dictionnaire Critique de Théologie*.

Fourier, Charles, *The Theory of the Four Movements* (Cambridge: Cambridge University Press, 1996).

Gerth, H. H. and C. Wright Mills (eds and trans.), *From Max Weber: Essays in Sociology* (London: Routledge and Kegan Paul, 1970).

Gibbs, Mary and Ellen, Gibbs, *The Bible References in the Works of John Ruskin* (London: George Allen, 1906).

Gill, Eric, *Art Nonsense and Other Essays*, (London: Cassell and Co., 1934).

Gill, Eric, 'Slavery and Freedom' (1918), in *Art Nonsense*.

Gill, Eric, 'Essential Perfection' (1918), in *Art Nonsense*.

Gill, Eric, 'A Grammar of Industry' (1919), in *Art Nonsense*.

Gill, Eric, 'Of Things Necessary and Unnecessary' (1921), in *Art Nonsense*.

Gill, Eric, 'Quae ex Veritate et Bono' (1921), in *Art Nonsense*.

Gill, Eric, 'Stone-Carving' (1921), in *Art Nonsense*.

Gill, Eric, 'Indian Sculpture' (1922), in *Art Nonsense*.

Gill, Eric, 'The Revival of Handicraft' (1924), in *Art Nonsense*.

Gill, Eric, 'Responsibility, and the Analogy between Slavery and Capitalism' (1925), in *Art Nonsense*.

Gill, Eric, 'Id Quod Visum placet' (1926) in *Art Nonsense*.

Gill, Eric, 'Art and Love' (1927) in *Art Nonsense*.

Gill, Eric, 'Christianity and Art' (1927), in *Art Nonsense*.

Gill, Eric, 'The Criterion in Art' (1928), in *Art Nonsense*.

Gill, Eric, 'The Future of Sculpture' (1928), in *Art Nonsense*.

Gill, Eric, 'Art Nonsense' (1929), in *Art Nonsense*.

Gill, Eric, *Autobiography* (London: Jonathan Cape, 1940).

Gill, Eric, *Last Essays and In a Strange Land*, (London: Jonathon Cape, 1947).

Gill, Eric, 'David Jones' (1930), in *Last Essays*.

Gill, Eric, 'Clothing without Cloth' (1931), in *Last Essays*.

Gill, Eric, 'Ruskin' (1934), in *Last Essays*.

Gill, Eric, 'All Art Is Propaganda' (1935), in *Last Essays*.

Gill, Eric, 'It All Goes Together' (1936), in *Last Essays*.

Gill, Eric, 'Eating Your Cake' (1936), in *Last Essays*.

Gill, Eric, 'Art and Business' (1940), in *Last Essays*.

Gill, Eric, 'The Human Person and Society' (1940), in *Last Essays*.

Gill, Eric, 'Art' (1940), in *Last Essays*.

Gill, Eric, 'Work' (1940), in *Last Essays*.

Gill, Eric, 'Private Property' (1940), in *Last Essays*.

Gill, Eric, 'The Leisure State' (1940), in *Last Essays*.

Gill, Eric, 'Art in Education' (1941), in *Last Essays*.

Gill, Eric, *A Holy Tradition of Working*, ed. Brian Keeble (Ipswich: Golgonooza Press, 1983).

Gurian, Waldemar, 'On Maritain's Political Philosophy', *The Thomist* V, 1967.

Gutiérrez, Gustavo, *A Theology of Liberation* (SCM: London, 2001).

Hauerwas, Stanley, 'Work as Co-Creation: A Critique of a Remarkably Bad Idea', in John Houck and Oliver Williams (eds), *Co-Creation and Capitalism*.

Hauerwas, Stanley, *Performing the Faith: Bonhoeffer and the Practice of Non-Violence* (London: SPCK, 2004).

Heidegger, Martin, 'The Origin of the Work of Art' (1936), in *Basic Writings*.

Heidegger, Martin, 'The Question Concerning Technology' (1953), in *Basic Writings*.

Heidegger, Martin, *Basic Writings*, ed. David Krell (London: Routledge, 1993).

Henry, Michel, *Marx: A Philosophy of Human Reality*, trans. Kathleen McLaughlin (Bloomington: Indiana University Press, 1983).

Hilton, Tim, *John Ruskin* (New Haven: Yale University Press, 2002).

Horkheimer, Max, *Critical Theory* (New York: Herder and Herder, 1972).

Horkheimer, Max, *Critique of Instrumental Reason* (New York: Seabury Press, 1974).

Horkheimer, Max, *Eclipse of Reason* (New York: Continuum, 1974).

Houck, John and Oliver Williams (eds), *Co-Creation and Capitalism* (London: University Press of America, 1983).

Innes, Stephen, *Creating the Commonwealth: The Economic Culture of Puritan New England* (New York: Norton, 1995).

Jameson, Frederic, *Postmodernism, or, the Logic of Late Capitalism* (London: Verso, 1991).

Jarvis, Simon, *Adorno: A Critical Introduction* (Cambridge: Polity Press, 1998).

Jay, Martin, *The Dialectical Imagination* (Berkeley: University of California Press, 1996).

John Paul II, *Laborem Exercens* (London: Catholic Truth Society, 1981).

John Paul II (Karol Wojtyla), *The Acting Person*, trans. Andrzej Potocki (Dordrecht: Reidel, 1979).

Jones, David, *The Anathemata* (London: Faber and Faber, 1952).

Jones, David, *Epoch and Artist*, ed. Harman Grisewood (London: Faber and Faber, 1959).

Jones, David, 'Art and Sacrament' (1955), in *Epoch and Artist*.

Jones, David, 'The Utile' (1958), in *Epoch and Artist*.

Jones, David, *The Sleeping Lord and Other Fragments* (London: Faber and Faber, 1974).

Jones, David, 'The Tribune's Visitation' (1958), in *The Sleeping Lord*.

Jones, David, 'The Tutelar of the Place' (1960), in *The Sleeping Lord*.

Jones, David, 'A, a, a, Domine Deus' (1966), in *The Sleeping Lord*.

Jones, David, *Wedding Poems*, ed. Thomas Dilworth (London: The Enitharmon Press, 2002).

Jones, David, 'Epithalamion' (1940), in *Wedding Poems*.

Jones, David, 'Prothalamion' (1940), in *Wedding Poems*.

Kittel, Gerhard (ed.), *The Theological Dictionary of the New Testament*, trans Geoffrey W. Bromiley (Grand Rapids: Eerdmans, 1964–), vols. II and III.

Lacoste, Jean-Yves (ed.), *Dictionnaire Critique de Théologie* (Paris: Presses Universitaires de France, 2002).

Lacoste, Jean-Yves, 'Travail: Théologie Historique', in *Dictionnaire Critique de Théologie*.

Lacoste, Jean-Yves, *Le Monde et l'absence d'oeuvres* (Paris: Presses Universitaires de France, 2000).

Lacoste, Jean-Yves, *Experience and the Absolute*, trans. Mark Raferty-Skehan (New York: Fordham University Press, 2004).

Larive, Armand, *After Sunday: A Theology of Work* (London: Continuum, 2004).

Lash, Nicholas, *A Matter of Hope* (London: Darton, Longman and Todd, 1981).

Lash, Nicholas, 'Marx', in Lacoste (ed.), *Dictionnaire Critique de Théologie*.

Long, D. Stephen, *Divine Economy: Theology and the Market* (London: Routledge, 2000).

Löwy, Michael and Robert Sayre, *Romanticism against the Tide of Modernity*, trans. C. Porter (London: Duke University Press, 2001).

De Lubac, Henri, *Paradoxes of Faith* (San Francisco: Ignatius Press, 1987).

MacCarthy, Fiona, *Eric Gill* (London: Faber and Faber, 1989).

MacCarthy, Fiona, *William Morris: A Life for our Time* (London: Faber and Faber, 1995).

Mandel, Ernest , *Late Capitalism* (London: Verso, 1999).

Maritain, Jacques, *Art and Scholasticism with Other Essays (1924)*, trans. J. F. Scanlan.

Maritain, Jacques, *The Things that are not Caesar's*, trans. J. F. Scanlan (London: Sheed and Ward, 1930).

Marshall, Gordon, *In Search of the Spirit of Capitalism: An Essay on Max Weber's Protestant Ethic Thesis* (Aldershot: Gregg Revivals, 1993).

Marx, Karl, *Economic and Philosophical Manuscripts of 1844*, trans. M. Milligan (New York: Prometheus Books, 1988).

Marx, Karl, *The German Ideology* (New York: Prometheus Books, 1998).

Marx, Karl, *Grundrisse*, ed. David McLellan (St Alban's: Paladin, 1973).

Marx, Karl, and Frederick Engels, *Selected Works* (Moscow: Foreign Languages Publishing House, 1962), vol. II.

Marx, Karl, *Capital: A Critical Analysis of Capitalist Production* (Moscow: Foreign Languages Publishing House, 1957–62), vols. I–III.

Marx, Karl, *Later Political Writings*, ed. Terrell Carver (Cambridge: Cambridge University Press, 1996).

Matthias, John (ed.), *David Jones: Man and Poet* (Orono, ME: The National Poetry Foundation).

Mauss, Marcel, *The Gift*, trans. W. D. Halls (London: Routledge, 2002).

McInerny, Ralph, *The Very Rich Hours of Jacques Maritain: A Spiritual Life* (Notre Dame: University of Notre Dame Press, 2003).

McLellan, David (ed.), *Marx's Grundrisse* (St Alban's: Paladin, 1973).

McLellan, David, and Sean Sayers (eds), *Socialism and Morality* (London: The MacMillan Press, 1990).

Mészáros, Ivan, *Marx's Theory of Alienation* (London: Merlin, 1986).

Milbank, John, *Theology and Social Theory* (Oxford: Blackwell, 1990).

Milbank, John, 'The Body by Love Possessed: Christianity and Late Capitalism in Britain', *Modern Theology*, 3:1, 1986.

Milbank, John, 'Politics: Socialism by Grace', in *Being Reconciled*.

Milbank, John, *Being Reconciled: Ontology and Pardon* (London: Routledge, 2003).

Mill, John Stuart, 'Utilitarianism' (1861), in *On Liberty*.

Mill, John Stuart, *On Liberty and Other Essays*, ed. John Gray (Oxford: Oxford University Press, 1998).

Miner, Robert, *Truth in the Making* (London: Routledge, 2004).

Moltmann, Jürgen, *Theology of Hope*, trans. James Leitch (London: SCM, 1969).

Morris, William, *A Speech by Mr. W. Morris from the Cambridge Chronicle 23 February 1878* (London: One Horse Press 1996).

Morris, William, *News from Nowhere and Other Writings*, ed. Clive Wilmer (London: Penguin, 1993).

Morris, William, 'The Lesser Arts' (1877), in *News from Nowhere*.

Morris, William, 'Useful Work versus Useless Toil' (1884), in *News from Nowhere*.

Morris, William, 'The Hopes of Civilisation' (1885), in *News from Nowhere*.

Morris, William, 'A Dream of John Ball' (1886), in *News from Nowhere*.

Morris, William, 'Gothic Architecture' (1889), in *News from Nowhere*.

Morris, William, 'Looking Backward' (1889), in *News from Nowhere*.

Morris, William, 'News from Nowhere: or An Epoch of Rest' (1890), in *News from Nowhere*.

Morris, William, 'Preface to Ruskin's The Nature of Gothic' (1892), in *News from Nowhere*.

Morris, William, 'How I became a Socialist' (1894), in *News from Nowhere*.

Mounier, Emmanuel, *Personalism*, trans. Philip Mairet (London: Routledge and Paul, 1952).

Murray, Patrick (ed.), *Reflections on Commercial Life: An Anthology of Classic Tests from Plato to the Present* (London: Routledge, 1997).

Nietzsche, Friedrich, *Beyond Good and Evil* (Oxford: Oxford University Press, 1998).

O'Donovan, Oliver, *Resurrection and Moral Order* (Leicester: Inter-Varsity Press, 1986).

O'Donovan, Oliver, '*Usus* and *Fruitio* in Augustine, *De Doctrina Christiana*', *Journal of Theological Studies*, 33, 1982.

Parsons, Talcott, '"Capitalism" in Recent German Literature: Sombart and Weber', *The Journal of Political Economy*, 36:6, 1928, and 37:1, 1929.

Pickstock, Catherine, *After Writing: On the Liturgical Consummation of Philosophy* (Oxford: Blackwell, 1998).

Pickstock, Catherine, 'Liturgy, Art, and Politics', *Modern Theology*, 16:2, 2000.

Pieper, Josef, *Only the Lover Sings: Art and Contemplation*, trans. Lothar Krauth (San Francisco: Ignatius, 1990).

Pieper, Josef, *In Search of the Sacred* (San Francisco: Ignatius, 1991).

Pieper, Josef, *Hope and History* (San Francisco: Ignatius, 1994).

Pieper, Josef, *Leisure as the Basis of Culture*, trans. Gerald Malsbary (South Bend, IN: St Augustine's Press, 1998).

Plato, *Theaetetus and Sophist* (Cambridge, MA: Harvard University Press, 1996).

Pontifical Council for Justice and Peace, *Work as Key to the Social Question* (Vatican City, Libreria Editrice Vaticana, 2002).

Preece, Gordon, 'Barth's Theology of Work and Vocation for a Postmodern World', in Geoff Thompson and Christiaan Mostert (eds), *Karl Barth: A Future for Postmodern Theology?*

Pugin, Augustus Welby, *The True Principles of Pointed or Christian Architecture and An Apology for the Revival of Christian Architecture* (Leominster: Gracewing, 2003).

Richardson, Alan, *The Biblical Doctrine of Work* (London: SCM, 1952).

Rose, Margaret, *Marx's Lost Aesthetic: Karl Marx and the Visual Arts* (Cambridge: Cambridge University Press, 1984).

Rosenberg, John D. (ed.), *The Genius of John Ruskin: Selections from His Writings* (London: George Allen and Unwin, 1963).

Ruskin, John, 'The Nature of Gothic' (1853), in Rosenberg.

Ruskin, John, *Unto this Last and Munera Pulveris* (London: George Allen and Sons, 1911).

Ruskin, John, 'The Roots of Honour' (1860), in *Unto this Last*.

Ruskin, John, 'The Veins of Wealth' (1860), in *Unto this Last*.

Ruskin, John, 'Qui Judicatis Terram' (1860), in *Unto this Last*.

Ruskin, John, 'Ad Valorem' (1860), in *Unto this Last*.

Ruskin, John, *Time and Tide*, 1867 (London: George Allen, 1904).

Ruskin, John, 'Fors Clavigera' (1871) in Rosenberg.

Ruskin, John, 'Praeterita' (1885–9) in Rosenberg.

Ruskin, John, *Sesames and Lilies, The Two Paths, and The King of the Golden River* (London: J. M. Dent and Sons, 1907).

Sayers, Dorothy Leigh, *Unpopular Opinions* (London: Victor Gollancz Ltd., 1946).

Sayers, Dorothy Leigh, 'Towards a Christian Aesthetic', in *Unpopular Opinions*.

Sayers, Dorothy Leigh, *The Mind of the Maker* (London: Continuum, 2002).

Schiller, Friedrich, *On the Aesthetic Education of Man: In a Series of Letters*, trans. Elizabeth Wilkinson and L. A. Willoughby (Oxford: Oxford University Press, 1967).

Schluchter, Wolfgang, *Rationalism, Religion, and Domination: A Weberian Perspective* (Berkeley: University of California Press, 1989).

Sennett, Richard, *The Corrosion of Character: The Personal Consequences of Work in the New Capitalism* (London: Norton, 1998).

Simmel, Georg, *The Philosophy of Money* (London: Routledge, 1990).

Simon, Yves R., *Work, Society, and Culture* (New York: Fordham University Press, 1971).

Smith, Adam, *The Wealth of the Nations* (London: David Campbell Publishers, 1991).

Solomon, Maynard, *Marxism and Art* (Brighton: The Harvester Press, 1979).

Sombart, Werner, *Die deutsche Volkswirtsschaft im 19. Jahrhundert und im Anfang des 20. Jahrhundert Eine Einfurung in die Nationalekonomie* [German Economy in the Nineteenth Century (1903)] (Berlin: Georg Bondi, 1912).

Sombart, Werner, *Der moderne Kapitalismus* [Modern Capitalism (1902)] (Boston, MA: Elibron, 2001).

Staudt, Kathleen Henderson, *At the Turn of a Civilisation: David Jones and Modern Poetics* (University of Michigan Press, 1994).

Staudt, Kathleen Henderson, 'The Decline of the West and the Optimism of the Saints: David Jones's reading of Oswald Spengler' in Matthias.

Stirk, Peter M. R., *Max Horkheimer: A New Interpretation* (Hemel Hempstead: Harvester Wheatsheaf, 1992).

Tar, Zoltán, *The Frankfurt School: The Critical Theories of Max Horkheimer and Theodor W Adorno* (New York: John Wiley and Sons, 1977).

Tawney, R. H., *Equality* (London: George Allen & Unwin, 1983).

Tawney, R. H., *Religion and the Rise of Capitalism* (Harmondsworth: Penguin, 1990).

Taylor, Ronald (ed.), *Aesthetics and Politics* (London: Verso, 1980).

St Thomas Aquinas, *Summa Theologiae*, trans. The English Dominican Province (London: Eyre and Spottiswoode, 1963).

Thomas, Keith (ed.), *The Oxford Book of Work* (Oxford: Oxford University Press, 1999).

Thompson, E. P., *William Morris: Romantic to Revolutionary* (London: The Merlin Press, 1955)

Thompson, Geoff and Christiaan Mostert (eds), *Karl Barth: A Future for Postmodern Theology?* (Adelaide: Australian Theological Forum, 2000).

Turner, Denys, *Marxism and Christianity* (Oxford: Basil Blackwell, 1983).

Volf, Miroslav, 'Review of Laborem Exercens', *The Scottish Journal of Theology*, 37.

Volf, Miroslav, *Work in the Spirit* (Oxford: Oxford University Press, 1991).

Ward, Elizabeth, *David Jones: Mythmaker* (Manchester: Manchester University Press, 1983).

Weber, Max, *The Protestant Ethic and the Spirit of Capitalism* (London: Routledge, 2001).

Weber, Max, 'Politics as a Vocation' (1918) in Gerth and Mills.

Weber, Max, *Economy and Society: An Outline of Interpretive Sociology*, eds, Guenther Roth and Claus Wittich (Berkeley: University of California Press, 1978).

West, Philip, 'Towards a Christian Theology of Work: A Critical Appropriation of the Thought of Jürgen Habermas' (PhD Dissertation, University of Cambridge, 1986).

Wheeler, Michael, *Ruskin's God* (Cambridge: Cambridge University Press, 1999).

Whitaker, Thomas, 'Homo Faber, Homo Sapiens', in Matthias.

Williams, Raymond, *Culture and Society 1780–1950* (London: Chatto and Windus, 1960).

Williams, Rowan, *Grace and Necessity: Reflections on Art and Love* (London: Continuum, 2005).

Yorke, Malcolm, *Eric Gill: Man of Flesh and Spirit* (London: Tauris Parke, 2000).

Zizek, Slavoj, *The Fragile Absolute – or, Why is the Christian Legacy Worth Fighting For?* (London: Verso, 2000).

Index